To Bob Hughes

for a job well done!

Thank you.

Cyril Ramaphosa.

HEAVEN ON A STICK

...the monster! He
unexpectedly leapt! He
was so big and so close he
nearly knocked Reg and me
over! I thought he was
going to eat us! He was
huge!...

Chris Hale.
1993.

HEAVEN ON A STICK

A self-illustrated anecdotal examination of fly-fishing and fly-fishing retreats around the world

Chris Hole

ROBERT HALE · LONDON

ISBN-0-7090-5362-2

Robert Hale Limited
Clerkenwell House
Clerkenwell Green
London EC1R OHT

Printed in Singapore

Contents

Acknowledgments

When I completed my 1991/92 travels I spent some time compiling an index of names, addresses and telephone numbers of all those who had helped me, and those I had met along the way. Whether it was early administrative support, travel planning assistance, companionship in fishing, advice about writing and artwork, later typing, editing and publishing help, or simply the offer of company—ships that pass in the night—all their cards (or addresses on scraps of paper) were deposited in a special part of my briefcase. It was these that I subsequently sorted to make the index, and it is those people who deserve my deep thanks for their contributions to this book.

In Australia it included Peter and Jill Blackman at the Outpost II, Ginny West and her Frying Pan hut, and Claudie and Dave, in between the two, at Adaminaby. Further south, Rowley Banks, the late John Sautelle, Howie and Anne Charles, and David and Libby Bright introduced me to the Basalt Plain, while across Bass Strait in Tasmania, Rob Sloane gave me good advice about the Central Highlands before I visited Jason and Barbara Garrett at their wonderful London Lakes Lodge.

Trans-Tasman, Brian and Christine Thomson and Phil and Marg Waldron have looked after me for years in New Zealand. So too have the Sargison family, Jimmie and Willie Collenso and Ron Jackson; while Bryan and Nancy Tichborne have helped immeasurably with advice about art and printing. Additionally, the companionship of John and Stephen Clayton, during my early New Zealand visits, was something I shall always value.

Daphne and Christopher Skeate, when he was part of the British High Commission staff in Canberra, were the ones (particularly Daphne) who introduced me to Patagonia and to Jane Wood. That was the beginning of one of my favourite visits and I thank them, Jane and all at Estancia Huechahue for it. My thanks also to Santiago, my Argentine guide, to Harry and Betty Thompson, Andino Grahn, and Pedro Larminat and his American and Canadian guests at Estancia Cerro de Los Pinos.

In South Africa, thanks to a Tichborne introduction, Fred and Peggy Pilkington looked after me wonderfully in Durban. Meyrick and Lola Hudson-Bennett at Himeville, and Michael and Gaye Youngleson at Nottingham Road, maintained these high standards as I moved into the Drakensberg, and Bob Crass was extremely helpful at the Trout Fishing Club.

I could not have chosen a better companion and organiser than Eric Jones in Zimbabwe, nor a better lodge than the Troutbeck Inn under Trish Lee's management. It was wonderful also to have the advice of Peter Turbull-Kemp and to meet United States Ambassador Gib Lanpher and his wife, June, again.

In England I was almost smothered in kindness. It started with Ambrose Streatfeild in Hampshire, and was continued by his friends and contacts; in particular, Bedrick and Carol Eisler and their family; John and Sue Phillips and their son, George; Andrew MacKean and his fiancée; the Featherstone-Dilkes, Ian Hay, Tony Barton-Hall and Bryan Clarke. Then, in Devon, Anne Voss-Bark was the charming hostess at the Arundell Arms where Roy and David looked after my fishing so well. And I could not leave England without paying tribute to Pauline Kennedy of the National Trust at Cliveden Estate.

Manfred Raguse was a wonderful host and

6

organiser in Norway and I'll never forget that hot summer, fishing in perpetual daylight with Simon, Yves and Herbert, while Lucy kept us so well fed.

There were so many anglers passing through Nordurá Lodge in Iceland I couldn't hope to thank them all individually for their companionship, but I do remember German, Norwegian, French and Italian being spoken in addition to English and Icelandic during dinner. They were wonderful people. Jon Borgthorsson has every reason to be very proud of his club and his members and staff. Ingo and Kristián looked after my fishing admirably and Gudmunder Vidarsson gavdlaxed my fish to perfection. It was an outstanding visit.

Inside the Arctic Circle in Baffin Island, Ross Peyton provided some of the best fishing of my travels. Thanks to an introduction by Graham Lochhead in Canberra, this went very smoothly, and Graham also paved the way with First Air for transportation and with accommodation at Donna Copeland's comfortable Auyuittuq Lodge. The days I fished in Clearwater Fjord with Jaco and his son, and with David Parker, were outstanding and I must say how glad I am that Jeff Peyton is going to keep it going.

Bill Bennett and his son, Noel, run a very taut, efficient and comfortable ship in their excellent lodges on the Labrador coast. I thank them and Reg, and Leslie and Alma for the wonderful time they gave me and my fellow anglers: the two Johns, Robin, Harry, Stuart, Doug, Paddy and Tarquin.

In Idaho and Montana, Don Haines pulled out all stops and I shall remain in his debt for a long time to come. Particularly his friends who extended the warmest hospitality: Bud and Ruth Purdy, Ralf and Harriet Stinson, Walter Monter, Bob and Betty Klemann, Don Siegel, Joe Brainard and Herb and Minerva Kunzel all did so much to help make my visits enjoyable, and I thank them very sincerely. The outfitters Bob Jacklin and George Kelly were also very kind and helpful people, and it was a privilege to fish with them.

Keith and Terry Corbould, and their Tweedsmuir Lodge in British Columbia, were introduced to me by an Australian army friend, David Fergusson, and I am extremely grateful for it. I had a wonderful visit to Bella Coola where they, and Keith's brother, Ken, looked after me so well and where I had, as charming lodge companions, John and Esmé Cope from England.

Susan Fitzgerald and Jo-Ann Poffel of Frontiers, and Andrew Brzoz of Australian Fly Fisherman, organised Kiribati and Christmas Island for me and I thank them for an excellent job. In addition, when my program had to be altered, Winona Anzalone and Donna at the Honolulu Airport Holiday Inn were very helpful and they, too, have my thanks. On the island itself I was very thankful for Big Eddy's organisation and for Tuna's guiding. My thanks also go to Darrell, Jerry, Tim, Richard and Edmund for advice and for their companionship on the flats and in the surf.

There were others, not necessarily along the way, but to whom, nonetheless, I owe a debt of gratitude. The retired publisher, Hector McKinnon, who gently introduced me to the world of publishing, and Jocelyn Milton of National Australia Travel who organised my very complex and detailed travel arrangements with total professionalism. In other trout-related matters, Peter Gibson, Fred Dunford, Richard Tilsey, Lofty Tottenham, John Turnbull and Rob Sloane gave me the benefit of their experience. In terms of tackle, Andrew Brzoz, Mic O'Brien, Gordon Winter and John McGinn helped markedly when Orvis and other priority brands were too distant; and Arttec Warehouse provided the best quality art supplies at discounted prices.

I would also like to acknowledge the much discounted rates that the majority of lodges and travel organisations gave me, without which the overall costs could have meant the termination of the project.

In the end I suspect it is probably the typist, the editor and the publisher who should receive the lion's share of an author's thanks. I have therefore thanked them separately in the Preface which follows. In production, however, there was one other who helped me greatly. My very sincere thanks go to Karen Lochhead (the wife of the fellow who sent me towards Baffin Island, no less) for her indexing and assistance with the Bibliography.

Finally, I would like to thank Collins/Angus & Robertson for permission to quote from *The Seven Rivers* by Douglas Stewart (c) Margaret Stewart, Peregrine Smith Books (c) Grace Voelker for permission to quote from *Trout Magic* by Robert Traver, and Aitken & Stone for permission to quote from *The Old Patagonian Express* by Paul Theroux.

If someone's card or details have slipped through my briefcase-to-index list and they are not mentioned here, I accept responsibility, I apologise for the omission and I thank them for their part in this book. There are, however, others who appear only in the text and who added to its variety.

My very sincere thanks to all of you for helping with my story.

Preface

At first it was only a dream.

It started in the middle of 1989 when the very talented watercolour artist, Nancy Tichborne, and her husband, Bryan, visited us at Brindabella on their way home to New Zealand, having been in Hong Kong together proofing the first run of their calendar *The Great American Fly-Fishing Calendar 1990* (now a collector's item). The talk naturally got around to international fly-fishing and I asked Nancy: 'Would you ever take on a world calendar?'

She seemed hesitant. I thought she might have been worried about difficulties with overseas distributors (particularly in the Northern Hemisphere where she'd had some less than satisfactory experiences). I probably said something about parochialism being a world-wide disease. Whatever I said, I found I was holding the embryo of an idea; a dream which simply wouldn't go away.

I realised its strength some months later when I found myself spending hours at my desk, pouring over atlases, maps, brochures and copies of *Fly Fisherman*; re-reading Farson, Haig-Brown, Schwiebert, Ritz and Pawson. Its persistency I acknowledged a little later when, casually questioning diplomatic friends in Canberra, I would, for example, ask a Canadian: 'I have this friend, he is thinking of going to Labrador to fish . . . could you . . .?'

As a spy or diplomat I would have failed dismally! It was starkly transparent, and eventually I had to come clean when one or two friends asked: 'When do you leave?'

Planning absorbed nearly two years and took the form, in the first instance, of listing in my order of importance based on my own reading and experience, all those places in the world where one *could* fly-fish for salmonids or saltwater game fish.

Next, and once again subjectively, I discarded those places considered to be too high a cost-to-achievement risk. For example, fly-fishing in Kashmir while living in a houseboat on Lake Nagin might seem very attractive, but was the expense justified on a limited budget when one might not be able to fish because of consistent spate conditions, or because of the need to dodge bullets? Similarly, it can be an awfully long and expensive trip to visit Tierra del Fuego, only to find oneself sheltering in a hotel for a week while blizzards rage outside and the rivers are unfishable. The third factor I applied was: if a number of places in one relatively small geographic area were famous for their fly-fishing and had already been written about at great length, perhaps it would be better to cover only some, tending if possible towards the more unusual and the less described. In the European theatre, for example, I covered only two places in England and a small part of Norway, omitting (obviously) Scotland and Ireland, also the rest of England, the remainder of Scandinavia and all of Continental Europe.

Finally, I took what was left in my list of subjective order of importance, I linked the places geographically, juggled the reality with my travel agent, found out I would need to make two circumnavigations to obtain the optimum fishing periods in both hemispheres, and began at the beginning all over again. This process was repeated several times, and it must have been a pretty good formula because it worked! Nonetheless, while doing this I tried to comprehend the mathematical need for a *control group*—a later requirement to visit some of those countries I discarded if only to verify my original hypothesis. The start of another dream, maybe?

By that stage I was well into the first dream and

knew there was no turning back. It was a fascinating, thoroughly enjoyable and absorbing task, not to mention a first-class revision of schoolboy geography—like time zones and distances, things I have always loved. Without my many friends, their contacts and my own, it would have been a much more difficult job. A friend in the British High Commission in Canberra with relations in Argentina would say: 'They can arrange . . .' Another in the Canadian High Commission: 'There's someone I know in the Northwest Territories who can . . .' There was a good friend in Hampshire in England . . . another in Sun Valley in Idaho . . . a third in Ranfurly in New Zealand . . . a fourth in British Columbia, and so it went on.

Then I learnt, very early in my research, that the world operates on a facsimile machine. Letters go unanswered; phone calls don't but they are expensive—one always has to discuss the aunt, the cousins and the weather—and there is no subsequent record. But the fax not only transmits a short message cheaply and quickly, but does so at any time of the day or night without inconvenience, and there is always a written record at the end. I installed a machine six months after I started dreaming and wondered, later, why I hadn't done so years earlier.

At the outset I decided that this was not going to be a 'How to' book. Thousands of these had been written already and it seemed illogical to travel the world with such an aim, when the same thing could be written locally from any one of a number of places, given enough experience, and when travelling for fishing could encompass so much more. While some may gain a little education from this book (if one wants to land a big salmon in Iceland, one does not drink red wine with a Norwegian until 3 a.m., then go forth with a trout rod) but that never was an aim.

Nor is it, intentionally, a 'Where to' book. Only a handful of them, covering the international scene, have been published; except for one or two, although very useful as references, they don't tell a *story*.

I like a good fishing story, and I like pictures.

So I guess I approached 1991 and 1992 in that frame of mind. I had my dream, I'd worked out where it was to take place, I wasn't exactly sure what would happen to me when I got there but, whatever it was, I wanted to tell the *story*—anecdotally if not whimsically. In a sense the result is a short autobiography, and if it throws up a number of places that others might like to visit and fish, then so be it. Such was not the intent, even though I have included an appendix of names and addresses in the back of the book.

Titles also are not always easy to choose. I started out with one which was both lengthy and obvious, one that had publishers looking for hiding places, especially when my manuscript had yet to cover their locale. I didn't blame them for thinking that it might be indicative of the content. It was like naming an amateur jazz concert *The Darktown Strutters' Ball*, or a book about shoes *Twelve Inches to the Foot*! As I travelled with this early and clumsy title on a copy of my part-completed manuscript, I found myself occasionally using old, forgotten childhood phrases to illuminate a particular point. They seemed to work for me and sometimes I tried them out on others to gauge their reaction. In Labrador, an English fly-fisherman with whom I was discussing these matters heard me quote one of these phrases and exclaimed: 'There's your title, it's right in front of your blessed nose. It *sings* and it's so easy to remember!'

So *Heaven on a Stick* it became!

I think it was Gini, my wife, who first used the expression in our house. Regrettably, she can't recall its origins, although I suspect that it probably came from a fair or sideshow background, where children could win toffee-apples and kewpie-dolls on sticks. Heaven, at that age, could have represented the otherwise inexpressible stick-supported apex of fairyfloss wonderland. Much as a child of the same age would address an envelope to another by name, street address, town, country . . . all the way up to 'Outer Space', 'The Universe', 'Heaven'.

The physical production of a book is also not easy, even if one has access to a fax machine. An obliging publisher (who believes in the author) has to be found and, preferably, a co-publisher if the book has international coverage and requires international distribution. Publishers, I am told, meet at annual bookfairs in Frankfurt and in Los Angeles where they peddle their wares; but I don't think they can win end-of-a-stick prizes at these meetings—which must be awfully disappointing for them.

I was also faced with the dilemma of choosing between metric and imperial measurements. Arguably it could be claimed that the international language of fly-fishermen talks in pounds for fish and breaking strain (although in America fish are often measured in inches). Similarly, rods are normally talked of in feet and inches, and so on and so forth. On the other hand, many countries were born metric, many have since become wholly metric, while others have only partly converted—leaving, for example, distances between towns in miles. Most pilots still talk altitudes in feet as do nautical men when describing fixing points on a coastline (although metres are preferred to fathoms when talking depths). It is very confusing and I visited so many different measurement zones that I have chosen to use what I believed at the time to be the measure most applicable. It is hard to break lifetime habits and even those many years my junior tell me they still can't visualize a 170-centimetre man being sought by the police!

Then there are the problems of design, colour content, printing, promotion and distribution.

Long before this, the author is blessed if he has the support of a good typing and editing organisation. In these things I was very fortunate.

Jo West, who astonishingly agreed to edit my manuscript, spent a difficult 12 months massaging my scribble, correcting my misspellings and reducing my comma-glut into prose. If, in doing so, this has produced a *story*, then she is the clever one and I am the better for it.

Those most in my debt are my own family. They lent support to a man with a disease which had long since become critical; they humoured him in his ups and downs (often at great distance), made excuses when he should have been somewhere when he wasn't, put up with his excesses, foibles and bad habits, remembered what fishing books they had already given him, accepted with grace his angling-oriented presents, were both critical and admiring in the one breath, and smiled when he paid no attention to their advice. They kept giving him their support when others would have long since abandoned a lost cause.

Particularly Gini, who purchased a very modern lap-top computer and spent thousands of hours typing and correcting my manuscript.

This book could not have been completed without her.

Life would be unbearable if we couldn't read stories, and it would be unliveable if we couldn't dream dreams.

C.M.G.H.
Canberra, December 1992

PART I

PRE-SAFARI DAYS

1
In the Beginning

Granite Island, a little off the shores of Victor Harbour in South Australia, connected to the mainland by a causeway and an antique, horse-drawn tram, was probably where I started fishing. Aged somewhere south of six, I was lured to its old screwpile jetty, once prominent in the grain trade, to fish with baited hook through small holes in the decking for what we called 'salmon-trout' (probably *Arripis trutta*).

In those days, during the height of the Second World War when we carried a piece of sponge rubber hanging on a string from our schoolbags (to bite in the event of a bombing attack), we stayed at Victor Harbour for two weeks during the May and September school holidays. And two weeks, when you are somewhere south of six, can stretch to eternity.

At the start of the holidays my brother and I would buy a whole crayfish (for two shillings and sixpence) which would last as bait apparently forever in that eternity—pungent at its unexpected end 14 days later. After nearly half a century I remember that extravagance in terms of present-day lobster thermidor prices.

But what a bait it was! A quarter of an inch of claw meat on the hook and the quickly snared salmon-trout looked so big I still find it hard to believe we ever squeezed them through the holes in that screwpile.

At home in Adelaide at the time, I had an old book (1910 or thereabouts) entitled *Sports and Leisure Pastimes for Gentlemen*. It was leather-bound (in deference to its stated clientele) and included very detailed pen and ink drawings of moustachioed characters, in what looked like long johns, playing cricket (with all the fielding positions prior to Jardine), fencing, hawking, shooting and even indulging in that sacred and secret-society stuff of angling with the artificial fly.

I'd never heard of Dame Juliana, Izaak Walton or Francis Francis at that stage, let alone Skues, Halford, Gordon, Haig-Brown, Wulff, Borger, Whitlock, Voss Bark, Farson, Schwiebert, Maclean, Leitch, Sautelle or Traver. But, having been brought up on a diet of crayfish through the holes in the screwpile at Granite Island, I found the whole idea totally irresistible and knew, immediately, that fishing with the artificial fly was the only way to take fish 'properly', and that I would fish, from then on, in no other way. In retrospect I find this awakening had an affinity with the singularly descriptive opening to Norman Maclean's masterpiece, *A River Runs Through It*, when he said:

> In our family, there was no clear line between religion and fly-fishing. We lived at the junction of great trout rivers in western Montana, and our father was a Presbyterian minister and a fly fisherman who tied his own flies and taught others. He told us about Christ's disciples being fishermen, and we were left to assume, as my brother and I did, that all first-class fishermen on the Sea of Galilee were fly fishermen and that John, the favourite, was a dry-fly fisherman.

My early attempts were dismal. The leather-bound book gave no instruction about tying flies, or patterns—it was maintaining its (then acceptable, even expected) mystique. So I tied fowl feathers to cork, and inserted monstrous salmon-trout hooks, and glued the whole mess together with Tarzan's Grip to produce something that would repel a grey nurse shark, let alone deceive anything attractively aquatic.

Then in the 1950s I visited Scotland; really to learn to fly Tiger Moths at Lossiemouth. But having 'gone solo', 'ground-looped' a couple of times, and learnt the meanings of 'auto-rich' and the cries of the young ladies at the Beach Bar at Elgin when they said: 'Y' din'na wan me y' jist wan m' bawdy!'

(perceptive lassies they were), as I motored south a stone bridge near Dunkeld jumped out and hit my MG.

I was lucky to be rescued by the laird of a nearby manor who, with added kindness and generosity, dispelled the leather-bound mystiques. He and his family taught me the simple pleasure of casting a rod on the waters, they taught me the names and the dressings of hundreds of flies and how to tie them, they taught me about fly-fishing tackle, they introduced me to the pleasures of single malt at the end of the day and, ultimately and most importantly, instilled in me a love of fly-fishing and an awareness of the need to protect the environment.

For these things I remain eternally grateful. The March Brown, the Blue Dun, the Pale Olive, the Teal series, the Nymphs, the Partridge series, the Watery's and the Spinners were conceived then for me and remain forever, as does the peaty aroma of Laphroaig. It was the beginning of something very special and irreversible.

But I was young then and beginning to enjoy what was to become, some said, a successful career in the Royal Australian Navy. Fly-fishing, except on a few occasions of remarkable convenience (and I admit I sometimes managed to orchestrate them), took second place to fleet programs, fuel estimates, exercise plans, astro-navigation, tactics, strategy and weather forecasts for the next three decades, during which I navigated, among other ships, two aircraft carriers (without being hit by a single destroyer), and eventually commanded my own destroyer (without hitting a single aircraft carrier), and won the coveted Gloucester Cup for efficiency. I also enjoyed the experiences of working for Her Majesty the Queen in the Royal Yacht *Britannia*, duty in the Australian Embassy in Washington, D.C., and commanding the Australian navy in Darwin where I caught barramundi and queenfish on the fly.

But I was always restless. In the early 1980s, with perhaps one (or maybe two) sea appointments ahead of me at best and with a life of desk-bound intrigue and politics to follow into the undetermined future, I decided to pull the plug on a world I loved and didn't want to see spoiled by the grey miasma of over-government and bureaucracy that, I was convinced by then, really ran the navy and all other government departments in greater or lesser confusion.

Around this time I came to the conclusion also that command at sea and the world of fly-fishing, although unlikely bedfellows, had a great deal in common. The exquisitely satisfying agony of success mixed with fatigue experienced at the successful completion of a major undertaking in mid-Pacific was a feeling not far removed from that experienced after stalking a given fish for two days in some high mountain stream, to have him finally accept the artificial fly tied some weeks before. I discovered there was similarity in isolation without feeling lonely; in being absolute master of one's domain for both success and failure; in the companionship of seniors, peers and juniors involved in a common and highly skilled undertaking; in the need to maintain equipment in excellent working order; in the demand for utmost accuracy; in respect for and understanding of the environment; and a common bond in the need to see things in black and white with little room for grey. In short, I concluded that the mountains and the fish offered for me as much as command of a ship at sea; what is more, both would accept and respond similarly in direct proportion to the effort put into them, and both had no place for a bungling bureaucracy hell-bent on pursuing the ultimate committee-forged consensus of eternal compromise.

While these thoughts were taking time to cohere, I found myself looking about for a mountain property with extensive trout river frontage, usable land, reasonable access to modern facilities, beauty and isolation, yet capable of making its own way at worst, and a reasonable profit at best. In 1981 I found this at Brindabella: 500 acres at the southern end of the valley with two and a half miles of river frontage and a carrying capacity of around two sheep to the acre.

For two years following this discovery I lived in Darwin and, during this time, a good friend and master builder, Laurie Woods, camped at Brindabella and, almost single-handedly, built a homestead-cum-fishing-lodge for me overlooking the Goodradigbee River where the quince trees grew.

I stocked the land with fine-wool merino sheep and the river with fish and, on leaving the navy and returning south late in 1983, with the assistance of a knowledgeable neighbour, Neil Seagrim, I started to run the place, improve and fence it and, ultimately, make a small profit while pursuing hours of pleasure with the fly rod.

My own rural background was non-existent. Although I had two uncles who were farmers and graziers, my father was a naval officer killed at Guadalcanal in 1942, and my closest uncle was a restless wizard at all things engineering (and a George Cross winner while serving in the Naval Reserve in 1945). Until 1983, I followed the maritime tracks rather than the rural and any successes I achieved at Brindabella were mostly attributable to Neil Seagrim, and also to Richard Lawson who transported his rural knowhow from the old days in South Australia.

By now, fly-fishing, which had grown from a childhood interest, had become a lifetime passion.

"Mallard & Claret"

Chris Hole 1992.

2
Brindabella

The lost valley of Brindabella, 40 kilometres west-southwest of Canberra, nestles astonishingly between peaks at the northern extremity of the Snowy Mountains. And if 'nestles' is the right word for the valley, it certainly could not be said of the road in and out—'squats with appalling discomfort on the brink of disaster' might be better. Indeed, it is a wonder that the likes of Murray and Mowle, in those early days when stock were taken from the Canberry Plain for spring feeding, ever found their way in and out of this ancient and once-secret part of Australia.

In the 1970s, nearly a century and a half after those early settlers first grazed stock at Brindabella, I found my way into the valley. I called the land I bought at its southern end Berinda (a shortened concoction of the original spelling of Berindibella), and for ten years, ran fine-wool merino sheep over its rolling hills, steep escarpments and fertile flats. And, always, the clear and glittering Goodradigbee River, splitting the middle of the valley as it poured out of the mountains, watered and maintained life: the sheep in the paddocks, the pastures beneath the blue hills, the habitations and, perhaps most important, the brown and rainbow trout in its depths.

And trout at Berinda were probably a much more important part of life than sheep. Certainly, the homestead was dedicated to fly-fishing; filled with rods, reels, fly-tying materials, books, photographs, diaries and seven original fly-fishing watercolours by the incomparable Nancy Tichborne. Indeed the formal dinner which heralded the opening of each trout season was at least equal to, if not more important than, shearing some two months later; even though the latter was most necessary in order to finance the former.

With few exceptions, the fish at Brindabella were wild mountain trout; old and not large in size. That very gifted writer, naturalist and trout fisherman, the late Douglas Stewart, noted in writing about the area in his classic, *The Seven Rivers*: 'But fish? . . . Certainly, there were enough small fish everywhere to keep one intrigued . . . There seemed to be good fishing downstream . . . where the trout in the fast current would take the fly with a bang and break the cast so that they all felt like two-pounders; but . . . I doubt it.' He also noted that the regular recording of two- and three-pounders at Brindabella was ominous because: 'Where two- and three-pounders are reasonably common, as in a really good stream they should be, you do not bother to record them.'

Still, there were those exceptions, and even Stewart noted that: 'Just once, away downstream . . . where the old quince-trees grew in the clear paddock, I saw a big fellow . . . He was the most superb three-pounder. Two-pounder? Four-pounder? He was the lord of the mountains.'

In January 1989, I took a six-pound brown trout from the Quince-tree Pool, immediately in front of Berinda homestead, using a size-12, hair-winged Royal Coachman!

Berinda had its share of visitors, both uninvited and invited. Uninvited were dingoes, wild pigs, foxes, rabbits and other vermin not to mention thistles, briar, blackberry, bracken and trespassing humans—those lost souls determined to stay without an invitation. The invited ones included diplomatic heads of mission from Canberra and their staffs, members of the New South Wales Rod Fishers' Society and of *La Confrerie des Chevaliers du Tastevin*, an ex-Flag Officer Royal Yachts and his Lady, numerous naval friends, the then Lord Mayor of Darwin (the late Alec Fong Lim) whom I had to cart out over that track of appalling discomfort when he suffered an angina attack (which resulted in a quadruple by-pass operation), as well as close fishing friends like Peter Blackman and Rowley Banks (more of them later).

United States Secretaries of State and Defense, Jim Baker and Dick Cheney, who visited in November 1989, proved knowledgeable fly-fishermen and, despite world pressures, excellent company. Lunch at the homestead was a very good humoured affair on that occasion, when they had hooked 15 fish during the morning, upstream in the gorge at Koorabri. Their entourage of secret servicemen and electronic toys, however, seemed unnecessary and sadly out of place among the green ferns, white sally-gums, grey-green granite cliffs and the peaceful bubbling flow of a trout stream.

Dick, who took the lion's share that day, was using President George Bush's split cane rod. Apparently the President had given it to Dick in the early days of his term, noting that it was unlikely that a president would have much time to use it in the future. I imagine Dick subsequently found himself in much the same predicament.

The visitors contributed to the place too. For my fiftieth birthday, in 1988, Australia's bicentennial year, Peter and Jill Blackman very kindly gave me a copy of Conrad Voss Bark's *A Fly on the Water* with the following inscription: 'All the very best on this your demi-century. It must feel good to reflect that you are only a quarter the age of Australia.' And for the same forgettable event, Rowley Banks composed the following poem which he had printed (surmounted by a size six-0 hook dressed as described in the poem) and framed for me:

To C.M.G. Hole, On The
Occasion of His 50th Birthday

The Dotted Slamdunger's the
name of this fly,
(Shrouded in mystery—don't ask me why).
The hackle's of toilet brush,
body's of string,
But it really is THE most
incredible thing.

When the weather's against you
and fishing is tough
And the water is low and you
can't do enough
To entice fish to rise to your
dun or your spinner,
Don't give it all up and go
home to dinner—
Get out the Slamdunger and
tie it on quick—

This remarkable fly, it will
soon do the trick.

From the depths and the top
and the tail of the pool
The fish will assemble, as one,
in a school.
Then cast the Slamdunger as
hard as you wish
At the head of the nearest
available fish.

The impact will stun if your
cast is direct
And you'll know (if my teaching's
had an effect)
That in spite of what's written
in fly fishing books,
The way to catch fish is with
VERY large hooks.
So don't fall for tall tales of
finesse or of skill,
Tie on the Slamdunger and go
for the kill!

RMB
1.5.88

Another remarkable contribution also came in the form of a poem. Andrew Parkin was, at the time, an expatriate Englishman living in Canada, a professor of English literature and an internationally acknowledged poet, who was visiting the Australian National University on sabbatical leave. My wife and I met him through a French friend living in Canberra, a wonderful girl whom Andrew subsequently married in Canada. While Andrew and Francoise were together in Canberra they visited Berinda one day for lunch, of home-smoked trout, naturally.

Lunch at Berinda (*l. to r.*) Secretary Baker, Gini, Secretary Cheney, the author.

Berinda Homestead and Andrew Parkin's poem.

The really remarkable thing about all this was that, until that lunch, Andrew had never been exposed to the world of trout and fly-fishing in any form whatsoever. And yet, three days afterwards, he managed to write a poem demonstrating quite clearly an extraordinary insight into the fly-fishing world of fur, feathers, silk, boron, graphite, Orvis and *Salmo fario* — an insight often not equalled by those who have flogged the waters for years.

He wrote it because, after lunch, when he was about to sign the visitors book, I presumptuously gave him my Hardy fishing diary (courtesy of the House of) and asked him to write a small poem in it instead of signing the VB. The result, reproduced here, is also superimposed over the watercolour of Berinda homestead:

Trout Catch

(for Chris & Gini)

Unseen hands ripple the river's skin,
a tickle to snatch her secrets out
into the gasps of words. Her crooked grin
and icy clarity approve the fatal wit
of solitary angler, fish's reflex guile.

Her creatures learn the accurate abouts
and tacks of her descent amount the shallows.
Here earth colours stipple sleek bed-stones
of river-race in Brindabella's shadows,
mosaic place of water-tinted grace.

Beneath the fallen tree the fierce-toothed
jack or hen dawdle near Quince Tree Rapid
or Upper Shifting Sands. Fish flow, flick back,
break cover to raid what rests in Boulton's Deep
unseen from basking slopes of mild Berinda's fields.

Curving to the glide at Camper's Flat,
the waters rub like a restless cat
around the waders as he casts for trout,
the rainbow or the brown. He skims
meticulous disguises of the barb:

Snowy Mountain Hopper's black and yellow fly,
or scarlet Royal Coachman or the Wulff,
or elegantly lethal Teal and Red,
all bound by fingers deft with thread
and feather, and the artist's brush.

Patience, craft, the strike's explosion
at the lure's bright sting; relief to rod:
these are virtue in the changing light.
The catch smokes, hooks our appetite.
I hang on my line the river's rush and flight.

Andrew Parkin 12.i.1989

I sold Berinda in 1991. Not because I had tired of that beautiful valley (God forbid!), but for many other reasons; some personal, and others practical and more obvious. The personal reasons remain exclusively mine; the practical included a dramatic fall in the wool market (not an overriding reason), the problems of increasing human pressures and pollution from nearby urban Canberra (an

Ambrose fishing the Goodradigbee.

Order Ephemeroptera — "The March Brown
(USA Style)

Chris Hole
1992.

unfortunately irreversible phenomenon not helped by extension of the National Parks), and a restless desire on my part to move on, particularly to sample fly-fishing over the remainder, often remote parts, of this planet (maybe an overriding reason).

I shall always love Brindabella and will try to remember it as it was when I left.

So I've tried, over time, to put together my picture of the area neatly and concisely, but that (for me anyway) seems an impossibility. Was it the first impressions of beauty: clear, Australian-blue mountains in that ever-changing light, and a bubbling trout stream partly overgrown by willows, sally-gums, tea-tree and berries? Was it landing the six-pounder from the Quince-tree Pool late that summer evening? Was it the isolation of winter with snow-capped hills on either side of the valley and a log fire burning at the hearth? Was it the heat, the dust and the flies, and the smell of sheep and lanolin at shearing? Was it the constant battle to repair fences and beat the spread of thistle, briar, bracken, berries and vermin? Was it the party we gave to herald the celestial transit of Halley's Comet on that icy night in April 1986 (when the clarity of the phenomenon, as predicted by Mount Stromlo Observatory, was very much less than two weeks earlier, when I was awakened by its incandescent glacial light, leaving its signature as it moved westwards on the eastern horizon before dawn)? Or was it the memory of the company of my fishing mates, particularly at the dinners at the opening of each trout season, that truly represented the place? It was, certainly, all of those things, and many, many more.

Perhaps I can sum up by giving the final word in this chapter to another teacher of English, Latin and Greek; another Englishman, a trout fisherman and cricketer, a retired member of the Royal Air Force, a gentleman from Winchester named Ambrose Streatfeild. Ambrose stayed at Berinda just before Christmas 1990 and we had some marvellous fishing and wonderful and exciting summer days. When Ambrose (who appears later in this odyssey on the banks of the River Test) wrote to me after that visit he said:

> There have been a few places in this world ('blessed plots indeed') of which the memories, whether past

or recent, have brought me constant joy and, occasionally, solace: the Trout Pond in the Isle of Wight where, aged 6, I caught my first trout, and the nearby cove, where the Romans transshipped their Cornish tin for Gaul, and where I learned to swim and to catch prawns; St George's Chapel, Windsor; Eton's and Pilgrims' cricket grounds; Lord's on the first day; the 7th and 18th at Rye; the Cerne and Frome Valleys in Dorset; the Sacramento Delta and its snowgeese; the marshlands of Bharatpur; and Winchester Cathedral. To this personal list I must now, with the greatest happiness, add Berinda—and especially Merlin's Grotto. Nowhere proves better the adage about 'fishing is rather more than catching fish' (and I admit that it's easy to be smug about this when you *have* been doing so!).

'Merlin's Grotto', as Ambrose renamed the pool on the Goodradigbee, I originally called 'Outward Bound Deep' for the rather obvious reason that it was beside this pool that summer courses from the Australian School of Outward Bound camped for the night before moving on downstream by canoe the next morning. I wholeheartedly approved of Ambrose's renaming, and Merlin's Grotto it shall remain, as far as I'm concerned.

3
The Quest for the 'Rakaia Monster'

Each November from 1985 until 1990, I made a pilgrimage to fish for wild brown trout in the South Island of New Zealand and, on return, would write an article about my fishing. These six stories, thanks to two kind editors, were published in *Tight Lines*, the journal of the New South Wales Rod Fishers' Society. I acknowledge the assistance and polite, but friendly, speed with which the editors gave me their approval to reproduce and paraphrase parts of those articles in this book, mostly in much edited form.

I begin with the tale of the quest for the 'Rakaia Monster' and, from there, meander my way through to the termination of my pilgrimages in 1990 when I gave them up to pursue my dream of a world fly-fishing safari. Before that, I ought really to expound at length about the wonders of the South Island: the astonishingly beautiful landscape, the monstrous trout, the splendid hospitality, and the seemingly endless days of pleasure on some of the greatest trout waters in the world.

But I won't.

Let these stories speak for themselves.

The Rakaia River rises in the Southern Alps in Canterbury Province of New Zealand's South Island, somewhere at the head of Cloudy Peak Range between the Gardens of Allah and Eden. From there it tumbles mightily as a glacial juggernaut towards Mount Hutt Gorge, being joined by the Mathias and the Wilberforce on the way. From Mount Hutt it continues unchanged in its southeasterly direction, broadening to reach the coast in delta formation just south of Christchurch. It is a trout river of great magnitude, but it is also a salmon river when those kings of sport run to spawn in March and April each year.

I first visited the area in 1985, and now I borrow from my *Tight Lines* article describing that visit . . .

We arrived at Mount Hutt Lodge that evening to find that our host, Nick Randall, had completely recovered from the flu and had organised a trip for me the next day to Mount Algidus Station; to the Hydra Waters where the springs feed the streams which feed into the Rakaia River; where we would go to search for monster trout.

Another good dinner and a moderately early night, then a knock on the door at half past five and we were packed into the Landcruiser by a quarter to six, heading up towards the Station. After an exciting crossing of the Wilberforce River, with water pouring over the bonnet, we reached Mount Algidus at about half past seven, then the fog came down. It looked as though I wasn't going to win. But, around nine, Nick said to me: 'Come on, we'll go and have a look anyway.'

We drove out to a prominent point which overlooked a main feeder river for the Rakaia itself. This feeder river was fed from feeder streams from the Hydra, or spring waters, in the high country. I looked down from the cliff and my heart almost jumped into my mouth. There was a hen brown close to double figures, cruising with nonchalance and feeding lazily close in by the bank.

By becoming a sort of mountain goat, and with Nick directing me, I managed to get into a position where I could backcast to the rough location of the fish. I put a Brown Nymph near enough to cause interest; the fish turned and inspected my fly closely, I was shaking with excitement when my very educated quarry turned slowly and, with disdain, sank into the aquamarine depths. About this time, its male companion (an even bigger fish) arrived on the scene. A period of exciting but fruitless casting with numerous fly changes followed before, in frustration, we gave it away for lunch.

After sandwiches and beer, Nick took me to another cliff which overlooked a sixty-foot diameter

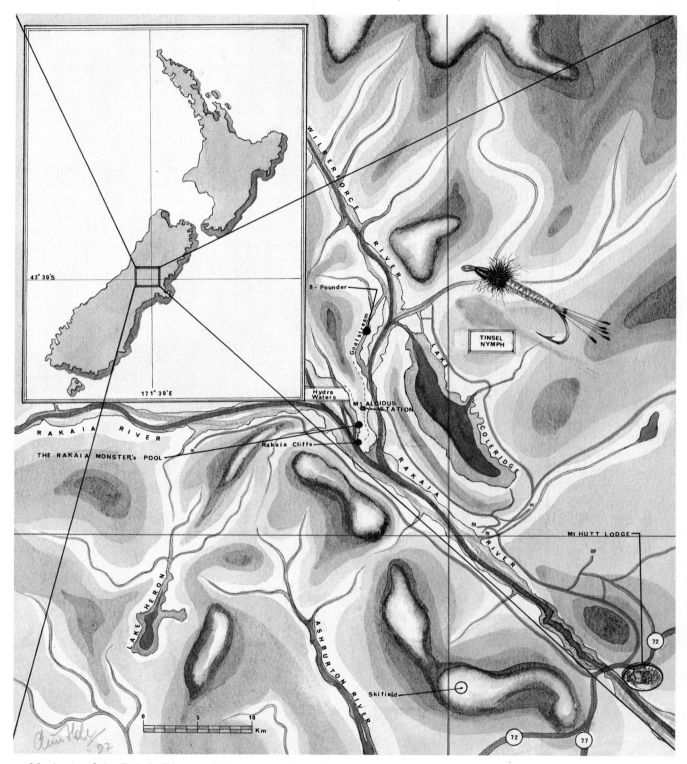

Mudmap of the Rakaia River and the monster's pool.

pool, probably twenty-five feet deep, which was just off the main feeder stream. As we reached the top of this cliff and peered down through the grass, I saw the greatest sight I have seen in all my years of trout fishing (if Scotland is included). There at the edge of the pool, feeding gently on nymphs, was a truly gigantic trout.

We studied him for a while, then I said to Nick that I would creep around to the back of the pool (some 500 paces) and come in from behind. Nick stayed on the cliff to spot. Almost a quarter of an hour later I came out on a sandspit over which I could crawl on my stomach to cast to the monster. Well back from the fish, I prepared my gear and stripped off everything except a pair of old jeans and a shirt because I knew that, if I hooked him, I would be towed by that leviathan down the feeder and into the Rakaia itself. And, quite honestly, I was fully prepared to do just that.

I crawled into position and, with Nick's help spotting from the cliff above, I started casting. I had probably 20 minutes of sheer, adrenalin-pumping excitement trying to get that fish to strike, but all to no avail—he took no notice whatsoever of anything I offered him and eventually became sick of my efforts and left the pool.

I rejoined Nick, who said that, while he had been spotting the monster, he had taken a relative transit of its nose position with a mark on the sand and a similar one for its tail. When we measured those marks on the sand-bank we found them to be an unbelievable 48 inches apart. Four feet and probably 25 pounds of fighting jack brown trout!

Nick also told me that the jack had two henfish with him in the pool, both of which were in the double-figure class; truly an amazing sight. I vowed to return the following year to try for him if someone else had not got there first.

In 1986 I kept my promise, but not before spending an exciting (if not agonising) winter and spring in Australia before being able to return to Mount Algidus to continue the hunt. I recorded my thoughts at the time and these became the introduction to my 1986 *Tight Lines* article . . .

But dreaming as always with trout fishermen leads to images of ghostly, behemoth browns lurking in deep pools or feeding in shallow tails at sunset. More often than not it reminds us of opportunities missed—occasions which always seem to grow in our memories. The late Douglas Stewart put it beautifully in the closing story of the first chapter in *The Seven Rivers*, when he told of a noble monster which he nearly caught:

I crept up to the edge of the backwater and dropped my Tup's Indispensable over the lilies; and with one almighty swirl he took it—and there he was racing across the pool, that magnificent seven-pound rainbow, only a few ounces lighter than David Campbell's, if that; leaping, surely an eight-pounder if not more—six times in all he leapt, with my heart in my mouth each time for fear I should lose him; rushing away over the perilous submerged rocks, across to the far bank where the dangerous wattles dipped their branches into the water, back into the centre of the pool with such a weight and drag on the line that I was certain the cast would never stand it; leaping again with his gigantic body silver over the blue water, racing off once more until there was barely ten feet of line left on the reel—and I had no backing.

Slowly he began to come in, inch by inch, ounce by ounce—I really do think he may have been up to ten pounds, but hardly more. I was afraid of the snags near the edge—nasty-looking submerged logs; I was afraid of the waterlilies; I wondered how ever I could fit him into the net.

But I needn't have worried about any of those things; for when he was so close that I could see him plainly, swimming in about six feet of water, a colossal shadow, dark-backed and silver-flanked, suddenly the line went slack.

And that was my fatal mistake. I thought he was off, and he wasn't. He had taken a sharp little run towards me, incredibly swift and sudden, and when I swung back on the rod to pull the fly out of the water he was still on. But one wag of his head, with the grip of the hook loosened by that momentary slackening, and he was gone indeed. I sat on the bank and shook.

If only I had not let the line go slack—if only I had allowed for his great power and speed even when he was coming to the net . . . But the sun shone on the white sally-gums and the wide blue pool; and was I so sorry after all that he had got away? He was the most wonderful fish I have ever lost; and roughly, I should say, a twelve-pounder.

Similar thoughts were my companions during the winter of 1986 although, in this instance, I had not even hooked the monster. But monster undoubtedly he was—in fact let us from now on call him the 'Rakaia Monster'. I wrote about him in *Tight Lines*, having chased him in November 1985, and John Sautelle (who died in 1991) had also fished for and written about him in the mid-1980s; and after a great deal of consideration both of us agreed, conservatively, that he measured in excess of three and a half feet and 20 pounds.

Thus, in my dreams during the winter of '86 I stalked this fish, in fact I positively lusted after him. I planned every strategy and, like Stewart, I pondered the wonder of hooking and losing him. If I caught him (what presumption), would it be more noble to release him and be elevated to a saintly plane, or to keep and mount him, to let him spend the rest of his days in my garage (not in the house, as my wife cannot stand stuffed animals)? It would depend on the fight and the circumstances (first, hook your fish) but I was sure he would not give up easily. More likely he would drown me in the high waters of the Rakaia, towing me like some waterskier downstream until (to misquote Stewart): 'Chris Hole entered the Rakaia; the Rakaia, not to be outdone, entered Chris Hole'; or perhaps, like Hemingway's 'Old Man', I would dream of lions and baseball as an uncontrollable force pulled me though the water.

I remember in November 1980—on the first of November (if my fishing diary is accurate)—I 'did a Stewart'. I hooked and lost an eight-pound—no, possibly a ten-pound—well, in the end, he must have been, conservatively, a 12-pound brown trout, in a secret part of the upper Murrumbidgee. In the same lunchtime foolishness that day, I lost three other fish of between three and seven pounds, one of which swam between my legs and pulled out the hook. That is another story, but each of these fish had really *hit* at a fly I shall call a Tinsel Nymph—basically a stick-caddis tied with a black seal's fur head protruding from a silver-tinsel stick, with pheasant tippet tail wisps and no wing cases.

I thought: Why shouldn't the Rakaia Monster, at the same time of the year and in the same latitude (give or take a few hundred miles, different weather and water conditions and a thousand other reasons), do likewise? My lack of logic, my dreaming, my strategy and my equipment were beginning to build up, or perhaps I was becoming paranoid; perhaps, like Ahab, I was obsessed with this Moby Dick, depending on one's attitude of mind. And so the next assault was mounted.

Together with John Clayton, I flew from Sydney to Christchurch on 8 November 1986 having (in the words of the 'Fisherman's Prayer') 'disturb[ed] the whole household with mighty preparations and hearts full of hope'.

Two new thoughts occurred to me as we flew east and south across the Tasman: perhaps I should write this part of the story in the belief that I had hooked the Rakaia Monster and build up a make-believe drama around this fable. The second thought was equally evil, equally ignoble, and equally dismissed—but it was also equally devious. What if Nick Randall had contrived to construct a mechanical trout—a clockwork colossus in the image of *Jaws*—a robot which he launched into the Rakaia to encourage (and bedevil) tourists? Was the Rakaia Monster radio-controlled? It would explain a lot of things.

While I dismissed these unworthy thoughts and scolded myself for belittling those involved in our noble sport, I made a mental note to check for oil-slicks if that Trident-class submarine, the Rakaia Monster, showed himself.

By the evening of 8 November all had gone according to plan. We were ensconced in Mount Hutt Lodge and the weather looked promising as we dined with our host and a number of other guests (from Queensland). The next morning, Nick drove John and me to Mount Algidus Station. At this juncture, let me point out that Mount Algidus is really a peninsula, lying in a north-south situation between two rivers: the Rakaia (and Hydra Waters) to the west and the Wilberforce (and Goatstream) to the east. The tip of the peninsula lies south at the confluence of these two great river systems.

Having set ourselves up in the shearers' quarters, we struck out for the Hydra with me, anyway, positively shaking with anticipation. But as luck would have it (I wouldn't mind a dollar for every time I've heard a fisherman use that expression!)—as luck would have it, things from then on did not go quite according to plan. Certainly, everything looked the same to me as we drove towards the Hydra; I could see in the distance Hydra Point where I had last seen the Monster. But Nick read my thoughts and said: 'I'm not taking you over there until you've worked off some steam on lesser quarry.' Torture, but probably sensible thinking under the circumstances; however, after that, events took an unplanned twist.

The first problem was the unforgiving north-wester. It came howling down the Hydra plain with unrelenting fury; it made spotting very difficult (although anything the size of the Monster would have shown up) and accurate casting well nigh impossible. Secondly, the Hydra can be a difficult area to fish: high, tussocky banks bordering beautiful water but with sudden drops into three or four feet of mud for the unwary. I did manage to entice a three-pound rainbow, nonetheless, by dapping a size-16 Caddis over a tussock. But fairly early on that first afternoon, as the wind became if anything stronger, we decided on an early night and a dawn start when conditions hopefully would be calmer. That worked in theory but there was no early rise and, by the time there was enough light to spot through the water, the wind had risen to gale force again. I thought: time to go and look for the Monster!

As we looked down from Rakaia Cliffs at the south end of the Algidus, when we made ground towards the Monster's pool, I noticed that the big fish were still there; double-figure browns, cruising and feeding in fast aquamarine water; very difficult to cast to and probably impossible to catch. But it was perhaps an indication that the Monster was still resident, and so off we went in pursuit.

As luck would have it (that's another dollar), when we breasted the hill at Hydra Point and peered through the grass into the Monster's pool, I can only describe my feeling as one of a fisherman's partly expected disappointment. The pool was discoloured; the Monster was no longer in residence. Had he been so, the eight-pound grandchild, which was nonchalantly cruising the pool would certainly have been banished elsewhere. Perhaps the Rakaia Monster is now swimming that big backwater in the sky? I hope so because, living to the size I remember him to be, he surely deserves to be; and what's more, I can now say confidently he was, *at least*, a 25-pounder.

So around 4 p.m. that day and in low spirits (as the blasted northwester continued), I suggested to Nick that we ought to try the Goatstream on the other side of the peninsula; not because it might be more sheltered but simply because it was the only area we hadn't examined.

Half an hour later, after a very rough drive, Nick and I clambered down to the stream while John stayed with his camera on the cliff top, some 20 feet above, to film the awe-inspiring mountain scenery. Almost immediately all of us together spotted a big rainbow feeding ravenously in a deepish run. With no prompting I crept in behind and tried, unsuccessfully, to punch a dry-fly into that 30-knot wind without having it blown back on the fly-line. Finally, in desperation, I told Nick that I would move away, cross over, and try to float something downstream. In position ten minutes later, I floated a weighted Brown Nymph down to the target area on a slack line. Both John and Nick, almost in unison, called out: 'She's interested . . . very agitated . . . she's going to take it' . . . and WHAM! The next words were a laconic statement from John on the cliff top to the effect that I had half an hour's hard work ahead of me. Obviously, by then, my companions had determined size, sex, strength, and my angling ability.

In most aspects they were right. I hooked up at 4.55 p.m. and finally netted at 5.25 p.m. But, unlike most rainbows, she was not aerobatic; she was a deep down slugger. Several times, in those 30 minutes I had her into the bank within feet of me, only to have her streak over to the other side down deep—and all this on a 4X tippet too. I thought of Doug Stewart as the line whizzed out on each powerful run, and I'm sure the hook started in the middle of her mouth but was well into the right-hand side when we netted her. And netting her was no picnic, either; it took Nick and me three attempts (while I spoke silently to our Maker about Stewart's loss needing to be offset by my gain) before she was safely on the bank and we took the obligatory photos. Eight and a quarter pounds of superbly conditioned hen rainbow shone amongst the tussocks. The feeling was one close to ecstasy and was fortified by a dram or two of single malt. Fishing may be rather more than catching fish, but the odd eight-pounder does help.

The next day we decided to return to Mount Hutt Lodge for the night before travelling south to fish with our friends in Otago country.

As we left Mount Hutt the next morning, an amusing incident occurred when Nick drove us in his 3.8 Jaguar to catch the bus to Wanaka from Ashburton. We were running late and, as we arrived at the bus depot, we observed 'our' bus pulling out into the traffic with its right indicator blinking.

We gave chase. But how would you feel, as a bus driver, if a Jaguar attacked you with headlights flashing, horn blaring and three evil-looking figures gesticulating with two-fingered signs (meaning—to them—two more passengers for you)? It took five kilometres before our message was understood, and plenty of laughs when the bus driver pulled up. In fact we were cheered onto the bus by the other passengers.

So, reluctantly, we departed the Monster's domain.

The Rakaia Monster may have eluded me, but it is probably better that way. After all, he was the most wonderful fish I have known personally but never hooked, and any trout that grows to *at least* 30 pounds surely deserves to win.

. . . hooked up! (*John Clayton*)

. . . playing. (*John Clayton*).

. . . to the net! (*Nick Randall*)

THE EIGHT POUNDER FROM THE GOATSTREAM.

. . . and an indication of size! (*Nick Randall*).

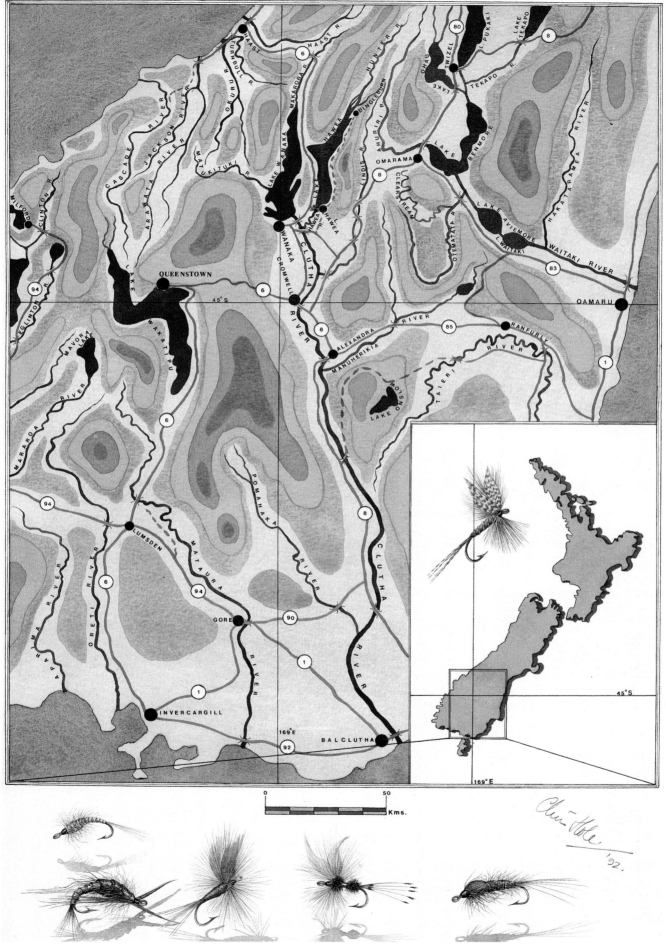

Mudmap of my favourite parts of the South Island of New Zealand.

4
Otago and Southland

I visited Mount Hutt only once more after the saga of the Rakaia Monster, in November 1987. Otherwise the remainder of my New Zealand tales, published in the *Tight Lines* series, all took place in my favourite provinces of Otago and, to a lesser extent, Southland. It was in those mountainous parts of New Zealand that I was lucky enough to meet some astonishingly kind and hospitable people, now good friends, who were prepared to share with me, among other things, the secrets of their rivers and streams. It is those good souls, and thousands more like them, who help to keep the trout fishing so excellent in their country of splendid hospitality.

Brian and Christine Thomson, from Lake Hawea when I first met them, and now from Ranfurly; Phil and Marg Waldron, from Ranfurly when I first met them and now from Dunedin; the late Ian, and Peg Sargison of the famous Dingleburn Station on Lake Hawea; Jimmy and Willie Collenso, who introduced me to the Otematata River and the Clearstream; and Ron Jackson of Gore and the Mataura, and his extraordinarily eccentric housekeeper (who used to clean house beautifully, but often short-sheeted our beds or filled them with Scotch thistle heads while we were away fishing!) all stand out in my memory for their kindness, humour, hospitality and (I must admit) for their angling ability.

The hotchpotch of tales in this chapter is dedicated to that noble band of hard-fishing, hard-living and over-generous souls.

God bless them all . . . 'The long and the short and the tall'.

My first story covers two trips to the Hunter River; one in 1986 (after 'coming second' in the search for the Rakaia Monster) and the other in 1987, when John Sautelle (the then doyen of Australian fly-fishing) joined John Clayton and me for our annual New Zealand expedition.

Perhaps, at the outset, I should establish that the Hunter River rises in Otago Province, very close to the northeast extremity of Mount Aspiring National Park in the Southern Alps. It runs in a southwest direction, ultimately entering Lake Hawea, with Dingleburn Station on the left. Now, having established the geography, I resume the pillaging of my *Tight Lines* articles . . .

In 1986, on the weekend of 15/16 November, to be accurate, John Clayton, Brian Thomson, Phil Waldron and I decided to drive around Lake Hawea, through the famous Dingleburn Station, to stay in a shepherd's hut and fish the Hunter.

What a sound decision that was.

The hut is part of the history of that area; it was used in the days before helicopters, when stock mustering was done on horseback in the high country, and when it often took several weeks to get the animals home. The very walls (with their fundamentally clever mountain graffiti: 'I thought a Lesbian was a French vegetable—until I discovered Smirnoff!') echoed this history and one could not ask for a better place (this side of heaven—and there were times when I thought it was, indeed, heaven) from which to go trout fishing.

There were fish there too. Mighty monsters in all the waterways; in the glacial mainstream and in the quiet backwaters and, to keep my record up, with Phil spotting for me on the first day, I hooked two good fish, both of which broke me, inspiring language which quickly became as colourful as the scenery. But some careful thinking about bloodknots and the power of the initial run of Hunter River trout (you must let these fish run unhindered when they first strike) put me back on track with two good fish.

Sunday 16 November, for me, was one of those

red-letter days. We counted between 60 and 70 good trout that day; I hooked ten and, twice during the day, John and I managed double hookups in a backwater; and (remember) they were all fish of four pounds or more!

It was demanding fishing over great distances of glorious high country; casting in warm but windy conditions into ice-blue water, with white peaks piercing a cobalt sky in every direction. So, taking sandwiches and beer for lunch each day, we would fish from about nine until four, then return to the hut for rest (and whisky) followed by the brewing of a big evening meal; then go back for the evening rise and wind our way home again afterwards for a couple of snorts before bed. Whether this full day had anything to do with the two-part (and sometimes three-part) snoring harmony at night, I really don't know, but accusations were levelled in all directions.

For the most part we used small Stonefly Nymphs, but some classic and highly visible hookups were achieved using small dry flies in the backwaters; the most successful being the Royal Wulff—size 14 or 16.

On the final evening at the hut we fished a backwater near to the Hunter's outlet into Lake Hawea—a backwater teeming with trout. I hooked a five pound rainbow early in the activity from a spotting stalk, a fish which gave me probably an even more satisfying fight than the eight-pounder at the Algidus—in fact I was still connected until shortly before returning to the hut. He took me out to the backing twice and put on an aerial display of which the Red Baron would have been justifiably proud. But this time it was: Hole 1—trout nil.

As we drove out of the high country the next morning, and crossed the Dingle on the way to Ian Sargison's Dingleburn homestead to say farewell, I looked down as the car crossed the bridge. I make a habit of looking down as I cross bridges in trout country—it often pays off, and it did so on this occasion. There was a rainbow of five to six pounds close in by the bank, darting out into the mainstream from time to time to feed. I made noises that sounded like I'd caught my feet in the transmission, Brian stopped the car and I scrambled down to do battle while the others watched from above. As I got down near the fish to approach from behind, I overheard a whispered discussion from above to the effect that even-money was being offered on Hole busting off again. As it transpired the fish was totally uninterested in anything I had to offer and was eventually spooked by a line-end. All bets were off and we continued on our merry way to Hawea.

Then in 1987, in *Tight Lines*, I wrote about the Hunter . . .

The team of ruffian Australian gentlemen, privileged to fish the South Island in November '87, ended up being a little bigger than that which sallied forth (or perhaps fifth) a year earlier. The party was increased from John Clayton and myself by the eleventh-hour inclusion of the doyen of Australian trout fishing, John Sautelle, whom we nicknamed the 'Doyen', not only because he deserved it, but to distinguish between the two Johns on that trip.

This time, as we flew south and east across the Tasman, I didn't dream, nor did I make-believe. I was more relaxed—a much better way to approach our noble quarry, as we all know. This was undoubtedly due to the experience gained during several previous South Island visits. How necessary it is to 'get the feel of the water' before fishing it. If anything, my thoughts turned towards our family doctor who, at my pre-departure and annual medical, told me to watch my bloodpressure. Fancy saying that to a Rakaia Monster hunter! On hearing details of life in the Dingleburn hut in 1986, the doctor nearly had apoplexy himself.

The memory restrained me from a third Gordons and Schweppes before lunch, but I debated with myself (and won) that a glass or two of riesling with the airline *Flambé Plastique* surely couldn't do any harm, especially with all the fresh air and exercise to come.

On this 1987 trip, the Australian visitors had in fact started in Otago on the Otematata River and Clearstream (more of that later); but I take up the story after that juncture, when we reached Dingleburn Station to stay in the shearers' quarters for three days and, once more, took on the ice-blue Hunter River . . .

On 18 November, Sarg (Ian Sargison) turned on his helicopter and his son, David, flew John and me way up the Hunter for an eight-hour walk-fish day, after which the helicopter would collect us to return to the Dingle.

What a great day it was: sunny conditions with a good breeze, breathtaking scenery, world-famous trout water, a six-kilometre walk-fish day ahead, and a can of beer and a sandwich to keep the wolf from the door. Unfortunately we didn't meet up with a great number of fish; as we progressed we realised that human footprints and the telltale marks of jet-boat keels had obviously taken their toll of a once-private domain. However, I hooked a good rainbow late in the morning on a Stonefly Nymph

Lunch by the Hunter (*l. to r.*) Brian, Phil, the author. (*John Clayton*).

John Clayton with a Hawea River brownie.

and she took me some 300 metres downstream before I could land her, prior to release.

Then, near lunchtime, John discovered a backwater which held 15 or 20 fish. We managed one each, only to discover that they were 'slabs', having just finished spawning. I hooked another good hen shortly before we left the river, then we lay in the sunshine, drinking in that beautiful landscape for 20 minutes, waiting for the noise of the rotors. What a great day, and well topped off by a delicious roast dinner with Ian and Peg and the family at the homestead that night.

We left the Dingle for Hawea after lunch on the next day and, on the way out around the point, stopped to look down over the cliffs for fish and were greeted by two perfect examples patrolling the edges, feeding off the top. Cameras were brought out and started to grind, particularly because the Doyen wanted shots of trout taking the fly for his next book (which was released early in 1991, thankfully before he died). I couldn't resist the opportunity and promptly offered to unpack my gear and scramble down to do battle.

Away I went, then nearly everything went wrong. I hooked a bracken bush on my first back-cast, John's video camera refused to function, I accidentally flicked part of the bush into the water, the air was becoming foul with oaths and, as the laughter from the cliff top swelled in volume, I didn't join in (after all, I was in-charge of oaths). Finally, after I managed to get a Royal Wulff out into position, the fun started again. Brian, up on the cliff road, began to count down the distance in feet from the fly to the fish as it closed: 15, 10, 9, 8, 7, 6 . . . Although I could see the fly I couldn't see the fish, being roughly level with it; the strain was unbearable. Somehow I withheld my strike until (what seemed like an eternity) after they said she'd taken it—and I was firmly connected. Then the fun started for a third time: I found that

I'd put my reel away in a hurry and there was a mass of loose, overriding turns on the spool. I plucked out as many as I could and managed to keep the fish at about 25 metres while Phil came down to provide the necessary third and fourth hands to get the reel running again. I eventually beached the fish to find a three-pound 'slab'!

Had it been a fit fish, I would have been broken off surely with that jammed reel.

And that was the Hunter—or 'The Tracker' as Sautelle once renamed it (to confuse belly-fishermen).

Backtracking to the start of that 1987 trip in Otago, to the period preceding the Dingle, on the Otematata River and the Clearstream, I noted in *Tight Lines . . .*

It all started in the Otematata area, inland and south of the Waitaki system, where the Clearstream joins the Otemata River and where there is a complex of ancient mustering huts belonging to Otematata Station. That country is dominated by steep ravines and gorges and, in one part, where the track looks down a thousand feet to the Clearstream and where a Land Rover has to be backed and filled around the corners, I re-christened the track the 'White-Knuckle Highway'. Someday I must present them with a signpost —it really was quite scary stuff.

But there was plenty of room for the seven of us (the Doyen, John, Brian, Phil, Jimmy, Willie and me) to fish there too: upstream on the Otematata where I caught three good fish mainly on nymphs; on the lower half of the Clearstream, where Phil and I fished the first day for seven noble creatures; on the upper reaches of the Clearstream where Jimmy and Willie pioneered the first day, joined by Phil and me on the second for a total of 11 fish; in front of the huts, and even downstream on the main river.

The Doyen made his usual mark. He started the

trip with a good dose of flu, which he passed on to all around him. But he was good enough to come up with two miracle cures (they really should be published in *The Lancet*). They were: several 'wee ones' in the evening, and an extraordinary elixir labelled Redhead's Tonic which, apparently, he found in Canberra. I can remember my uncle using Buckley's Canadiol Mixture to run his car during the Second World War, but this Redhead stuff could power a Sherman tank!

The Doyen's second mark came on day two on the Clearstream when he was really low with flu (we must have run out of Redheads and 'wee ones') and decided to have a morning in bed. Phil and I had told everyone about five fish we had missed on the lower Clearstream, close to the hut the day before; well, the Doyen was so 'ill' that he managed to crawl out of bed, spot and catch those five and one other, all in two hours' fishing!

Unquestionably, though, my most exciting day in that part was the day up the Clearstream Gorge with Jimmy, Phil and Willie. The White Knuckle Highway was followed by very steep, rocky, gorge country bordering a fast-running stream filled with trout. It was mountaineering (let alone trout fishing), and when one hooked a six-pounder while perched high above the water, one knew one faced a good half-kilometre trail, up and down rock faces, through briar and bracken and around outcrops and pinnacles before any hope of reaching a stony beach. We lost a few (fish that is).

It was a full 12-hour day, and the first 'wee-one' back at the hut was the most heavenly nectar imaginable. But I couldn't get my boots on the next morning—I found that I had fractured a big toe and, what's more, I was getting the Doyen's flu.

My first year of fishing-failure in New Zealand—relative failure in that sportsman's paradise, of course—was 1988. The west coast had been experiencing unprecedented rain (up to 60 inches a month for three months on end in parts). The rivers were running dangerously high and very discoloured, all dam taps were open so as not to impede the flow and there were cases of larger rivers backing up smaller ones for miles (I never found out how they handled the excess generated electricity—perhaps they just turned off a switch!) This weather pattern moving subsequently east over the mountains had brought near-drought conditions to the eastern side and strong west and northwest winds howled over the entire South Island.

It was very unfortunate that this happened to be the year I persuaded Peter Blackman and Rowley

Banks to join me—both they, and the reputation of the New Zealand trout fishery, deserved better. But it was on this trip that we visited the North Island first, for two or three days, to make very firm contact with Nancy Tichborne's highly skilled watercolours of New Zealand trout scenes and flies. Later, in the South Island, we visited Lake Onslow which I described in *Tight Lines* thus . . .

On Wednesday, 2 November, we arose at 4 a.m. and drove for two hours south through frozen tundra to a place called Lake Onslow which, reputedly, has excellent fishing (and I'm sure this is true). But, when we arrived, it was sub-zero and snowing with a bone-chilling breeze blowing in. Rowley went on a penguin hunt, Peter said he was sure he had seen an Eskimo and an igloo on the way in and went back to investigate, and I tried to persuade the others that we had found the ideal location to build a single-malt distillery to rival Laphroaig.

Anyhow, we gave it a go (fishing that is), with some remarkable results. John landed one brown after chasing it for two hours; Peter hooked one and a half (something about losing one, and the other being too small); and, I think, Rowley caught one. Later in the morning Brian, Phil and I were examining a small bay when fish, astonishingly in those freezing conditions, started to feed, close in, off the top. It appeared that every now and then, when a zephyr of iced easterly blew from the cliff tops, clouds of hatching black spinners were being blown onto the lake. When the easterly dropped, the predominant westerly system would bring the activity close inshore for our pleasure. I tied on a size-14 Twilight Beauty and cast to a close-in position, indicated by Brian, to have a magnificent brown gulp down my fly and turn on mighty aerobatics. After its third jump I was so elated to be connected to a good fish again that I let out a war cry. How careless! That can only have one result: at the very next jump he threw the hook and I was left contemplating another five-pounder lost.

Then the northwester reached gale force, there was surf on the lake and we decided to go home to Ranfurly—via the Waipiata Hotel where we lost $50 through the poker machine playing some ridiculous system of Fives. That night, as the wind moaned outside, we held a small party at the motel and I demonstrated a devilishly clever raw-egg trick that didn't work, resulting in a much increased laundry bill.

As Bryan Tichborne (of the Itchenborne fame) wrote in *Anglers' Paradise*—the composite book of the best of his wife, Nancy's, calendar paintings of New Zealand trout waters: 'It must be a very monastic angler who has not heard of the Mataura River. To many, including a regular caravan of overseas anglers, it is the epitome of the ideal trout stream.'

I first fished the magnificent Mataura with John, John's son, Stephen, Brian and Phil in 1989, mainly in the Nokomai Gorge area between Balfour and Athol. It is an area of outstanding beauty with steep, often snow-clad, pink-sienna cliffs slumping down to bubbling, swirling trout water, bordered by flax, gorse bush, matagowrie and macrocarpa trees, and overhung with willows. And I said in *Tight Lines* . . .

On Tuesday 14 November we packed up and motored south to the Balfour area to fish the famous Mataura River. I had always been fascinated by stories of this purist, dry-fly stream; the Garston Hotel, George Ferris' 'Parawa Monster' and other tales. To have three full days on this heavenly stretch of water in the Nokomai Station Gorge area was absolute bliss. But it is not an easy river; the trout are fussy and well educated; exactly the right nymph or dry fly has to be chosen and presented accurately to get any response.

On the first day I missed two good fish down deep on the nymph and ended up a wiser man with no fish. By the end of the day, however, we had worked out that a small Copper and Hare Nymph was the daytime fly, and a size-16 (or smaller) Red Spinner the thing for the evening.

On the second day I suffered from sunstroke! Very foolish of me indeed. Until then, I had hardly ever worn a hat (but always do so now). A week of solid fishing in the sun in dry wind at altitude had taken its toll. As I sat down under a willow at lunchtime on that unfortunate day, with a can of ale and a sandwich, the world started to spin before my eyes and I broke out in a cold, sickly and clammy sweat. Somehow the others managed to get me back to the house and into bed, with no assistance from me, and with Brian muttering as he smoked foul tobacco during the drive back: 'We ought to bury him here, beside his favourite river'. I was in no condition to disagree. After three hours out cold in the dark, I awoke recovered if not a trifle weak and the very next cent I spent was included in $25 for a hat!

Nonetheless, just to prove I was a true fisherman (and probably a little foolish) I returned to the river that evening with the others to a spot where Brian had seen a classic rise previously—me with hat and J. H. McGinn split-cane rod (the Mataura, under the circumstances, I believed deserved the best). Anyway it resulted in the classic spotting dry-fly

hookup for me and a four-pound brown was successfully netted. My first fish from the Mataura, caught in copybook fashion after paying a considerable price and learning some important lessons.

It was also during that evening that we ran out of whisky beside the river and I committed the cardinal sin of throwing away Phil's cup (of whisky) because I thought it was cold tea! I must say he displayed superhuman restraint. Then, a little later, Brian felt the need to relieve himself beside the river and, in midstream (so to speak), heard a female voice say: 'How's the fishing?' Thomson nearly jumped out of his skin, confronted by two girls walking their dog, and was heard to mumble something about the fishing being not so good because of the wrong flies (as he did one up).

Penultimately, let me take you to the west coast of the South Island of New Zealand, to Haast; to an area which is about as far south as it is possible to go by road before entering impenetrable Fiordland, and where Brian Thomson shares a weekender with other hardy anglers and hunters. The first time I stayed there (again, with John, Stephen, Brian and Phil) was shortly after the Mataura adventure in 1989; we were fishing mainly the Turnbull and Jackson Rivers and, in *Tight Lines*, I commented . . .

On Tuesday 21 November it was back to the Turnbull in good conditions. We sighted a number of fish and, with Brian spotting for me, I connected to a hefty brown with a weighted Stonefly Nymph. After a short struggle, the fish went deep under some rocks in about 30 feet of water and I was broken off.

Later in the morning we passed the impossible backwater where the lusty one had been sighted the day before. Brian stopped the car and suggested that I should have a go. As it transpired the fish was in a slightly more accessible (or less impossible?) position; that which followed was storybook stuff.

I clambered (fell?) down a mud-eroded cliff into position behind some tussocks; I was facing downstream, the fish was upstream of me, facing upstream some 15 feet over my right shoulder in about 25 feet of crystal clear water, some six feet below the surface, surrounded by a million snags.

By backcasting I could easily put a nymph in the right position but it took two changes of fly to find a nymph with enough weight to sink down to the fish rapidly without having to cast so far ahead that I would spook him with a line-end. Once this was achieved the fish saw the fly, turned almost

By the front door at Haast (*l. to r.*) the author, Brian and Phil. (*John Clayton*).

in slow motion and followed aggressively. His huge white maw opened and shut quite obviously over the fly. In what must have been one-tenth of a second I thought: one should wait until the leader moves! But he has the fly in his mouth! Let's strike!

I was connected firmly with no apparent leader movement until the weight was on. Then all hell broke loose!

The others had been observing, commenting and eventually cheering from the cliff top but, showing considerable forethought, Brian rapidly joined me with a net, saying that we ought to net him 'green', otherwise the snags would win. Easier said than done, but after a few heart-stopping minutes we had him (or her as it was). She was 30 inches of very old, brown henfish. She weighed a little over five pounds but, had she been younger and in her prime, she must have topped seven.

The intriguing follow-up to this story is that, when John Sautelle was fishing for the Rakaia Monster some four years earlier, his companion-spotters on the cliff at Mount Algidus swear to this day that the Monster took John's nymph into its mouth! But John, like many other nymph fishermen, being a 'leader-movement-strike man', saw no leader movement and therefore did not strike. In the light of my Turnbull experience it is agonising to ponder what might have happened at Mount Algidus . . . Fishing is certainly more than just catching fish.

This chapter finishes with an explanation and a closing story.

Two of my favourite rivers in Otago Province

of New Zealand are the Hawea, that magnificent, often-overlooked, short-run stream between Lake Hawea dam and the river's confluence with the mighty Clutha at Albertown; and the Taieri, a slow-moving, tea-coloured, multi-meandering brown trout haven that starts south of Lake Onslow in the Lammerlaw Range, passes Ranfurly and eventually enters the sea south of Dunedin, having run many miles over an intriguing half-circle.

But, as these are my most favourite places I shall leave them for Chapters 10 and 11 in this odyssey, when I begin the overseas section of my world fly-fishing safari in New Zealand.

My ultimate story of those earlier days in New Zealand is one I feel compelled to share. It happened on our 1988 pilgrimage when Peter Blackman and Rowley Banks came with me to share that awful weather and the wonders of Lake Onslow, and I told it in *Tight Lines* thus . . .

We flew via Wellington on Sunday 23 October and then, by internal airlines, to Rotorua.

Our arrival in Wellington was both exciting in the extreme and then side-splittingly funny! We broke through appalling cloud and rain at about 900 feet on the final northerly approach to the airstrip from Cook Strait, passing over tempestuous seas and jagged rocks. As we flew into that northerly gale, the 767 struck a downward wind-shear, hurling us at the rocks short of the strip. Extreme power, the counting of rosary beads and the rapid consumption of brandy miniatures all helped somehow to save us, and around again we went. This time we just made it, with what we in the armed services used to call a 'hard landing'—one which puts so much stress on the undercarriage that the aircraft must be hangered for inspection of its landing gear before being cleared for further operations. When we pulled up at the terminal, the entire passenger congregation burst into spontaneous applause, thankful just to be alive.

Once inside the terminal, relief was quickly replaced by hilarity. Most will be familiar with the New Zealand accent: the lazy vowel, when an 'i' becomes a 'u' and an 'e' something between an 'i' and a 'u'. Well, there at the customs counter was a gorgeous, tall, blonde, shapely New Zealand customs girl who looked Banks up and down and said: 'Show us your dec!' She meant, of course, his customs dec(laration)—but remember the accent? Banks thought all his Christmases had come at once and had to be physically restrained by Peter and me as we reminded him of the New Zealand accent.

It was, without doubt, my most memorable arrival in the Land of the Long White Cloud.

5
Other Times and Other Places

Some of my earliest memories of fishing date back to Kangaroo Island off South Australia in the 1940s when, as a young schoolboy, I used to badger the likes of Frank Chapman and Maury Munt to take me out during the summer holidays in their clinker-built fishing boats to the sandflats off Kingston, to fish with cockles and handline for the incomparable King George whiting. Filleted fresh from the sea, dipped in egg and self-raising flour, then speedily deep-fried, these are still my favourite eating fish. Salt, ground pepper and lemon add to the experience, but are not really necessary.

In later years, particularly in the late summer months in the high country, when the mercury climbed towards the forties, when the rivers were low and warm, when there was a terrible fear of bushfire, and when it even required an effort to emerge in the comparative cool of the evening for the rise, I used to remember those carefree saltwater days.

So much so that on two occasions, again kindly recognised by the editors of *Tight Lines*, I took my family to saltwater paradises and managed to sneak a fly rod into the luggage each time and, on return, scribble a few paragraphs. The first venture took in that wonderful and secluded resort north of Cairns on the Great Barrier Reef, Lizard Island, when I had this to say . . .

In June 1988 I took my family to Queensland during the school holidays, and having somehow survived the 130,000-a-day crowds at EXPO in Brisbane for three days, I thought we needed ten days or so on (at, in, under or above?) the Great Barrier Reef. We flew to Lizard Island, in my opinion one of the greatest holiday places in the world, and that's where this story begins.

We had visited Lizard in 1984 and I was sorry then not to have taken a fly rod with me. I did

this time: a Hardy #8/9 with Hardy Sunbeam reel, WF9F line and simply miles of backing. I confess I also took some spinning and bait-casting hardware and booked the game-fishing boat for a couple of outings as well . . . when in Rome, etc.

One of the pleasures Lizard has to offer (as well as exclusiveness, good food, privacy, sailing, tennis, fishing, water-skiing, archery, lizards, scubadiving, sun, warmth, top-quality staff and luxury), is the provision of 12-foot, six-horsepower, outboard-driven dinghies on the beach that guests can take at will for fishing, picnics and the like. I took one on several occasions to fly-fish for saltwater monsters. I had tried this sport previously during a two-year sojourn in Darwin and had caught barramundi and queenfish on the fly, but was by no means an expert. Rather, I looked on it as a holiday relaxation; one certainly did not spot and stalk and so forth. It was not surprising, therefore, that this rather carefree tropical attitude resulted in my losing all my flies in the first 48 hours.

I calculated I needed three things: greater application (sterner stuff), more flies, and some superfine piano-wire leaders to overcome the impact of sharp pelagic teeth.

The beach at Lizard is run (discreetly organised would be a better description) from a hut which looks after fishing gear, boats, water-skiing, bait, picnics, cut feet, boring guests and anything else one cares to imagine between sunrise and sunset on a tropical island. The 'king' of the hut, at that time, was a fellow called Billy Beach—you wouldn't believe it! My family renamed him 'Sir William Beach'. Anyway, Billy and his offsider, Steve, provided superfine piano wire, pliers and a bench to work at complete with garage-sized vise. This left me to hunt around for fly-tying materials. For tying-silk I found that Johnson's Dental Floss was excellent; for tinsel I cut strips from a Nobby's Nuts packet; for feathers I unbraided a couple of inches of half-ton, white nylon berthing hawser, and for ribbing Steve gave me some thin mousing wire. Finally, Gini came up with nail varnish for cement.

I had my own hooks (two to six range) and the result was half-a-dozen presentable flies connected to superfine piano wire leaders.

Then the fun really began; and (having met with considerable success) as I subsequently tied more of those monsters at Sir William's hut, guests and staff alike would wander in, during the odd hour when tropical showers removed them from the aquatic environment, to watch this crazy southerner manufacture his exotic lures.

I caught a number of fish casting these flies but most came from trolling behind one of the little dinghies. Species included mackerel, queenfish, spotted perch and coral trout. It is very exciting to be struck by a 15-pound mackerel, a momentous event which will nearly empty the reel before one has any chance to think, let alone do something about it. It may not have been true fly-fishing but it was wonderful fun.

My son, Sam, and I had some excitement in the game boat too. Sam caught a 40-pound turrum (similar to a giant trevally) on 15-pound gear and

'Water Taxi' off Matamanoa.

I confess I spent two hours (a broken harness and a sprained back), using 30-pound gear connected to a 500-pound shark before (thankfully) I was broken off. However, I never summoned up the courage to suggest to the crew that we ought to trawl one of my flies (which by then I had christened the 'Lazy Lizard'). But I did present one to Sir William's hut at the end of the holiday.

There was one thing I did discover in all this activity and that was the need to take great care of one's equipment in a salt-water environment.

Sam's Lizard Island turrum.

'Totally environmentally green fishing!'

Each evening after fishing and before pre-dinner drinks, I would indulge in a hot bubble-bath together with my rod and reel and a large whisky and soda. The Hardy gear was cleaned from the outside in—the body was cleansed from the inside out. This, followed by a three-course Lizard Island dinner and a bottle of claret, was enough to make one consider that one had indeed found heaven on earth . . .

The other memorable salt-water occasion was a family visit to Fiji in 1990 when I wrote . . .

The first week of July 1990 produced so much snow and ice in southeastern Australia that Orange and Dubbo were cut off, stock losses were severe, skiers cheered and my own area of Brindabella lost power and telephone for three days and was isolated for a week. This never worried me unduly, not only because I happened to be in the fighting chair of a game-boat off Matamanoa, some 30 kilometres northwest of Nandi on the outer northwest reefs of Fiji at the time (well timed, Hole!), but because I firmly believe that if one looks for and accepts the private, unique quality and beauty of a place like Brindabella Valley, then if those qualities are to be maintained and not replaced by bitumen, traffic lights, people and pollution, one must accept a degree of isolation and inconvenience. Easy to say from a tropical distance? Maybe, but I've been through it before, and been cut off too.

But back to Fiji, which is far more pleasant at that time of the year.

Having mentioned Matamanoa's location, let me add that a reef system lies some five kilometres out from the western side of this little island, only three kilometres around, then nothing but Pacific Ocean— apparently forever. There are many inner reefs as well as the outer and all have good drop-offs where wahoo, Spanish mackerel, yellowfin, barracuda and sailfish swim the depths.

On the southwest corner of the island, the inhabited areas includes a central dining, drinking and swimming complex with 20 outlying *bures* facing a steep, curving, white, sandy beach. The lifestyle is totally relaxed but, as ever, I just happened to take a fly rod with me and on day one started some semi-serious work. My first attempts were to persuade one of the beachboys that he should convince his uncle (living on the next island) to bring over his 40-horsepower, outboard-powered, carved longboat to take me fly-fishing for the afternoon. 'Water Taxi' duly arrived. I christened him 'Water Taxi' because every time he became bored with my casting flies around ('You useum

spear, Sir , or bait—him much better'), he would grin and shout: 'Let's play water taxi!'

He must have seen films of Manila or Hong Kong harbour, because I would then have to reel in quickly and he would twist the throttle wide open and we would wave-bash for five minutes with him yelling 'We big water taxi', while the tribe of accompanying children would shriek with delight. Then he would slow down and I would start fishing again. When, at last, I hooked a small wahoo followed by a silver trevally, and gave the fish to him, 'Water Taxi' thought it was magic and kept muttering: 'Him catchum big fish with feathers from water taxi.'

Then I went totally, environmentally green fishing with my son, Sam. This meant using hand-made flies from discarded animal parts such as feathers, trolling with a fly rod from a Hobie-cat powered only by the wind, sailed by Sam and with me stretched out 'tween-hulls on the canvas in the sun. The fact that we didn't catch anything (but rose a few) didn't really matter. We just switched off, enjoyed it, felt righteous and revelled in the sunshine so badly lacked by those poor souls at Brindabella.

The final big excitement came with a couple of outings in the big game boat. Both took place in the morning as the fish really do go off the bite in the afternoon in that tropical haven. On the first occasion there was just me and the skipper as Sam had taken an extra day scuba-diving at the 'Supermarket'—so called because divers actually hand-feed sharks in that cavern, 30 feet under water. Not my cup of tea. Anyway, when the boat arrived for me from a nearby island I was somewhat stunned. Expecting a Bertram or the like, I was surprised to find an 'improved' water taxi, the same as my friend's but with added central console, rod holders, canvas dodger and icebox. I need not have been too worried. This boat handled the big Pacific swells near the outer reefs well and, apart from cramped conditions (and no chair) when fighting a big fish, and the need from time to time to keep one's toes out of the way of barracuda teeth, although slim, it proved to be a remarkably seaworthy machine.

That morning we accounted for some good wahoo among the dreaded barracuda before trolling between the reefs to pick up a brace of yellowfin tuna before lunch. Most of these fish were in the 15- to 20-pound class with one or two nearer to 30.

For day two in the gameboat I persuaded the owners to provide the 'Fishing Machine', a reasonable-sized Bertram with a good reputation which was normally berthed inshore for the Regent

Hotel trade. I took Sam too, which was foolish of me, as you will read.

We started trolling for scad bait early in the morning and I gave Sam the first hour/strike as I'd already had a fairly successful solo day. For 40 minutes nothing happened, which was encouraging in that it might have meant that the scads had been eaten by bigger fish which could still be lurking in the deep. Just then, with me as usual caught the wrong way and about to reach for a sandwich, I heard the first reel go off. With some difficulty we got Sam into the chair as line stripped out at an alarming rate, and I quickly recovered the other trolls. Sam hadn't gained an inch, indeed he had lost over 100 metres, and things looked decidedly non-scaddy by the time he was fully in control. I grabbed the chance to duck forward and collect my camera and started filming the budding Zane Grey from the billfish platform, whereupon the skipper suddenly yelled: 'Big sail!'

I turned quickly to see the classic tailwalk of well over 100 pounds of sailfish some 200 metres astern.

It was all too much! The sail soon threw the hook and Sam started down that dreadful 'primrose' path of becoming a true fisherman: by the time the swearing stopped, that fish had grown to over 200 pounds, it was on for two and a half hours, and when Sam is now asked to indicate its length, he asks me to stand beside him and join hands, then move as far apart as possible, with our outer arms raised horizontally to the typically over-exaggerated fisherman's position.

But we did account for some fine wahoo and yellowfin that morning, including a 15-pound wahoo that arrived chopped in half by a bigger brother. What a day, and with crumbed tuna pieces around the bar with drinks before dinner that evening, Sam's imagination grew and grew.

It is of subsequent interest that Sam and I call in on Mick O'Brien at Manuka in Canberra, from time to time, for a haircut, to buy flies and to lie about fish. On return from Fiji I was the first to Mick's and immediately briefed that worthy barbershop, tackle store and meeting ground of noble Canberra fishing folk about Fiji. They were warned to remark, on Sam's next and imminent visit, that they'd had word from friends in Fiji about a young Australian teenager who hooked a 50-pound sailfish early in July up there and who lost it through carelessness.

Two days later, while having his hair cut and listening to the locals retell this fable, Sam casually remarked: 'Dad's been in here, hasn't he.'

The remainder of that article was a short, and mainly unrelated, story about John Sautelle's eightieth birthday party held at Merimbula, New South Wales, in July 1990. It was a wonderfully happy family event but was sadly followed, some nine months later, by John's death—fortunately after his final book, *Champagne Fly Fishing*, had been released with success.

If I may borrow from *A Fly on the Water* and the words of Conrad Voss Bark when he wrote about the American journalist and fly-fisherman, Negley Farson, paraphrasing those words to apply them to John:

> Say a prayer for the soul of John Sautelle, an Australian fly-fisherman, who lived hard and drank hard and had the heart of an angel. Has anyone ever done more for Antipodean fly-fishing? I doubt it; he was a legend (and a wily one at that) in his own lifetime.

His memorial service was held at Bombala, New South Wales, early in April 1991 where, on a small table in the chancel of the church, stood his slouch fishing hat, one of his fly rods, and a Grant's Glenfiddich container. I attended the service, having buried my young sheepdog the day before. Waldo, as was the dog's name, died about the same time as John when a 'backed-up' member of the kangaroo species lured him into the river one night and drowned him when he became less mobile in the water—not a unique phenomenon I understand.

Although John and Waldo never met, I'm sure they would have been good mates had they done so. Neither of them ever thought other than good of all those they met. And I'm also sure (although I never met him) that the same could be said of an American who died around that time in 1991 too. He was John Voelker (better known to trout fishermen as Robert Traver) who wrote *Trout Madness* and *Trout Magic*, and who also just happened to pen a bestseller called *Anatomy of a Murder*. Based on a 1952 murder for which Voelker was the defence lawyer, it was made into an Oscar-winning movie in 1957. To fishermen he would be best remembered for his often-quoted passage, 'Testament of a Fisherman', which first appeared in *Life* magazine before it came out in his 'Anatomy of a Fisherman', and which Sautelle used in his first book and his son paraphrased in his father's memorial eulogy:

> I fish because I love to; because I love the environs where trout are found, which are invariably beautiful, and hate the environs where crowds of people are

Hooked up in the big game boat . . . father . . . and son.

found, which are invariably ugly; because of all the television commercials, cocktail parties, and assorted social posturing I thus escape; because, in a world where most men seem to spend their lives doing things they hate, my fishing is at once an endless source of delight and an act of small rebellion; because trout do not lie or cheat and cannot be bought or bribed or impressed by power, but respond only to quietude and humility and endless patience; because I suspect that men are going along this way for the last time, and I for one don't want to waste the trip; because mercifully there are no telephones on trout waters; because only in the woods can I find solitude without loneliness; because bourbon out of an old tin cup always tastes better out there; because maybe one day I will catch a mermaid; and finally, not because I regard fishing as being so terribly important but because I suspect that so many of the other concerns of men are equally unimportant— and not nearly so much fun.

Enough is often more than enough; by which I mean that while it may certainly be foolish not to learn from both the mistakes and the successes of the past, it can be counter-productive to dwell for too long on bygone, halcyon anecdotes, especially when one has set out to write and illustrate a book about a world fly-fishing safari as one travels. Let me therefore move on to Part II of this book, taking fly rod, paints, camera and notebook with me, when I tour, fish, describe and illustrate the Monaro in southeast mainland Australia and then some of the wild country of Tasmania.

At the outset (and even before I packed the car) I felt that I must point out that, in such an undertaking, one cannot possibly cover everything. For example: Victoria has excellent trout fishing, as does to a lesser extent South Australia, the West and the Armidale and Oberon districts of New South Wales, yet they are not covered here. Similarly, within the Monaro there are hundreds of favourite haunts which I do not mention—maybe to the disappointment, but more probably to the relief, of those fly-casting custodians who guard their secrets. No, my travels in Part II were restricted to less than half-a-dozen areas which I have fished and have come to love, which I have always wanted to paint, which have provided me with endless anecdotes—some of which I would like to share— and which, above all in my view anyway, represent a collective (if incomplete) panorama of fly-fishing for trout in Australia.

I make no apology for this, and similarly, when I swapped the car for the aeroplane for Part III of this book covering some of the Southern Hemisphere, and for Part IV when I switched to the north, my *modus operandi* was likewise constrained by time, travel, equipment cartage and ability. Again I make no apology for singling out some areas and missing others. Maybe someday I will be in a position to cover a fraction of those areas I missed; but I doubt very much if one could ever cover them all in a lifetime while, at the same time, allowing time to explore, fish, write, paint, photograph and record.

Negley Farson came close to it in his beautifully written *Going Fishing*, but he was a travelling journalist by profession who just happened to be a fanatical fisherman (although he would have probably preferred it put the other way around, and he would certainly have used a more gentle adjective than 'fanatical'). He had almost endless opportunity for writing and fishing, and had his book beautifully illustrated with pen-and-ink drawings by C. F. Tunnicliffe.

Another 'biblical' reference I used repeatedly

when planning my safari was Tony Pawson's *Fly-Fishing Around the World*—an extremely well written and comprehensive guide for the international game fisherman. But, once again, it was not constrained by the need for the author to paint, and in some cases photograph and record. He often in fact very sensibly relied on local knowledge being supplied.

On the other hand, Ernest Schwiebert has not only travelled and written extensively about fly-fishing, but has provided his own detailed illustrations as well; his *A River for Christmas* is a good example. Those intrepid, travelling author/illustrators, however, are not numerous, although, as I started travelling in 1991, *World's Greatest Flyfishing Locations* was released—a beautifully produced 'where to' book covering 40 locations, compiled by 18 authors and 20 photographers (the majority of whom doubled as the authors).

I simply wish to establish my constraints. If my book goes one-tenth of the way down the fishing and literary path that Farson and Schweibert pioneered and Pawson detailed I shall be surprisingly happy. So I have bypassed vast areas of Australia and, if I read Farson, Pawson and many others correctly, I have also regrettably sidestepped Chile, Tierra del Fuego, the Falklands, Ethiopia, Uganda, Kenya, Malawi, Zambia, Tanzania, Sudan, Lebanon, Turkey, Kashmir, Pakistan, Japan, Sri Lanka, the Azores, Czechoslovakia, Romania, Yugoslavia, Poland, Finland, Switzerland, Germany, Italy, Austria, Portugal, Spain, France, Luxembourg, Belgium, Sweden, Ireland, Scotland, eastern U.S.A., Alaska, Papua New Guinea, the former U.S.S.R., Belize—and probably more. On the other hand, at least I managed Greenland and Baffin Island (there won't be many in that club) and, someday, I hope to make a dent in the rest.

My mudmaps were also constrained: by my mind's eye of the areas drawn, by the need to preserve a modicum of secrecy, and by the length of my experience in each area. I remember I once sketched a private map of Berinda's fishing holes in 1981 which bears little resemblance to how I see the place (complete with Merlin's Grotto) today—and that, I believe, is healthy. So those fishermen who are sticklers for accuracy (especially when it comes to cartography) will find plenty of mistakes—most of which are deliberate or the fault of the mind's eye, but all of which should allow the visitor to find and fish my areas with success and, above all, with happiness.

PART II

SAFARI BEGINNINGS IN SOUTHEAST AUSTRALIA

6

Monaro Country Around Adaminaby and Yaouk

He used to buy my cast-off sheep after shearing each year—culls we called them, but they certainly weren't second-rate discards. In fact they were excellent fine-wool merinos, sold to make room on my small acreage for the next drop of lambs, sold because of their age (I never kept sheep after their fifth year) and sold to maintain the character of my flock. In all other respects they were damn good, 18-micron sheep.

He used to truck them down to Yaouk (pronounced 'yie-yack', as in 'kayak'), feed them on a diet of sticks, shale and granite, and turn them into 17-micron superfines without (apparently and miraculously) reducing the quantity of wool. Indeed, when he wrote to me to acknowledge the safe arrival of some wethers I sold him in '91, just before I sold Berinda, he said: 'They are being trained in the river paddock, where there is no feed. Next week they will be moved to the scrub paddock where there is no feed at all, and then they should fine up nicely with their brothers and kin.'

And after shearing these culls each year, he would invite me to Yaouk under the pretext of some good fishing but with the ulterior and secret (until the second time) motive of being able to gloat over the high price his (my?) woolclip raised at auction; really quite unbecoming conduct for a fly-fisherman.

'He'—a good friend, my fishing companion of long standing and one-time fellow naval officer—is Peter Blackman who, with his wife Jill, lives at The Outpost II, in my opinion the best fishing lodge on the Monaro, on the banks of the Murrumbidgee at Yaouk, among the mountains of southern New South Wales. They bought a thousand acres there

in 1984, left them while they were in England for two and a half years, and returned in 1988 to build the homestead, run Jill's flock of cashmere goats, the sheep, and perform a mass of other activities.

The house welcomes guests into large comfortable living and dining rooms with wide windows that bring the river almost indoors and allow glimpses of kangaroos, platypus, wombats, rabbits and rising fish. Jill loves to cook and Peter has a notable cellar. Guests are accommodated in two separate twin bedrooms with private bathrooms, both of which have direct access outside to the fishing so no one need ever disturb anyone else, not even before each day starts nor well after it finishes—the most sacrosanct of all fishing hours. Which presupposes, of course, that the annual, summer daylight-saving problem has been solved: whether to dine at seven before the evening rise, or at ten afterwards. And, if the latter timing is more sensibly chosen (good food and wine are better enjoyed after an expedition rather than rushed before it), the question remains whether to take in the next morning rise at five having had only four hours sleep. There is little doubt that The Outpost II can handle the choice whatever it may be; the place is a credit to Peter and Jill's dedication and work. The dream of 1984, now a reality, is in harmony with the fisherman; Peter's sympathy with and understanding of the sport is evident in his guiding, while Jill not only knows the way to a fisherman's heart, but ties flies as well.

The house looks over the river a little downstream from Yaouk Bridge in hilly, eucalypt country. But, if one follows the track out to the property entrance on the Shannons Flat road, one finds one has left

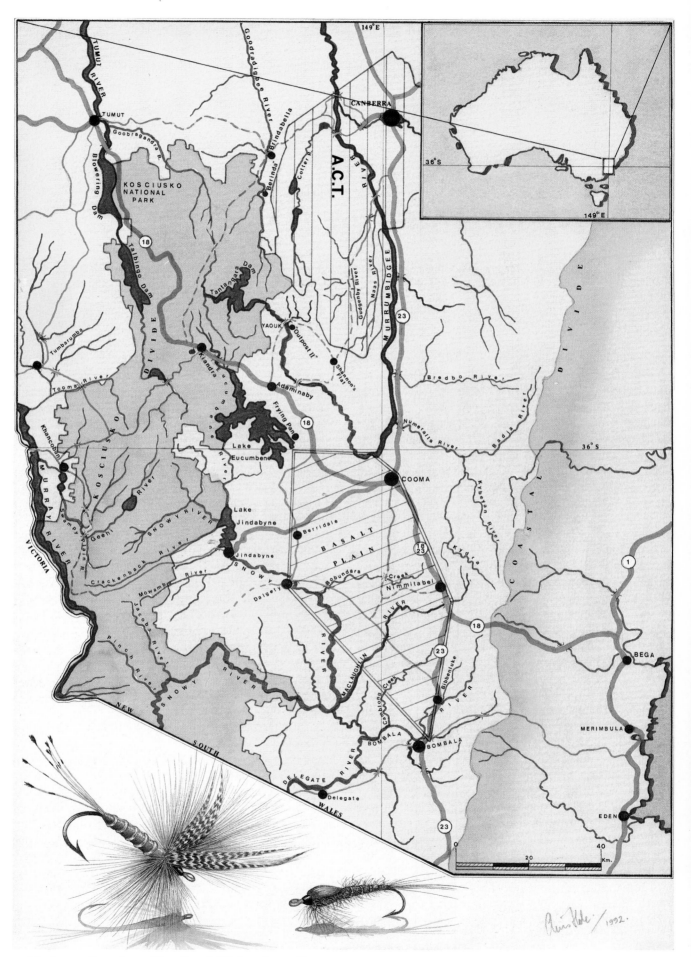

Mudmap of southern New South Wales, Australia.

The Outpost II on the banks of the Murrumbidgee River.

the hills temporarily to gaze out over the bowl of Yaouk Plain. This harsh yet fascinatingly beautiful playground is surrounded by the homestead hills to the south, and mountains in the distance to the north and west and, to a lesser extent, to the east. It is a drowsy place in summer, yet exciting when the Murrumbidgee's feeder streams are full of fat brown trout and the grasshoppers smack their yellow and black wings, while in keeping with the haze and the heat, the whole plain seems content to retire. Winter, by contrast, is bitterly cold with a mantle of frost and snow from early autumn waiting until late spring before the tussocks begin to thaw, the next generation of winged wildlife hatches and the stacatto call of plover mates warns of an incoming dive-bomber attack. It differs from the rest of Monaro in climate, soil and rainfall yet it is similar in that it is an area of character, contrast and extremes.

It is also, unquestionably, an area of exciting brown trout fishing, especially in late summer and early autumn when the activity in the small feeder streams is at its height. They bubble through the plains, past ups and downs of tussocks. Only three feet wide and two deep at most, they twist and meander with such drunken haphazardness that often the only way to fish them is to cast a nymph on a short line blind over the next corner and wait for the audible splash of the take, or watch to see the line jolt out. And when the fish at the other end is three or four pounds of wild brown, the results can be anything but predictable.

I motored down there from Canberra in '91 to absorb the place, perhaps to fish, but certainly to start my safari by writing this chapter and to do some painting.

The trip from Canberra (itself only three and a half hours' drive or 40 minutes by air from Sydney) takes a little under two hours if driving via Honeysuckle Creek (Space Station), the Gudgenby River, Namadgi National Park and Shannons Flat on predominantly dirt roads; or a little over if driving the Monaro Highway (23) through Cooma and the Alpine Highway (19) through Adaminaby, mainly on bitumen. Both routes are equally interesting in their own way; the former for its views of the Australian high bush country and wildlife as it climbs from the beauty of Naas Valley into the dense, alpine bush west of the Murrumbidgee and Naas systems, to emerge in desolate pioneering country east of Yaouk. The bitumen route represents the corridor to the ski country in winter. The long southward run to Cooma reveals the Murrumbidgee Valley to the west with hills in the distance, a veritable kaleidoscope of colour in the changing light. After Cooma, the skiers would normally take the left fork to Jindabyne and Kosciusko, while the track to The Outpost II is to the right through undulating country to Adaminaby and then north to Yaouk. Adaminaby, a regional centre for agriculture, skiing and fishing, is the second town to bear the name; the first, an old pioneering and mining town, was partially submerged when Lake Eucumbene was formed in 1958.

On the way down to Yaouk on each visit, or on the way home, or at some time during my stay (and often all three) I call in at the old Snowgoose Hotel at Adaminaby, a famous haven for skiers, fishermen and local characters like Claudie, who 'oddjobs' around the hotel, and Dave, the scar-faced fellow who leases the local sandwich shop and owns the fishing tackle store. I have a beer or two with Claudie, and buy a bottle of cold hock before picking up sandwiches (smoked trout pate and turkey with cranberry sauce) at that 'Best Goddam Sandwich Shop on the Monaro', almost next door. That delicious combination has long been my ritual lunch whether fishing the Murrumbidgee or its feeders, the Eucumbene River, Tantangra or Nungar Creeks, or Lake Eucumbene itself. I cannot imagine fishing that area, or even passing by, without it.

The Murrumbidgee at The Outpost II is made up of a series of fast runs spilling into wide, deep pools, then narrowing again at the tails before repeating itself, but with a very definite and separate character to each beat. It is tea-coloured and inviting with its banks changing from impossible cliffs to easy, grassy verges abundant in eucalypt and tea-tree. I don't recall the names of all the pools—Peter has named them and I once promised to do a mudmap for him (perhaps next visit if he doesn't boast about his woolclip)—I generally think of them numerically upstream or downstream from the house.

My favourite is the third upstream, a wide pool, deep only at the head and tail, and shallow and weedy over the rest of its length. It shimmers magically in the summer evening light, with spinners and circles from head to tail. It always holds good browns, frequently in the shallow gutters between reed beds, but these super-sensitive fish require a very careful approach. I think I've caused more bow waves than hooked fish in that stretch and maybe that's why I keep going back for more—in the hope that, someday, I'll reverse the order.

A further pool of great charm, character and confusion is almost equidistant downstream from the house. At the tail of the second downstream, where it runs into the head of the third, lies an island, with a fast run on one side and a trickle on the other (except in spate when both sides run fast). The tail, the head and the runs all hold good fish and, at the opening of the 1990 season, a house guest had this to say in my fishing diary:

> Between 80- and 100-pounds of energetic fury on a Green Nymph landed on the island with the help of Eric (The Outpost dog). A remarkable fighting animal, great strength and a strong swimmer, this grey kangaroo never looked like losing but my bent Green Nymph is now called the Kangaroo Nymph.

Away downstream the character of the Murrumbidgee changes. It leaves the hills, discards most of its rocky outcrops and, near Adaminaby, before turning eastwards towards Cooma, it changes character again, broadening to flow quietly through cultivated plain country. There it has ripples and runs between long pools, contained by a few shallow embankments but mainly by muddy edges held together with pebbles, tussock and waterlilies. Midstream the water is clear and tea-coloured, abundant throughout in those food sources so tempting to trout.

I made my way down there very early one morning when the washed-ink sky was just visible in the half-light through gaps above fog which clung to the black surface of the water, silencing its ripples. Although nothing was moving, I felt a sixth sense of the presence of fish—an experience, if proved accurate, not all that common among truthful fly fishermen.

I chose a place on the edge of the river among weeds and shallows where, without having to alter my position, I could cast into the backwaters surrounding me, to the edge of the main river nearest me, or across and upstream just short of the lily patches on the far side. I had been there before in the fog and caught trout, blind, on weighted nymphs. But this time for some good reason I remained motionless, rod with weighted Tinsel Nymph held loosely, carefully watching for telltale bulging among the weeds, or for any sign of pupal life.

I don't recall how long I waited thus, and I'm sure it was only the changing light, as the growing warmth of the sun diffused the fog, that sustained my concentration. At last I saw, across in the waterlilies, telltale bow waves and bulges of fish feeding on nymphs. I waited a little longer to allow a regular pattern to develop before stripping line in preparation for casting.

A multiplier reel on an eight and a half foot, six-weight rod controlling a weight-forward, six-weight line, probably nine feet of cast tapering to a four pound tippet with a single size-12 Tinsel Nymph at its end, was about to be propelled towards the lilies, exploding what was left of the mist, when I changed my mind.

There was something bigger close to my feet—at least, in that microcosm, I convinced myself it was bigger.

Inside that circle of immediate backwater was a speckled black back and dorsal fin. Had I missed its camouflage earlier through more total colour concentration elsewhere in that changing light? Whatever the reason, it had to be three or four pounds of brown trout, grovelling for pupae, oblivious of me in my stagnation, seven feet in front of me in the four-inch deep backwater at my feet.

Thank God I hadn't moved my cast over him; thank Him also that I didn't move too quickly; and thank whomsoever was left in the Trinity to observe my gyrations, that I managed to persuade a good length of flyline, with its long cast and weighted nymph, to drop the artificial lightly near (but not too near) to my changed target. In fact, somehow, most of the stripped line remained inactive at my feet while just enough was out in front to allow the nymph to bounce off a lily stalk into the water with the precision of *trichopteric* orchestration.

The trout moved with total dedication, nothing would have stopped it, and battle was joined.

As expected, his initial run was to clear the backwater and make for midstream, requiring split concentration on my part. I wanted to watch him accelerate through the mud and weeds with half his back out of the water, at the same time I knew I had to control the fly line piled up at my feet. For once it all worked, the fish finished his first run in midstream and finned the current with the hook still in place, and I could keep pressure on him while recovering the slack line onto the reel.

His second run was to turn and race downstream, so quickly that the line was left behind as I paid out slack, the weight in the water keeping the hook firm. Then he turned and faced upstream and I

had to recover quickly. A lull followed and I took the chance to recover line and apply more pressure when he started surface-flopping, and I kept the rod tip high as I moved downstream towards him recovering rapidly as I went. But he wasn't finished.

As I drew near and could see him plainly in the water, he equally saw me and made one last frantic dash for the lilies on the far bank. I held him up short and slowly worked him towards me, at the same time moving backwards to a pebbled stretch where I knew I could beach him. Round One was mine as I slid him over the stones, unhooked him, weighed him at four and a quarter pounds and gently released him for another day.

It was 9 a.m. and I knew that the backwaters and the edge nearest me were too disturbed to produce another fish for a little while. But the lily pads on the other side hadn't been troubled and I moved a short distance downstream from where I could cast up and across into a gap between them. It was a relatively easy cast and, with the rod held finally at 10 o'clock, the weighted nymph plopped into the water on target and started to sink and move downstream in the current past the lilies. Without bouncing off weeds it is very difficult to get a weighted nymph into the water without that telltale 'plop'.

But it didn't matter. The nymph had moved only a foot or so from the point of entry when the line went tight. It didn't just hesitate, the fish took aggressively fast and immediately jumped clear of the water, spraying the lilies for yards all around, dragging the line with him. It was a smaller fish and a rainbow but it fought well before I grassed it.

I took time to consolidate, to check my knots and to study the lilies upstream on the far side before further commitment. All was clear and bright in the morning sunlight; the narrowness of my fog-blinkered vision was replaced by a wide-angle view, and a gentle breeze was blowing enough to ruffle the water at the edge of the lilies. Perfect conditions, and the sixth sense was still with me.

Even so I was worried about the splash the weighted fly made when it hit the water; I couldn't be sure of bouncing off weeds every time, and I was certain the increased light would lead to a greater awareness in my quarry. Despite the ripple on the surface, I changed to a size-12 Stick Caddis Nymph—dark seal's fur protruding from a yellow, floss-silk 'stick' with pheasant tippet tail wisps. As it was not weighted, I soaked it thoroughly at my feet.

Upstream a little, and then back to watching the

Young Nick fishing the Murrumbidgee.

lilies. There it was again, the bulging of a feeding fish! Take your time; do it right; get the line out until the trace appears to be above the target; check it, and watch the fly drop. Gently it touches the water just short of the lilies and, because of the soaking, it breaks the surface meniscus and starts to sink slowly.

The fisherman's concentration is total, focusing on the end of the cast as it enters the water and out to no more than a metre beyond. Yet, without having time to fully register, I realise a bulge has passed through my circle of concentration and taken the cast downstream in less time than awakening realisation can be transposed into muscle movement. The tightening of the rod is automatic and, anyway, the fish's attack has caused enough drag to set the hook before I am fully aware.

Already 20 metres downstream, and with a belly of fly line astern helping to keep the pressure up, the fish leaps!

If it is a big fish, something almost alien happens to a fisherman at that time. Regardless of the adrenalin level, he tries hard to estimate size fairly accurately. His actions with rod and line continue automatically while he weighs and measures his fish in his mind's eye.

I had seen double figure browns before and watched them in many circumstances. I put this one well above ten pounds in the knowledge that, in all probability, it would go beyond the stretch of my little spring balance in the pocket of my fishing vest (which stopped at 11).

With the rod tip taking the strain, and the reel humming as the dacron backing joined the flyline in the water astern of the fish, I started to move downstream.

Until then I had completely forgotten my legs!

I kept him at 50 to 60 metres as he continued, thankfully in midstream. Then, in a twinkling, he turned about, forcing me to run backwards through the mud, weeds and backwater, regaining line with rod held high as he powered upstream. It was a further miracle that I remained upright.

Opposite the lilies again, and he jumped once more! Maybe to get a fix on me and his surroundings? Whatever it was, he seemed to like the idea and left the water in flying spray three more times as I tried to cushion the pressure with the rod tip and, perhaps, throw him off balance. I badly needed to get some of the loose backing and line under control and to ease the work on my left hand.

He must have been attuned to me; after his fourth leap (or fifth since he was hooked), for some seconds he remained almost motionless in midstream, finning the current. I wound all but a loop back onto the reel and applied side strain. This sent him fast in the opposite direction, at right angles to the stream, straight for the lily pads. I backed up with as much strain as I imagined a four-pound tippet could take and, at the last second, forced him into another downstream sprint.

Again the line looped behind him, and again the faded blue dacron shot out from the tip of the rod as he seemed to disappear into the distance. I worried about my flyline-to-backing knot, and I worried more about the connection of the backing to the spool. I have a recurring nightmare vision of the fish turning when all my backing is out, and me being unable to recover because the loose connecting loop is spinning ineffectively round the rotating spool.

But I am lucky. He finishes his run before the backing disappears and the connecting knots hold firm. Again I have moved downstream to recover line and again he turns and powers back towards the lilies forcing me backwards through the mud and tussocks.

By now, I figure, he has 'done the hundred in evens' three times and, with two further jumps on the return run, 'competed for the bar at the six-foot level' seven times. What an athlete! What an Olympian! He stops again midstream, out from the lilies. I recover line and try to ease him towards me; he is close to the surface now with his dorsal fin and tail breaking clear at times, his head yawing from side to side in the current, trying to throw the pressure from his mouth.

I ease him closer. He is huge! Undoubtedly far too big for the spring balance—I imagine the butcher's weighing machine at Adaminaby.

Then he sees me. In one almighty swirl he is off, downstream again, bending the rod tip alarmingly and making the reel wail in protest.

'PING' and the rod comes upright, trailing slack line!

'YOOOO—NEVVAHCUMDOWNAGIN-SUNNUVABITCHINGBAARRSTUD!'

I drop the rod at my feet and my arms and legs shake visibly as I gaze downstream at the silver shape jumping clear and crashing back into the water 50 metres away.

It is over. Finished. There is nothing more. My vision expands from a spot which is nothing but fish to take in the river and the plain again.

I recover my rod and notice the Stick Caddis Nymph still at the end of the tippet! The fight must have been right, my four-pound tippet held and my knots couldn't be blamed. On closer inspection I find the hook has straightened completely—and obviously pulled out. A faulty batch of size-12 longshanks? Who knows?

The strength of my weighted Tinsel Nymph is still buried deep in the woolpatch on the left shoulder of my fishing vest.

I figured it was an easier track home through Adaminaby and, anyway, the pub lay in that direction.

I entered the bar and saw the usual crowd: Claudie; Dave, the scar-faced fellow who runs 'The Best Goddam Sandwich Shop... etc.'; and some others. No one said anything much until I'd ordered a whisky; then a voice:

Claudie: 'How'd you go?'

Me: ' I lost a bastard!'

Nothing else was said.

Nothing else needed saying.

We got down to the serious business of drinking and telling lies which, by the time twilight had settled softly over the Monaro, helped cushion a loss I shall remember forever.

7

Lake Eucumbene—Anxieties about the Future

The Snowy Mountains Hydro Electric Scheme (SMHES), which began in 1949 and was 25 years in construction, is one of the world's greatest engineering and social achievements. The latter, because it represented the beginning, in Australia, of the integration of the migrant population and everything which that has come to mean. Volumes have been written about the social significance of this part of our history; I'll not delay to add to it here.

In engineering parlance, however, the achievement includes 17 major dams, reservoirs, pondages and intakes, spread between 290 and 1,550 metres above sea level; seven power stations, one dedicated pumping station, 12 inter-connecting tunnels stretching 145 kilometres, and 80 kilometres of confined aqueduct. It covers a total area in excess of 3,200 square kilometres and can produce 3,740 megawatts of power, upon which a great deal of southeastern Australia depends, including a guaranteed 30 per cent of the power requirement of the nation's capital, Canberra, undoubtedly resented by some at times of parliamentary ugliness.

The official death toll during construction was 121, staggering by present-day standards, and this did not include off-duty road deaths largely attributable to speed, alcohol, shocking roads and extreme weather conditions. Nor did it include a number of suicides caused by post-Second World War traumas, loneliness and other associated stress conditions.

It would most probably be impossible for such a scheme to have been undertaken—even contemplated—post-1974, due to environmental and human constraints. It was a one-off masterpiece built in juxtaposition to an era that allowed it, indeed welcomed it. New Zealand, by contrast, continued much later with the construction of additional major hydroelectric development, often without providing fish ladders for migrating fish, among other ecological mistakes—one of the few follies in her remarkable salmonid fishery history.

When full to capacity, the lakes of the SMHES hold 13 times the volume of the vast Sydney Harbour. In the middle of these lakes lies Lake Eucumbene, holding, when full to capacity, the largest volume of water, 4.8 million megalitres, or nine times the volume of that harbour. Construction of Eucumbene Dam was finished in 1958 and resulted in the Eucumbene River being dammed from west of Providence Portal, where Alpine, Swamp and Gang-gang Creeks join, for 25 kilometres south to where the 116-metre high earthfill wall, 579 metres across the top, holds the water before the then controlled river trickles downstream to Lake Jindabyne. The damming also extends the lake a further 24 kilometres to the east and south, including seven major arms and inlets.

Originally the settlement strategy around the lake foreshores was generally confined to existing settlements at Anglers Reach, Old Adaminaby, Buckenderra and Providence Portal. Later, two further areas emerged, but more about this and subsequent development later.

Predictably, pre-1950s fishermen tend to expound on the 'good old days' before the SMHES and the dams, when trout fishing was said to be much better than after completion of the scheme. Certainly the fish taken from those rivers (the Tumut, Murrumbidgee, Eucumbene, Snowy, Geehi and the

Swampy Plains) before the scheme, according to the written and photographic record, were on average, bigger and arguably more plentiful. But the number of fishermen, and fishing pressures were then markedly less. The additional fishing area created by the lakes in the scheme has given more room for more anglers; the initial fishing bonanzas as new lakes took over soil rich in trout food were spectacular; and today's number of trout, in Lake Eucumbene for example, remains significant.

Whatever the reality, since completion of the scheme the fishing, measured by any yardstick, has been good. It is more accessible over a larger area, and it can still produce excellent results around the lake edges when water levels rise, allowing the fish to move close inshore to take an abundance of new food and to chase emerging dragonflies in summer and autumn. Additionally, and in my opinion unfortunately, the fishing is promoted as being good in the lake feeder streams during brown trout spawning migrations when, controversially, all inlets are left open until much too late.

Nevertheless, the SMHES, and whatever good or bad its creation did to the local salmonid fishery, are now matters of history. The real challenges endure as how to manage these matters to provide the best sport while preserving the resource in the face of ever-increasing fishing and other human pressures.

And management has been at the hub of the challenge since trout were first introduced into New South Wales in 1887. From that time, until the mid-1930s, the Department of Fisheries was responsible for hatching, rearing and distribution, aided by anglers and bodies such as the New South Wales Rod Fishers' Society. The acclimatisation societies were then formed, and became responsible for these matters—indeed management of all salmonids and their waters was vested in the societies under *The N.S.W. Fisheries and Oyster Farm Act (1935) Section 45*. In 1959, hatcheries (only) were resumed by the Department of Fisheries, apparently reluctantly, and this was followed, ten years later, by regulation allowing the commercial cultivation of trout for profit through private hatcheries, by which time government hatcheries were reduced to two. Subsequently, total salmonid management was transferred to the then New South Wales Department of Agriculture and Fisheries by amending the 1935 Act in 1979 (*Act 112, 1979*).

Over the years, various institutes, councils and assemblies were created in addition to the acclimatisation societies, with the aim of presenting a unified voice to advise government on fishery management, together with other tasks. The Institute of Freshwater Anglers (then 'Fishermen') was formed in 1958, and the Freshwater Fishermen's Assembly in 1966. The institute initially provided direct advice to the New South Wales minister responsible for fisheries. However, with the formation of the New South Wales Amateur Fisherman's Advisory Council in 1968 (retitled the Recreational Fishing Advisory Council, after gazettal as a statutory body in 1979), advice to the minister was subsequently given in conjunction with this advisory council. The assembly, as a non-statutory body, represented the interests of the States and, from 1984, became a founding member of the Australian Recreational and Sport Fishing Confederation with input thereby to the commonwealth government—whose interest seems largely political on an 'as available' basis, although the confederation is lobbying hard for federal government support for recreational angling both in terms of policy and funding.

If you think that is complicated, consider further that the other states where salmonid fishing is a prime sport, namely Tasmania and Victoria, have their own inland rules (or lack thereof), regulations and advisory bodies. And all three states have dozens of individual clubs and organisations, all with their own views and policies.

Moreover, there were additional factors of a less tangible nature that influenced the conglomerate in New South Wales.

From the mid-1960s onwards, an ever-increasing number of the vast recreational fishing public began to realise that there were trout in the mountains; that (with the sort of reverse-snobbery so admired by Australians) one didn't have to be a rich fly rod waver to catch them; that they were good eating, and (with double-reverse snobbery) a special attraction on any dining table. In short: 'Let's go get 'em!'

Maybe it was the fault of the societies, assemblies, institutes and advisory councils for failing to educate this influx in the real joys of trout fishing and the need for conservation, but I doubt it. I think that any attempt would have been brushed aside with accusations about a privileged few trying to guard their domain, and the influx would have come anyway.

As the numbers grew, the voting potential of such a rapidly increasing majority could not have gone unnoticed by those in authority. It was then, I believe, that some unfortunate management decisions were made. Credence was added to my view that the two were connected when a fisheries management official, trying to explain new regulations in 1990 to a group of dedicated Monaro fly-men, finally concluded by saying in desperation: 'But isn't fishing really only about catching fish?' The sad thing was that he actually believed it.

The first unfortunate decision was made when salmonid management was finally transferred from dedicated acclimatisation societies to government departments, and by preceding this legislation with regulations to allow the commercial exploitation of trout through licensed hatcheries. In the first instance it resulted in control being removed from those dedicated to the sport and its preservation, and delivered into the hands of those capable of being influenced, rightly or wrongly, by a need to appease an increasing voice in the voting public. In the second, it resulted in the predictable exploitation of a sport resource for purely commercial gain, with the side effects of slaughter (and slaughter not necessarily contained within licensed hatcheries) to maintain profitability, and the dangerous possibility of the introduction and spread of disease through commercial hatcheries where, again, profit was the overriding motive.

Next, and once more apparently for reasons of political gain, this time by an incoming New South Wales coalition government, inland fishing licences were abolished in 1988 for National Party reasons. This resulted in a little less revenue which might have otherwise been used to support the sport, and which, had licences been retained and perhaps increased (and even been supplemented by consolidated revenue), could have been used to secure the fishery in a viable manner. As it was, fishery officer numbers were reduced to offset the loss in revenue and the need to administer it, thus further compounding the inability to secure the resource—quite probably to the satisfaction of the influx.

In 1935, the closed season to protect spawning trout in the Eucumbene River was gazetted as 1 May until 30 September. Over a period of time it was amended, bit by bit, until, in 1975 (and re-affirmed in 1990), it was reduced to close from the Sunday nearest 1 July to the Sunday nearest 1 November each year. The reasons given by government management were: To protect the later spawning migration of rainbow trout, which were said to be otherwise heavily exploited in October; and to allow exploitation (and those last two words must be hard for anyone to swallow) of the brown trout spawning run in May and June, as it was stated that the browns were an under-used resource. It was claimed that these arguments were sustained by 25 years' research costing $500,000 and rendering Lake Eucumbene arguably the most thoroughly researched and best documented freshwater fishery in the Southern Hemisphere. I say 'arguably' because that figure represents $20,000 annually—hardly enough to pay the salary of one research scientist and to provide his equipment and support (even after allowing for indexation). It was further argued that droughts and the lack of suitable spawning areas controlled trout stocks, not a shortage of brood stock.

On the other hand, it has always been widely accepted that rainbows are much easier to catch than browns. Furthermore, the influx, adding to and comprising the majority of the freshwater fishing fraternity—the majority who vote—are irregular weekend and holiday fishermen, whose collective character may or may not be exemplary, but whose aim, nonetheless, is to catch fish easily, almost regardless of any other consideration. And why not, they may ask, if the fish are there? Sadly, this majority, in their enthusiastic naivete—even carelessness—are egged on and maintained, maybe increased, by a minority of fishing journalists (steeped in 'quickfisho' cliches) whose very bread and butter comes from keeping their readers flush with fish regardless of any conservation considerations.

Thus the swapping of the rainbow exploitation for the brown would seem to satisfy that voting majority while, at the same time, the exploitation (or slaughter—it can be applied regardless of genus) of migrating-run browns could be justified by 25 years of research which apparently indicated we have too many of the species anyway!

May I be forgiven for thinking that, although the scientific research may have been commendable, the results in terms of regulations smell of politics? I think so.

In the armed services we used to conduct extremely complicated exercises (of the mind), where one was given a particularly complex situation and asked to deduce, with step-by-step presented logic (at call later), the best solution to the dilemma. It was called 'Appreciating the Situation'. The smartarses, to save time, or for a number of other reasons not related to the truth of the matter, used to begin at the conclusion (the result they wanted regardless of logical argument), then construct their arguments in reverse to arrive at the beginning of the problem! 'Situating the Appreciation' it was called—a dangerously illogical shortcut (or a useful tool, depending on one's point of view).

Perhaps I could be further forgiven for thinking

that management may have entered into this trap to appease the influx in the 1970s and 1980s. The question poses itself: if 25 years of research was made evident around 1990, it means it must have started in the mid-60s—the time of the beginning of the influx. Why? To 'prove' we should protect rainbows for the masses?

I would like to know: What's wrong with protecting both species anyway?

But there is more. In 1990, again apparently to appease the influx of 'born-again belly fishermen' at the expense of sport fishermen and the resource, but with the excuse of simplifying management, further regulations were introduced into the 1990/'91 season (and beyond). The fact that, despite some adverse comments by a number of freshwater sport fishermen in the various societies, institutes and assemblies, the regulations were still adopted, suggested to me at the time that either the influx had bought up a controlling share, or management had made up its mind again anyway. I was later informed that, although some members of the institute initially opposed a number of these regulations, as a body they became bogged down in detail during the consultative process, and the old *Schedule Regulations* were dispensed with, undoubtedly to the glee of management and to the subsequent sorrow of the institute. My misgivings were partly confirmed.

The principles underlying the new regulations, in addition to those already discussed concerning the Eucumbene River, were: to refine the closed season to a single closed season where possible; to open impoundments all year round; to abolish 'fly only' waters (keeping but a few for 'fly and lure'); to redefine 'downstream limits'; to allow fishermen to carry two rods in most impoundments; and to remove all restrictions on trout baits other than live fish and actual roe or products containing it.

In effect, the influx, through management, appeared hell-bent on turning all of a once magnificent and delicate sporting resource into a Saturday afternoon, beer-swilling mudflats expedition to fill the belly for tea . . . and the ballot boxes at voting time?

Old John Sautelle foresaw many of these future problems, and had it pretty well right when he argued for greater control but better access; for a more complex fishery that catered for all tastes. He was in favour of stocking only to meet the requirements, primarily relying on Australian-acclimatised wild trout. Wild browns could satisfy the sportsman and wild rainbows give others enjoyment. Put-and-take stocking could be undertaken in certain areas to satisfy food requirements, and appropriate stocking of both wild and stock-bred fish could be used sparingly to make up shortfalls. He further argued for certain areas for certain types, and closed seasons to protect spawning and to support the overall requirement. Policing and funding were to work hand in hand to support his concept; appropriately charged licences supplemented by consolidated revenue to administer the scheme, coupled with adequate policing and realistic fines to maintain its security and to add to revenue.

Whatever the truth of the matter, it must be put right so that all can have a go, each to his own taste, and not be biased towards one side or the other just because of a current majority, or to ease administration. A number of overseas countries, where salmonids have been native for millions of years, have sensibly tight controls and concomitant management practices developed over a long time. We would do very well to learn from them—not copy, as some practices may not suit us and others may be wrong—but certainly learn.

I would like to see Sautelle's concept pursued; I would like to see inland licences resumed and at an appropriate cost; commercial exploitation of salmonids severely restricted and tightly policed; closed seasons regulated so as not to interfere with spawning migrations; bag and size limits adjusted to maintain fish stocks; certain areas left to natural wild trout sustenance, others stocked (but only to make up shortfalls), and yet others stocked for put-and-take. I would be very much in favour of both wild and stocked areas being dedicated to certain types of fishing; I would do away with the two-rod concession and limit anglers to one only; specify particular fly, lure and bait areas; prohibit certain baits totally; and introduce barbless hooks and a catch-and-release policy in many specific areas. I would like to see this properly policed with effective penalties for offences. I would be very much in favour of paying for the administration of such a scheme through marked increases in inland licence costs. I believe that government supplementary financing would be needed and ought to be provided commensurate with the numbers participating in the sport, noting that a proportion of revenues received from taxes on sales of recreational fishing equipment ought to be used for this purpose. Finally, it is my fervent hope that management, whoever it may be, might always be driven by a need to preserve, enhance and control the resource for the benefit of all users as to their tastes, and never by the wants of one group (even a voting majority). I also wonder whether it would be too much to ask that all states involved in the salmonid fishery were similarly controlled.

That, unfortunately, is not all!

Let's dwell for a moment, while discussing the complex and controversial business of management, on the potential for commercial development of inland fishing and its infrastructure. Do we really want our lakes and rivers to be surrounded by a mass of hotels, motels, caravan parks, camping areas, marinas, airstrips, villages, roads, and their associated support; administration, garbage, sewerage and waste disposal; newspapers, telephones, Neighbourhood Watch committees, Harper Valley PTAs and all those other things (often hidden underground) on the dark side of civilisation?

Fly-fishermen need not refer to Robert Traver or his mermaid to answer that. But consider for a moment, please: perhaps to beat them we must join them? Maybe—just maybe—we should accept the unpalatable truth that development of some sort is inevitable for the very good reasons of increased leisure time, aligned with much increased fishing popularity.

Surely, therefore, *before* such development has a chance to gather pace, outside existing controls, in a haphazard nightmare of designer-striped four-wheel-drive beer-can disposal, toilet papier mâché tents, born-again wildlifers, shark-hook brandishing trailbike riders determined to mount siege on our waterways, concrete highrises with en-suite condom dispensers and push-button pollution, Zen-thinkers freaking out on the dollars possible in condos and subdivision, macho trout bums ready to finance the Zen-thinkers, and ultimately, those who will undoubtedly commit the final atrocity of trying to correct it all *after* it has gone wrong; surely *before* the chance of that creeping nightmare, proper and very much controlled development should be encouraged and, where necessary, development prohibited—to protect what we have, even in its development. After all, the environment and the resource are the reason for development, and thus they become the reason to control it. Developers, and state and local governments must be educated to understand that to kill the former is to kill their attraction and, therefore, the need for the latter.

The alternative, to stand back and let it all happen uncontrolled and then to say: What a pity, but I told you so, is nothing less than a cowardly reversal of responsibility for the crime.

In the end, true trout fishermen will always seek wild, untouched country, and weekend anglers their own easier accessed areas where they can relax and catch a couple of fish for dinner. Why should there be a fight about it when the two objectives are miles apart and yet in juxtaposition sufficient to find answers that might satisfy most while not upsetting the environment?

A development problem, ongoing at the time of writing, is worth examining briefly.

In August 1985 a proposal was put to the Snowy River Shire Council (SRS) by a business consortium to develop a village for 800 people including 125 rural residential holdings at Muzzlewood Inlet on the Frying Pan arm of Lake Eucumbene. Initially, it was strongly supported in principle by the SRS. The Monaro Acclimatisation Society (MAS), however, lodged a written objection to the proposal and consequently attended a council meeting in November 1986, only to find that council seemed poised to approve the proposal with only minor modification, but with no mention of a study of its possible impact on the environment in general and the aquatic habitat in particular—as requested by MAS and Fisheries.

Arguments followed, resulting in the SRS shelving the village part of the proposal in May 1987 and applying to the Minister for Lands for the 125 rural residential holdings only. But, lo and behold! One month later, the minister gazetted *Local Environment Plan No. 35*, specifically including both the village and its rural holdings! MAS followed with legal action seeking rescindment of the plan; in September 1987, the SRS unanimously rejected the entire proposal on the grounds of public interest, but the minister received concurrent legal advice to the effect that *Plan 35* could not be revoked.

To complete this recipe in the witches' cauldron, the developers then appealed against the SRS rejection and threatened legal action if the SRS sought rezoning of the land back to its original status—something requested by MAS in their original written objections in the first place.

The scene was thus set for a multi-directional legal and bureaucratic struggle of file-bursting proportions which, had proper controls over the processing of development proposals been invoked in the first place, might well have been avoided.

The outcome was messy and incomplete. Various interested individuals, bodies and media groups joined the fray; conflicting legal opinion grew, lobbying became an art form and, in February 1989, Judge Steiner, in the New South Wales Lands and Environment Court, handed down a judgment to the effect that *Plan 35* was null and void and of no effect.

This, although almost a return to the beginning, was important in that it ensured that any further plans for development in the area would have to be open to scrutiny and proper environmental planning and, therefore, unlikely to succeed.

It was a midpoint victory for MAS and its supporters and, in particular, for their leader in the fight, Fred Dunford, who had put so much into it; indeed he resigned as secretary of MAS in order to give his unencumbered attention to the matter. MAS (with considerable support) also continued to push for exclusion, at that stage, of further urban development in specific areas. Thus, in March 1989, when it came to processing the Muzzlewood II Development Application, numerous and rigid parameters were placed on the environmental study. This raised the question of costs and, after some argument between the SRS and the developer, SRS agreed to pay some of the costs of the environmental impact study. Finally the developer indicated that, because of the withdrawal of internal financial support, the study would not be needed at that stage.

Could the developer return to the marketplace? Quite probably when the dust settles; anyway he has a perfect right so long as he remains within environmental and other constraints. Would development without appropriate control be allowed in the area? Probably not, but it was an unnecessary and arduous lesson. And what of the future? A fair chance of other mismanaged developments must remain unless proper controls are applied from the outset. Ultimately, alternate sites for development must be chosen in properly serviced regional growth centres, distanced from the rivers and lakes, whose foreshores should be zoned 'non-residential'.

During my safari I shall be keen to study how they control and manage these things overseas. In the meantime a fly-fisherman's look at Lake Eucumbene—in the centre of it all—would seem very appropriate.

I don't normally go fishing in winter, except maybe at Lizard Island or Fiji.

Although the lakes remain open, I prefer the streams and, anyway, I enjoy a winter of tying flies, and writing and painting while I look forward, eagerly, to the glorious opening of the season in spring. Many fly-fishermen I know are of similar mind (although some skip the writing and painting).

My rods, reels and lines are cleaned and stowed away in May and are not normally resumed and rerigged, in great anticipation, until September.

However, a young Englishman, Nick Wolstenholme, used to arrive in Australia for his school summer holidays in the middle of our winter. In doing so, of course, he missed some great Northern Hemispherian fishing; and I do mean missed, because he has a devotion to fly-fishing which exceeds almost my own. I took him once to Lake Pejar, near Goulburn in New South Wales, nearly froze to death, caught one rainbow, broke a lug on my Princess Multiplier and vowed never to fish in winter again.

Then, in the middle of writing this chapter, I realised he was in Australia once more in winter. We had a family friend with a wonderful rustic shack on the edge of Lake Eucumbene at Frying Pan, where the flowering bulbs were just coming out. Why not complete this chapter, *in situ*, with a few days there when Nick could fish and freeze to death and I could write and paint—and probably freeze to death also?

Moreover, I thought, if I was going to such extremes, it would be very foolish not to take a fly rod with me—just as a precaution. After all, one takes whisky to New Zealand in case of snake bite, and everyone knows there are no snakes in New Zealand!

The night before we left Canberra, an intense low-pressure centre moved into the area accompanied by a series of four cold fronts, upper-air disturbances and isobars so tight together that a pin couldn't separate them. It rained all night and, as we turned westwards at Cooma the next morning, we drove into 50-knot winds, horizontal sleet and snow, occasional driving rain and sub-zero temperatures. On the way in, trees had to be chainsawed and towed aside from the track where they had fallen; I was genuinely surprised to see the rustic hut still standing; and the lake was an unbelievable maelstrom of spindrift, horizontal snow, 80-knot winds, two-metre waves, and totally unfishable!

After chopping a pile of wood, thawing out and having lunch, Nick with the indomitable spirit of a true fly-fisherman, had the nerve to suggest that we should venture out into 'Titus Oates' country to 'have a look'!

Have a look, I thought; if one could open one's eyes out there—presupposing, in the first place, that one could stand upright—the eyeballs would have been seared by driving ice! Then I thought that if I'd had to visit England in the midst of our summer, when they were freezing to death in their winter, and I had a chance to stay in a hut beside impounded trout water, I, too, would be urging my

Frying Pan Hut and Lake Eucumbene in winter.

host to have a go—even in extreme conditions.

So I took him to the water.

One hour later, after facing very real dangers and nearly getting crushed by the car door as the wind applied pneumatic force, we returned to the hut, me to continue writing and Nick to stoke the fire.

By chance I remembered it was the evening of Australia's six-yearly census. I had no form, we were miles from nowhere, not even King Herod could

have found us, and one of us was an alien on a short visit! I have never before laughed so much about the apparently serious business of counting heads; it was the first and only time I became, officially, a non-person.

The snow hit the windows and the wind moaned outside and I thought I probably deserved whatever I got. Lakes Onslow and Pejar were summer tranquillity in comparison, and it was only Tuesday.

the fire. Although I never would have taken it on myself, and gave Nick strict instructions about being back by lunchtime, with warnings of hypothermia, I didn't have the heart to suggest he shouldn't do it. He was young and a damn sight more fit than I was. I went back to the shack, to my pads, pencils and watercolours; to work inside for the day, and to get a weather forecast which suggested similar conditions for the rest of the week.

At midday, lo and behold, as I went outside to get some photos of the hut for later sketching, a triumphant, ice-clad figure emerged from the frozen tundra, yelling at the top of his lungs and holding a magnificent three and a half pound brown trout on high.

Total dedication deserves its own.

Total dedication was filleted for a delicious dinner that evening.

Thursday morning was a complete whiteout. There was half a foot of snow outside and a raging blizzard that even Nick had to admit was a fishing-stopper. I braved the elements to drive (slide?) into Adaminaby for more film, victuals and grog. I rang Peter Blackman at Yaouk, he cancelled his proposed visit to us: 'Snowed in and stock to look after', he said. I watched some girls skiing down the main street, rang Canberra to tell them we were still alive and slid back to the hut in four-wheel drive to find Nick still huddled around the fire. At least, I thought, I was getting some good practice for Baffin Island. But more was to come.

That afternoon Nick made me believe things were marginally improved. We examined a couple of reasonably sheltered bays without success, then moved on to the inlet where Nick had caught his fish. A fresh blizzard welcomed our arrival, which prompted me to remark how effective those fishermen's black oilskins are. Except for face and hands they really cut out that penetrating cold in

The Snowgoose Hotel at Adaminaby.

Overnight I thought the roof would go, and we arose on Wednesday morning to persuade ourselves that the winds had eased by about 20 knots—from 80 to 60. Outside was a scene of total desolation: banshee sub-zero winds, driving sleet and visibility down to 50 paces at best. After breakfast, Nick persuaded me, as I knew he would, to drop him at a place where he might fluke a few casts before making a four-kilometre slog back to the shack and sub-zero conditions. I made a mental note to include silk gloves and a balaclava in my overseas packing list.

By late afternoon, with visibility down to 50 paces, driving snow and the wind-chill a minus factor that I didn't want to even contemplate, I indicated to Nick that we ought to get back to the hut while we could still find it. As we approached to ford a little peaty stream at the head of an inlet, I tried one more cast into the outflow.

You guessed it. In blizzard and whiteout conditions I was connected to a very healthy two and a quarter pound jack rainbow. But I couldn't claim any measure of sporting success: I'd fluked it, blind; the fish did the hooking and, in my frozen state, I think he did the playing and pulled himself ashore with me doing very little about it. It was the most appalling weather in which I have ever taken a fish.

Miraculously, Friday dawned a glorious day, with even better weather following on Saturday and Sunday. Nick put in hours of enthusiastic but surprisingly unsuccessful fishing; I caught up with sketching and painting, until then prevented by the conditions, and Peter Blackman arrived one lunchtime with pies, chops and a bottle of hock—rather like a John Wayne Seventh Cavalry relief column. The final days of our visit were, thus, relatively normal and I took the chance to look at the problem areas around Lake Eucumbene.

I visited the museum at Happy Valley, just outside Adaminaby, to see what (if anything) I could find of interest. It was worth the visit because, hidden in other remarkable exhibits, was a copy of page 21 of *Pix* magazine dated 17 December 1949. It was a half-page artist's impression of Adaminaby of the (then) future entitled 'Adaminaby Today'. It depicted a thriving tourist town of about 8,000 on the banks of (the yet to be constructed) Lake Eucumbene. The water was covered in yachts, water-skiers, people swimming, fishermen and speedboats; it was a blatant attempt to whip up recreational support for the SMHES, again relevant to the time; a time before environmental impacts were fully understood, even if they were considered.

Later, on walking the edges of the lake, I found it was impossible not to notice the disgusting condition of the foreshore. Empty tins, bottles, used lavatory paper and all the other muck usually associated with very careless picnicking or camping was in abundance. In almost every instance—and I mean every 50 paces or so—this refuse was in proximity to forked sticks stuck into the sand at the water's edge. Ever heard of a fly-fisherman resting his rod on a stick?

Which leads me to the next point: when the weather cleared over the weekend and the fishermen arrived, they were all bait or spin casters. On enquiry I found they were also all irregular, weekend belly-fishermen. On later observation, Nick and I estimated they were using up to five baited rods apiece, and most of these were left sitting in forked sticks. Finally, on the Sunday morning, Nick came back to the hut for breakfast after a stint of early fishing, to say that he hadn't felt too comfortable when he heard rifle shots and the zip of bullets nearby. A team of rabbit hunters? Possibly, but more likely a team of beer-bottle target shooters.

In six days we saw not one ranger nor one Fisheries officer in the area.

I didn't have to go to extremes to make these observations, they were all blatantly obvious, and obvious at a time of little recreational pressure following very bad weather conditions; it defies imagination to think what it might be like in summer. My views were reinforced: first, any further development must be confined to regional growth centres well back from the lakes; Adaminaby, at six or seven kilometres, should be the absolute inner limit in this instance. Second, tighter and, if necessary, more complex fishing regulations should be brought into force. Third, much more stringent rules covering camping, picnicking and other recreational activities ought to be considered. Finally, the policing of such rules and regulations must be sufficient to make them effective.

There are plenty of examples throughout the world where such steps have been effective and have provided very popular, well-managed and environmentally sound recreation areas.

Robert Traver (again) said it all in *Trout Magic* when he told of his friend, Hal, who had returned to his favourite and secret water one year to find developers working to the rhythm of chainsaws:

'Did you try fishing the creek?' I managed to say.
'Lacked the heart,' Hal said, sadly wagging his head. 'When I got there and saw the old beaver dam full of trailer-camp suds and beer cans floating in garbage I almost knelt and wept. The loggers came in from the other side and have unerringly built a hauling bridge over the hottest [trout] spot. From this bridge I beheld two immaculate characters spin casting and monotonously hauling in chubs. I didn't even rig up.'

8

The Basalt Plains of Southeast Monaro

Every time I thought that I'd started to finish a chapter in writing this book, something happened to prove me wrong or forced me, later, to acknowledge some omission or another. In Chapter 5 I thought I'd 'killed off' all the good guys in 1991: Sautelle, Traver, Waldo, but that was, as I found when I read *Fly Fisherman* for September 1991, far from the truth. There, on page 4, written by the editor for all to see, was an obituary to the master of the master of all masters of fly-fishing, the great Lee Wulff (1905–91). And when I say 'great', that is how he appeared to me and to thousands of others: revered almost, as the great Joe DiMaggio was to Hemingway's 'Old Man'.

Lee Wulff died on 28 April, 1991, when his ancient Piper Super Cub crashed into a hillside near Hancock, New York State.

It was not a good year. Following this sad news, my editor hacked into my first draft of Chapter 6 with such unbounded enthusiasm that, although her criticism was well-founded, I was left reeling and literally praying for 1992 to arrive. I knew that all was not entirely lost, nonetheless, when I heard her say (through a fog of self-pity; mine—and with attractive innocence; hers): 'You know, I didn't understand that you could get so much enjoyment out of *losing* a fish; you don't land that many anyway, and those you do you seem to put back. You really don't go fishing just to catch fish do you?'

I could have hugged her. After only six draft chapters, the gospel was evidently at large, the word was apparently understood, and the dawning of knowledge among the proletariat looked possible.

So, with reborn enthusiasm, I travelled to southeast Monaro to open the 1991/'92 trout season,

vowing to provide her with a story of a respectable fish landed; perhaps even to present a monster to her with the first draft of Chapter 8.

Southeast Monaro, in New South Wales, lies, as far as I'm concerned, roughly to the south and east of Cooma. It includes the villages of Nimmitabel, Kydra, Kybean, Bibbenluke, Bombala and Delegate; and the trout waters of the Kydra, Kybean, Bombala, Delegate, MacLaughlin and Little Plains Rivers, Bobundara and Campbalong Creeks and, maybe, the eastern part of the Snowy River near its confluence with the MacLaughlin. The centre of the area is about two hours' drive south from Canberra.

The famous, low-rainfall, basalt rock segment, however, does not cover all this area. The basalt, or treeless plain as it is known, is roughly confined to the country contained by a meandering line joining Cooma, Nimmitabel, Bombala, Dalgety, Frying Pan and the Murrumbidgee River at its southernmost point, although there are pockets of basalt outside this and gaps within. It is also significant that a great deal of the southern part of the basalt lies in a rain shadow (less than 24 inches annually) between the coastal and the Kosciusko sections of the Great Dividing Range.

All these geophysical phenomena, created just after the Ice Age, are particularly important to trout fishermen (whether they are aware of it or not), because the native and natural food sources in this area are capable of maintaining a sporting, acclimatised brown-trout fishery which I consider to be one of the best in the Southern Hemisphere and which, if it is managed properly, could remain

Adams Irresistable
Chris Hole / 1992.

one of the best in the world.

Understandably, this is an area of delicate fishing for very wary, large brown trout. Indeed, fly-fishermen, and particularly those who write about the sport, often preach a philosophy in which there are three stages in a fisherman's life. Stage One, when he tries to hook the greatest number of fish; Stage Two, when he pursues the biggest possible fish; and Stage Three, when fooling only the most educated and difficult fish will satisfy him. Southeastern Monaro, and particularly the basalt segment, is undoubtedly an area for Stage Three fishermen, while, at the same time, the entire area is home to some very large creatures—a recipe for wonderful fly-fishing.

I arrived at Nimmitabel around lunchtime on the day prior to the opening of the 1991/'92 trout season. From there, it was only a 15 minute drive to Rockybah, the delightful grazing property of Howie and Annie Charles whom I first met in 1983 when our daughters attended school together. From that

first introduction, Howie made it plain that he wanted me to visit them, to try the fishing over their six-kilometre frontage on the MacLaughlin River, and (although it was left unsaid at the time) to begin to understand that part of Australia. Very stupidly, it took me eight years to accomplish this.

Howie was in the middle of his monthly computerised accounting for the property when I arrived but broke for lunch and, afterwards, very kindly gave me a guided recce of the fishing spots supporting this with a mudmap (which will remain exclusively mine). The MacLaughlin (or Mac) at Rockybah flows through steep, rocky country, 30 minutes by four-wheel drive from the homestead, with commanding views, on the track in, of the Snowy Mountains as far as Mount Delegate, some 70 kilometres to the southwest in the state of Victoria.

That short statement, however, goes nowhere in describing this most unusual place. It is old; very old. The geophysical battles over past millennia have evolved a humped and tired moonscape which is so steeped in delicate colour that it defies any accepted perception of light while haunting the artist with a vision that very, very few have been able to express. The treelessness somehow avoids harshness, except perhaps under the midday sun. But it is not until one breasts the top of a rise to gaze over this small part of Australia that one begins to understand the true size of the country. When one realises that this is also trout country in a remote class of its own, then it's time to rig up.

The weather was exceptionally warm and balmy as I arrived on the Mac that afternoon (as it was on the previous year only to be followed by a most unwelcome change with rain at midnight on 'opening'). And, because there were nine hours or so before opening, I carried no rod, only a camera and polaroids. In the absence of the excitement and pressure which I knew would surely follow on the morrow, I examined all the pools in a relaxed and careful manner. Thus I spotted over 30 trout (between two and four pounds), one eel, one fox and one huge eastern grey kangaroo.

All the pools appeared to be in good condition; Ti-tree, Toopeller, Floodgate, Cliff and Commissioners; but I noticed that, until mid-afternoon, the trout seemed to like the faster water at the head, keeping deep and feeding on nymphs. After 4.30 p.m., with plenty of chironomids and mayflies in the air, they moved to quieter water and began to feed off the top.

I knew I would be too excited to fish skilfully the next day and was sorely tempted. Nevertheless,

Bibbenluke Lodge on the banks of the Bombala River.

I awarded myself a halo by managing to keep Satan astern of me that afternoon.

Next morning at daybreak, Howie and I made our first casts in those prehistoric conditions.

But I *was* too excited! I spooked the first two fish as the sun rose into our eyes, blinding us with its intensity as we cast upstream to the east, scattering fish with reflections from sunglasses and untreated rods, something I should have foreseen on my recce the previous day. These lessons come hard but, what the hell, I wouldn't miss any of those exciting opening moments for anything in this world.

Luncheon that day was a barbeque in the enjoyable company of the Kydra–Kybean branch of the Monaro Acclimatisation Society on the banks of the Kybean River. Afterwards, in the late afternoon, we returned to the Mac in a much more relaxed frame of mind.

I chose Ti-tree Pool, a very fine tippet (three-pound) and a small Brown Nymph. On the third cast I was well connected to a three-pound brown trout which I landed a few moments later, thereby announcing to myself a very satisfactory opening to the 1991/'92 trout season. Before returning to the homestead for dinner, I hooked two more good browns of roughly the same size but one threw the hook and the other swam under a log and broke me off.

The next morning I arose with the sun and worked happily at writing and painting watercolours until well after lunchtime. At that stage, Annie's parents arrived to fish and to stay for dinner. Her father, Mark, a most likable and capable fisherman, her son, Andrew, and I piled into my pickup and headed for the river. But all good things must come to an end: ugly, black cu-nimbs were piling up in the west and steadily marching towards us; a front and a change after some remarkably warm spring weather. We should have moved out earlier to catch the often-fantastic fishing ahead of the front, but what one should do and what one does in the world of trout fishing are often not the same thing.

As we slid our way down the mountain to the flat beside the river the rain hit us hard. Quickly putting on oiled fishing jackets, we held a deliberate council of war and decided we had better return to wait at the top of the track in case we couldn't get up if we stayed at the bottom. We made the top with considerable difficulty over the wet and slippery basalt, and then, a few minutes later, the sky cleared. Down we slid again, sideways, putting doubts in my mind whether we would ever get up again, but Andrew read my thoughts and said: 'It is remarkable how quickly basalt dries out!'

Fishing after the passing of a front is never as good as fishing just before it. I saw hardly a fish, Andrew similarly scored a zero, and Mark managed only two small ones (around one and a half pounds each). So, as twilight descended, we clawed our way back up the track and, having made the top, called on the CB radio for martinis to be ready for our arrival back at the homestead. Fishing can really be an awful lot of fun—even without fish.

That night there were ten of us for dinner (very tasty home grown Murray Grey beef), and for pre-dinner goodies, Annie soused my opening day trout as follows:

Two fillets of trout (about one pound each)
One and a half tablespoons of common salt.
One tablespoon of brown sugar.
Two teaspoons of chopped mint.
One cup of gin.

Rub the mixture well into the fillets.
Place the mixture & fillets into a bowl.
Cover and place in the fridge for six hours.
Slice thinly (as with smoked salmon).
Serve on brown bread, sprinkled with lemon juice and
    pepper
Accompany with martinis made from the leftover gin.

Notwithstanding the celebrations of that night, at 5 o'clock the next morning (the day I had to leave Rockybah) I was on my way down to the river, to miss a good fish at the head of Toopeller before moving upstream to Floodgate where Howie had recommended that I should try. The sun was still below the eastern ridge on the far side of the pool as I fished upstream from the west bank and, on approaching a beautiful run at the head of the pool, I noticed two things: a good trout working in the run, and a mass of willows and briar bushes 'protecting' my casting position. Somehow or other

I managed to lean back into the willow branches with my toes gripping the basalt edge of the bank, looking down into eight feet of cold water, and backcast a nymph up to the edge of the run.

The fish took it like an angel and raced downstream on the far side, with me immovably enmeshed in willows and briars.

I untangled myself somehow and stepped behind some obstructions, passing my rod from hand to hand around them in front of me, and ducked and wove in front of others. When, at last, we made open ground, the fish turned and raced back upstream and the obstacle course had to be repeated in reverse. He was tiring, however, and I said to him: 'You are going to be mine, fish, at least temporarily, after which you will be my editor's, so make it easy on yourself; after all, you've had a good life and your sacrifice to me and my editor is a far, far better thing . . .'

So he came to my bank, I tailed him with a handkerchief onto the grass, and gazed down at four pounds of well-conditioned brown trout, a moment of pure happiness in one of the most beautiful parts of Australia.

Later that morning, and with a great deal of regret, I said my goodbyes and left Rockybah for Bombala, crossing the Mac and Campbalong Creek on the way. I didn't fish because it was a holiday weekend and the waters nearer the inhabited areas were overcrowded with anglers.

Bibbenluke, ten kilometres northeast of Bombala, is the location of Bibbenluke Lodge, an old and comfortable homestead situated on the banks of the Bombala River, where Rowley Banks introduced me to trout fishing in Australia many, many years previously. The lodge used to be a mecca for Sydney and Newcastle trout fishermen, mainly doctors and dentists for some unknown reason. It has sleeping accommodation for about eight, a drinks room, a dining room with an open fireplace and a long, polished table which supports a fisherman's dinner until about 10 o'clock, then becomes a fly-tying arena; and a large and comfortable sitting room overlooking the beautiful wild garden and the Bombala River. In those early days when Rowley first introduced me, the owner was a model train fanatic and one room was dedicated to his addiction. In fact, if one was asked to view this holy of all holies, it was a herculean effort even to get past the door, which had to be opened by radio request. The opening removed the east London skyline; then several cross-beams at waist level had to be raised to allow human passage, thereby removing most of

Victoria Station. But, once inside, with the London landscape and skyline restored, I haven't met a trout fisherman yet who was not prepared to play stationmaster, even if it meant missing the evening rise.

I arrived at the lodge at about lunchtime, having left Rockybah, and spent an hour with the new owners, exploring, taking photos, completing a recce, and obtaining kind permission to fish their country on the Bombala and to do some sketching and painting. They told me that, although they still provided very comfortable accommodation for four, this was only available to friends or by introduction through friends on an as-available basis. I hope it is continued and augmented as a fishing lodge as it is one of the best I have known.

So I drove on to Bombala where I took up residence in the local motel as a two-day base for the completion of my coverage of the basalt plain. After lunch, the old haunts began to beckon to where Rowley Banks and John Sautelle had initiated me on the Bombala River. The basalt plain in that part, however, suffers from its proximity to the eastern seaboard: in the afternoon the prevailing sea breeze from the northeast gains speed and its effect can be felt for a considerable distance inland. As everyone who has fished in southeast New South Wales can tell you, once the easterly starts, the fish disappear and the angler may as well return to his wife, his books, his writing, his paints, the hotel, or whatever his fancy may be.

The breeze was blowing by the time I reached the river, but it was pleasant to return and examine the area and I managed one brownie of about two pounds on a Brown Nymph from a sheltered run—for the family this time. I also indulged in some nostalgia and visited John Sautelle's place, five minutes from Bibbenluke, where I made a few casts into his lake, with prearranged permission from his son. Although the wind had died by then, and a big fellow was rising just outside casting range in a regular position near the island (as he had done for years), without the old man around the feeling was just not the same and, after a short stay, I returned to Bombala to put the family fish in the freezer, for dinner and an early night.

Tuesday 8 October I wrote, and painted Bibbenluke Lodge from first light until mid-afternoon, and then fished for a couple of hours in fairly cold conditions without success. Having packed away my notes, paints and camera, I walked slowly upstream at twilight towards the highway bridge. Under a particularly impossible run by a bankside overhung with willows, three good fish were 'slurping' flies; they were spaced about ten paces apart, in line up the river. Each could be seen through a hole no bigger than an arm-span in diameter through the willows, working a run of about the same length. I managed a bow-and-arrow cast at each of these as the darkness descended; each apparently went for the fly, as I could both see and hear the splashy attacks, but I felt no weight. I was left wondering what on earth I would have done if I had hooked one of them.

That's fishing, and it was the end of a remarkable four days in one of the best fly-fishing areas in Australia—at the opening of the season too.

Oh, incidentally, I filleted the four-pounder and, on return to Canberra, gave the fillets to my editor and her husband together with Annie's recipe. Sometimes, but not all that often in fly-fishing, things turn out as planned.

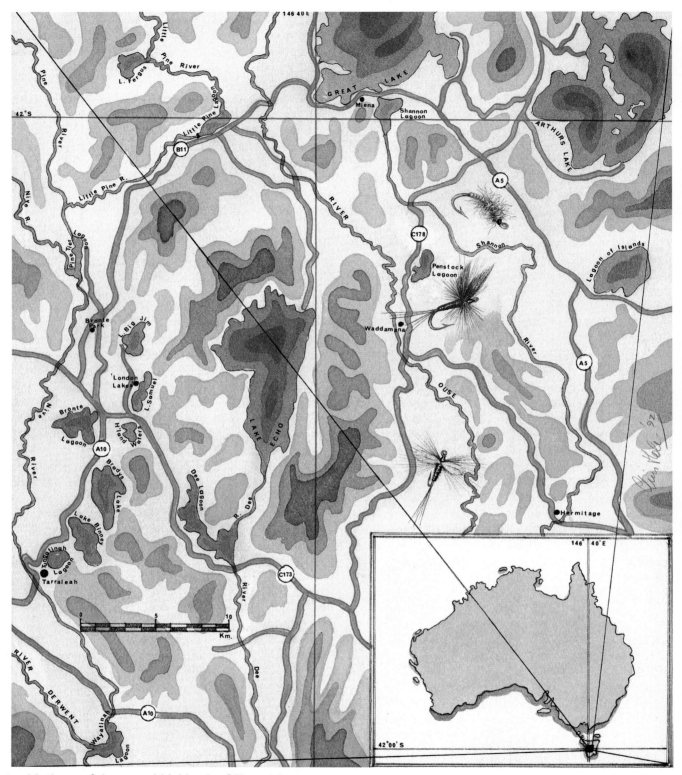

Mudmap of the central highlands of Tasmania.

9

The Central Highlands of Tasmania

When the weather is fine and the fish are rising it's very easy to put off the toil of writing and painting until conscience forces the pace, but that is unusual. It is more likely that a change in the weather for the worse or the unpredictable sullenness of trout force the conscience much earlier.

When, however, the weather is so appalling that there is no fishing at all, it leaves little to write about, and watercolour painting in the field becomes an impossibility. That is how it was in the Central Highlands of Tasmania when I arrived there in mid-December 1991, having flown to Hobart from Canberra, via Melbourne, and motored north to the Great Lake region. It is a simple flight of 55 minutes from Canberra to Melbourne, and an hour from there to Hobart. Direct from Sydney to Hobart is about an hour and a half's flying time.

Rob Sloane met me at Hobart Airport. Rob was, at one time, Commissioner for Inland Fisheries in Tasmania. He is an avid and very competent trout fisherman, a Doctor of Philosophy, having followed his BSc in Zoology and Botany with First Class Honours, specialising in Freshwater Biology. He has written and published a number of books about trout fishing. He is also a much sought-after speaker and writer of articles on all aspects of the sport. When I arrived that morning in sticky, humid and threatening weather, I could not have been put in better hands to be directed and sent on my way with mudmaps and advice.

After Rob's briefing I drove north from Hobart along the banks of the Derwent estuary, through Bridgewater and then inland on Highway 1 to Melton Mowbray. From there my route lay northwest on Highway A4 through Bothwell to Miena at the southern end of Great Lake. This was about two hours' easy drive from Hobart through rolling plains at first, then climbing through rain forest in one of the few predominantly green areas of Australia; an area of streams, tarns, lakes and runnels, where fly-fishing is conducted mainly in still waters for large brown trout which have become acclimatised and wild.

At Miena (or Haddens Bay), I booked into The Compleat Angler Lodge. This, together with the Great Lake Hotel nearby, offers an ideal and inexpensive base from which trout fisherman can explore the lakes and streams of the Central Highlands. These two establishments accommodate the majority of the tourists and fishing visitors to the area. Both establishments are very ably run by their managers in a partnership with Jim Allen, of The Compleat Angler tackle shops; hence the naming of the lodge.

Unpacking and rigging up took a little while, so it was not until around three-thirty that afternoon that I reached Little Pine Lagoon, my first stop on Rob's advice, for chasing the legendary Tasmanian browns.

Like many of the Central Highland lakes, Little Pine is shallow-edged and weedy, thus providing ideal cruise-feeding for big browns chasing caenids, nymphs, duns and spinners. It is easily wadeable out to good distances from the shore, and funnel-wind effects create many wind-lanes over the surface. This man-made lagoon was created by the damming of Little Pine River as it flows southwest to join Pine River.

It is a fundamental truth that all trout areas

require thought, concentration and experience. To the stream fisherman, lakes appear very daunting at first sight: where could the fish possibly be in that huge area of water? By studying the wind, the wind-lanes, the insect activity and the whereabouts of other anglers among other obvious and some less obvious things, the field can be narrowed significantly in 15 minutes' observation. A relatively sheltered spot, with duns blown onto the water near wind-lanes, might be a good position for the first observation and, if trout are observed to be taking the duns, the question is partly answered.

It took a little while before I saw my first rising trout in Little Pine that afternoon, rising so delicately that the movement on the surface was barely discernible. Using a small Blue Dun, my first cast (to this fellow) was on target; he came fast to the fly, pushing water in front in an obvious bow wave but, at the last moment, he flipped and sped away at right angles. It was the last movement I was to see for some considerable time and, thinking back, I believe the Blue Dun was too pale in colour. Then the humidity turned into spots of rain, the spots turned into heavy rain, and the heavy rain turned into a torrential downpour that continued with ferocity throughout the night. So that was the end of it.

I was told later that the oppressive weather on the morning of my arrival started the dun hatch at eight-thirty and the trout had fed heavily until about 3 p.m. If only I had arrived earlier, if only, if only, if only . . .

So, as the downpour continued and, in the comfort of my Compleat Angler cabin, I wrote what I could, painted some watercolours of trout flies and dwelt on what might have been. I unrigged and rigged my rods, sorted out my flies, made lists of amendments to my safari packing lists and thought back to the previous week, when I visited a world-renowned rod-builder in Brisbane, and I recalled that, even then, the monsoonal weather was beginning in the north.

The rod-builder, John Hugh McGinn, was born in Scotland but lived for a long time in the Lakes District of England where he was taught rod-building by his grandfather who worked for the House of Hardy at Alnwick. John worked freelance at his rod-building in England, which included work for Hardy, before emigrating to Australia where he continued his work in Queensland. His split-cane trout rods are individually and beautifully hand-crafted and sought after world-wide and I was lucky enough to become the owner of one in the 1980s but that's another story. Since then, at his factory

in Brisbane, John has been experimenting with hexagon-section graphite rods, perfecting them for salt-water fishing.

John's hexagon engineering, unlike other well-known styles where the six individual pieces are triangular in section, is made up of six T-pieces where the tops of the Ts join at their extremities to produce the hexagon cross-section, and the bottoms of the T-uprights join at the heart of the rod.

Working up to 12 hours a day, seven days a week, the small McGinn team has perfected and patented this technique to produce magnificent game, spinning, bait- and plug-casting rods, but trout rods were, at the time of my visit, still being further researched. These more delicate instruments apparently required reductions in their power-to-length ratio and in their overall weight. At the time it was expected that these problems could be overcome by experimenting with graphite modulus and rod taper, and by eliminating much of the gusset material between the upright and crosspieces of the individual T-sections. The results could well be epoch-making!

During the visit, John gave me an experimental model with which to start my world travels, and a promise of improved models along the way.

So, as the rain persisted, I decided that, at the first sign of clearing, I would take the experimental hexagon to Little Pine—with a heart full of hope and a dream in sore need of realisation.

But when the weather cleared marginally at lunchtime after 20 hours of downpour, I was so keen to get going again that I left the hexagon at the lodge and had to make do with the other graphite rods in the back of the car.

When I arrived at Little Pine, the fish were rising spasmodically to dark duns in the shelter of the dam wall. Plenty of duns were being blown down onto the water but the feeding trout were only taking one in every 30-odd, and then in widely dispersed positions. After watching for a while, I observed that they were not only feeding on those duns but on emerging nymphs as well. So, tying on a size-16 Copper and Hare, and greasing the cast to the eye of the hook, I started after them.

The Copper and Hare was immediately effective; I had chosen the right fly for once. The passage of the duns over the water was related to short and irregular lulls in the wind, and trout feeding only followed their passage. It was a tricky but sporting and exciting contest which finished with three trout chased and three trout being hooked. The fish were around four pounds each and all were in good condition with deep red-orange flesh. Two were allowed to remain in the lake and one was kept for dinner.

There is no doubt that, like any other fly-fishing, this type of lake fishing requires knowledge and practice.

My contentment at dinner in the lodge that evening was only disrupted by a phonecall from the mainland concerning changes in my planned internal flights in Argentina, and a possible loss of 24 hours' fishing time in Patagonia. A matter, I decided, better handled on return to Canberra. Inga, the chef at the lodge, had made a gastronomic masterpiece of my trout, and Argentina was quickly forgotten (for the time being). Inga's recipe was so good that I must share it with you (she said I could):

Brown Trout With Fresh Pea Sauce

One brown trout filleted (.75 kg)
20g butter
freshly ground pepper and salt
50 ml white wine
50 ml fish stock
40 ml thick velouté
Six fresh peas in pods (reserve the pods)
20 ml cream
Lime slices for garnish

Melt the butter in a frying pan. Season the trout fillets with salt and pepper and fry them for three minutes each side.

In a small saucepan, combine the white wine and fish stock and add the pea pods. Simmer for about five minutes.

Discard the pods. Add the velouté, cream, frying juices and peas, and simmer for three minutes. Pour the sauce on a plate and place the fish fillets on top. Garnish with lime slices.

The next day the weather was still marginal so I worked in my room until 11 a.m., then ventured out to Penstock Lagoon (Rob's second recommendation), remembering this time to take the hexagon with me.

Whether the hexagon had a hex upon it or whether it was just the Australian weather pattern, I don't know, I suspect the latter. A strong northeast wind was blowing when I arrived; the rain was continuous, the water very muddy and impossible to polaroid, and the only fish I encountered I managed to spook at my feet to produce a very healthy bow wave. So back to Little Pine where the weather was no better but where there was a significant hatch of duns, which the fish were totally ignoring.

After I had spent two tiring hours pushing through the reeds in waist deep water, trying to find a spot where the trout might attack a dun, the rain cleared and the wind dropped. The fish started to feed, bulging the surface but apparently still ignoring the duns.

Tiredness melts away when fish feed, but it was one of those times when, no matter what artificial fly is chosen, the fish won't take it—frustrating in the extreme. The rise stopped 45 minutes later; the wind increased and swung to the north and, as the rain started once more, I stopped fishing. I had one minor victory, nonetheless: as I slogged my way back to the bank I saw what I believed to be one of those old, flat 20-cigarette tins floating on the water near the edge. Being a good garbage-cleaner-upper I thought I'd better pick it up, only to find it was a very neat, six-compartment fly box with 40-odd well-tied dry flies inside! One is sometimes lucky, particularly if one helps clean up rubbish!

I put a couple of 'Found' notices in the hotel and the lodge with my telephone number, but made it evident to the proprietors that any claimant had better be able to describe the box in detail (indeed to the last millimetre) in order to have it returned.

So back to the lodge for one of Inga's magnificent dinners—unfortunately my last of hers on that visit to Tasmania.

Incidentally, I found the hexagon rod to be one of astonishing power. Only seven and a half feet long, it could, if necessary, power an eight-weight line over great distances. It was, however, a heavy and tiring rod to use and I look forward to the day when those modifications I mentioned are incorporated to produce lighter and more supple rods of extraordinary power and strength.

I left early next morning and drove southwest on the Marlborough Highway (B11), stopping to fish again at Little Pine Lagoon (without success), to Bronte, where I turned left onto the Lyell Highway (A10) and left again onto route C173 and thus to London Lakes. In all, it was a total distance of about 50 kilometres, or two hours' easy drive, with time to explore and fish.

I arrived at London Lakes Lodge after lunch to be greeted by my hostess, Barbara Garrett, whose husband and my host, Jason Garrett, was sadly absent in Hobart for a couple of days, visiting a sick friend.

The place immediately reminded me of a Scot's highland house, totally dedicated to the pursuit of fly-fishing. The lodge is handcrafted by Tasmanian artisans. Walls of field stone and celery-top pine logs enclose a richly panelled interior. Huge

London Lakes Lodge in the central highlands of Tasmania.

fireplaces, log slab tables, central heating and tartan carpets provide an atmosphere of wildlife elegance. It caters for ten guests in luxury; there is a rod room at the entrance, and a fly-tying area and conference room upstairs. It is also the home of the owners who take great pride in their achievements and who go out of their way to fulfil their guests' every whim.

The property covered 4,200 acres when first purchased by Jason in 1973 from 'Big' Jim Hall, when it was known as London Marshes.

Jason set about construction of the two major

lakes in 1977, Lake Big Jim (named after the previous owner) to the north, and Lake Samuel (named after the Garretts' son) to the south. In 1974 the name of the property was changed to London Lakes for obvious reasons. The lodge itself was started in 1983 and became habitable in December 1984. In 1988 a further 800 acres, to the south of the original holding, on the other side of Victoria Valley Road, were purchased and a third lake, Highland Waters, established in 1989. This new area was subdivided and offered for sale from that time.

I mention this background because it was the dream of one man, an enormous dream, a dream which came to reality; the dream of Jason Garrett.

Jason, Tasmanian by birth and a licensed land surveyor by profession, once lived and worked in private practice at Madang in New Guinea. A totally dedicated fly-fisherman of half a century's standing, he would 'disappear south' a couple of times each year to pursue his beloved browns in the Central Highlands of Tasmania. As the years went by he became less and less enamoured of the state of 'his' waters: rubbish, pollution and lack of conservation were becoming more and more evident (shades of Lake Eucumbene?). Anyway, such was his concern, combined with his ambition to build a lodge of international standing in Tasmania, that the idea, which became the dream and finally the reality of London Lakes, was conceived. Barbara kept saying to me during my short visit: 'Jason is a dreamer'. To which the only reply was: 'If that is the case, he is one of the very few dreamers in this world who has made his dreams come true.'

Down to the last nut and bolt, the whole place is a statement on conservation of fly-fishing; from the brass trout knocker on the front door to the library; from the painted trout on the tiles in the bathrooms to the awards on the mantelpiece; and from the photographs in the sitting room to the lakes themselves. This place, to me, is very close indeed to Paradise. The artwork on the walls in the lodge also carries this theme with considerable force and expertise; at the time it made me think twice about my own undertaking.

Jason's ultimate plans at the time of writing included the construction of a six-kilometre trout stream and breeder run between his two major lakes.

London Lakes is, in my opinion, one of the finest lodges in Australia and must rank amongst the best in the Southern Hemisphere. What is more, its very existence makes a bold statement for the preservation of wild trout in Tasmania; a statement which could well be taken on board by the other Australian states where salmonids remain.

After I settled in, because of the master's absence, Barbara (who is not a fisherman) phoned one of their guides, Lonsdale Smith, on the other side of Lake Samuel. Lonsdale was introduced to me so he could advise me about the best areas to fish. I was tickled that Barbara introduced me as a journalist, and pointed out that I was really a retired naval officer, grazier and artist who was crazy enough to embark on a project of writing and illustrating a book. Later, when I looked up 'journalist' in the dictionary, I found it had two meanings: 'One who keeps a journal', and 'One who edits or writes a journal as a means of earning a living'. From my own point of view, I think I would prefer to be associated with the former group.

Lonsdale Smith and I hit it off immediately. I found him to be a retired dairy farmer, trout fisherman and fishing guide, and also an artist of considerable ability. I told him that I used to run fine-wool merinos, did a little painting, and loved trout fishing myself, and the ice was more than broken, only to be thoroughly smashed later when he started telling his stories.

His immediate advice was: 'Forget London Lakes (temporarily) and make the ten-minute drive to the western side of Bronte Lagoon!' He said that the lagoon had filled rapidly with the heavy rain, that the lakeside rushes had been covered by the rising water, and that the trout were voraciously feeding on a mass of spiders which had been washed off the rushes. Off I went in hot pursuit, remembering, fortunately, that fishermen exaggerate—if not lie like crazy! The weather looked clear for the first time in three days or so and, in shirtsleeves only, I trudged the three kilometres from the car to the marsh area, almost shaking with anticipation. As I drew near to the rushes and saw three fish in action, two things happened at once. I noticed a marked lack of spiders (had they all been eaten?) and a mass of dark rainclouds building up in the northwest. I had a five minute stalk after one brownie before the deluge hit. The rain turned the surface of the lagoon into a froth resembling a freshly shaken and opened bottle of champagne and, within seconds, I was soaked to the skin. Visibility was nil, and by the time I had found the car I knew that I had been very lucky to find my way back to my starting point. I probably looked like a fish.

So, back to London Lakes and Lake Samuel, to two areas recommended by Lonsdale. I found nothing at one, and managed to prick two cruisers in the other. Not a very good start in one of the world's great trout fisheries.

I was up at five next morning only to find Lake Samuel completely dead. I had breakfast and spent the rest of the morning writing and painting until about 3 p.m. when Bronte Lagoon began to beckon again. In the spider area there were certainly no creepy-crawlies left, and not a fish moving.

I came across another fisherman (in a bright red jacket!) We exchanged pleasantries and I found out that he was a Canadian fishing journalist. We chatted on. He told me that he was camping in a pup-tent nearby and had nearly been washed away by the previous day's rain. I commented that I was out in it trying to fish and he observed: 'Oh, you must have been the crazy guy out there being soaked to the skin and swearing his head off! Swearing carries over water you know!' I sheepishly admitted guilt, and he replied: 'I was swearing just as hard as you but it doesn't carry over land!'

We quickly became friends and swapped a lot of fishing lies. The truth was, however, that there were no fish feeding close-in that day and I suggested to my new-found friend that bright colours turn trout off. He smiled and said that he quite understood the need to blend into the background, but his red jacket was the only serviceable and dry protection he had left.

Back to my favourite spot on Lake Samuel and to stalk another fish, again without success. By then I'd had three sessions in the London Lakes area with zero results.

Jason Garrett arrived late that evening after dinner and we talked until midnight. At 7 a.m. we started for Lake Big Jim where we found nothing, then returned to a bay on Lake Samuel in front of the lodge, to chase three or four fish. On Jason's advice I tied on a local caenid artificial and cast in front of a fish, close to the shore. The fly sat badly on the water due, I thought, to superglue strengthening and other modern affectations and, from the surface movement, I was strangely convinced that the fish had ignored it. I lifted the fly from the water to check the knot and a bow wave shot out towards deeper water! The fish must have been stationary under the fly, inspecting its abnormal attitude and, when I moved it from the water, he took fright.

We then each chased another fish out into deep water, but their feeding pattern was too fast and irregular for us to entice either of them. Much the same thing happened with a final fish of significant character; it came past Jason fast, sipping caenids. He made several casts to it without success before it sped outside his range and into mine. It was so fast, however, that the same thing happened to me. It was a frustrating morning so we returned to the lodge where, at breakfast, one of Jason's guides spoke of similar problems. In a rather silly way I was relieved to deduce that my low score was not entirely my own fault, after all the locals had no better batting averages.

The weather that Saturday was markedly improving. After breakfast, I wrote for an hour or so and then took the first opportunity since my arrival in Tasmania to start some watercolours outside.

At lunchtime, two groups of guests arrived and the place moved into overdrive top. Three extra guides arrived (including Lonsdale), and fishermen were rigged up and briefed before disappearing in all directions. I continued working and sketching until about 4.30 p.m., then went after the browns again with (like the others) another nil result in much-improved but cold weather.

Dinner was taken early that evening so we could disappear afterwards in various ways for the evening rise. The dinner was relaxed, enjoyable and chock-full of fishing talk. The fishing was, regrettably, not so successful (nil all around again) because,

although the skies had cleared totally, the temperature had dropped and there was no discernible hatch. I operated with one of the guides so that we could continue to 'talk fishing' (he said), but I suspect, on the advice of 'The Taipan' to get me a fish before my departure the next day.

The Taipan? Yes, that's what the guides call Jason . . . because he strikes hard and fast (like the deadly Queensland snake), and runs his empire like the famous fictional Mandarin of Hong Kong—all said with a great deal of respect and affection.

But once again, my final evening was a non-event: too cold and no hatch. I did have a go at one fish, nevertheless, in the bay in front of the house with a fly my guide called a 'Black-Winged Caddis—to be used when all else fails'. I would have called it something else, but who was I to argue with the local experts? I chased a monster. The fish rose close to my fly; my guide said he'd taken it and maybe he had, but being a stream fisherman, I probably tightened too late and found there was no weight on the line. As the guide said at the time, 'Strike hard and fast in the lakes—like a Taipan!' . . . on the other hand, it could have been just encouraging chat!

The next morning we made one more attempt before I departed. In cold, blustery weather we sallied forth with the same results of nothing. I found that it didn't matter very much because Lonsdale came with me and a fellow guest at the lodge (who happened to be rod-builder J. H. McGinn's accountant). Lonsdale spent the short morning telling guide stories that had both of us rolling around in the swamps, doubled up with uncontrollable laughter. Fishing didn't matter; we were too convulsed to fish anyway.

Didn't I once say that fly-fishing is rather more than just . . . etc?

I was extremely sorry to leave London Lakes. Even with very few fish to my credit, I left Tasmania knowing that the Central Highlands provide the best lake fishing in Australia and that the management of inland fishing in that state also sets an example which others would do well to follow.

And, if fishermen are contemplating visiting Tasmania: fish the Central Highlands, get to London Lakes if you can, and if that state is suffering from drought, continuous high temperatures in the middle of summer and a total fire ban to prevent bush fire, don't forget to pack your raincoat, your umbrella and your thermal underwear!

PART III

THE SOUTHERN HEMISPHERIAN SAFARI

10
Burnt Toast But No Fish at Hawea

During the two weeks before my departure for the first of my two world circumnavigations, I took stock of my achievements towards the goal of publication. I listed the lessons I had learned in fishing, recording and painting; I dwelt upon my mistakes and what I had gained from them, and tried to formulate ideas to correct them. I also took time to update the lists of equipment I would need on my travels.

The Tasmanian trip was the first occasion when I had to take all my gear with me by air. I had to operate 'overseas' with sufficient equipment to fly-fish, to paint, to photograph and to write, while taking the minimum amount of clothing and accessories to keep warm, dry, cool, comfortable and, at times, presentable in differing climates and circumstances. In planning I allowed for: one large suitcase (for clothes, waders, reels, overflow fishing and art equipment, notebooks, toilet gear and the like); one large, flat rugged folio case with inserts (for watercolour paper and blocks, paint tray and completed artwork); one rod bag holding up to six rods in individual metal containers and with additional pockets for boots and so forth; and one airline pilot's briefcase (for writing material, safari and personal files, stationery and other administrative paraphernalia). These four pieces were all marked for the aircraft hold while, in the cabin, I planned to carry my camera case holding a Nikon AF601 and lenses for slide work, and a Minolta Weathermatic for rough work and quick prints, together with films and accessories; and, finally, a personal briefcase for travel documents, papers, tickets, travellers cheques, duty free booze and the block of A4 upon which I was scribbling the current chapter.

Six pieces and about 63 kilos weight in all!

Learning from the Tasmania experience, I managed to reduce the content but I was still left with six essential items, probably acceptable in hire cars, taxis, hotels and lodges with a minor security risk, but with a strong and unfortunate likelihood of creating excess luggage penalties when flying. I really had no other choice and, armed with plastic cards, I departed—to find out the hard way.

Next, I realised that, in my fishing, I had always been drawn to streams and rivers and had developed a prejudiced preference not to fish the lakes. My Tasmanian experience had fortunately brought home to me just what I was missing. Also, three weeks before I left Australia I found myself in the Adaminaby area again (just for practice mind you) only to find that a recent three and a half inches of rain had turned the local rivers into torrents of mud.

I was forced to fish Lake Eucumbene!

It was my good fortune, however, that in the Frying Pan area I had to make myself concentrate on the shallows and the rushes; I had to match the hatch, and I had to polaroid and stalk fish carefully in crystal clear summer conditions if I were to achieve success. And, by applying myself accordingly, I did achieve it. I grassed 23 good fish (releasing most of them) on my best day and learned a great deal more about hooking fish in the different circumstances of still-water fishing.

From this experience I made a list of many other mistakes and prejudices. At the time I was re-reading *A Fly-Fisher's Life* by the world-famous Swiss hotelier and superb fly-fisherman, Charles Ritz. I found, not surprisingly, that many of his early mistakes were also mine, and that his work offered me a number of solutions. He observed, among other things:

- that the charm of fly fishing lies in one's numerous failures and in unforeseen circumstances;
- that, even if no apparent faults are committed in any one instant, one still has a great deal to learn;
- that red-letter days are few and far between, and they inspire an increased confidence which leads to an increased ability—often an illusion;
- that disappointing days are frequent, they decrease confidence and, therefore, ability;
- that, if all days were red-letter days, the allure of fly-fishing would rapidly fade;
- that laziness, and lack of concentration and patience are frequent and contagious failings;
- that strikes are often made too early, too late or too hard;
- that tackle collecting and examination, like fly-fishing itself, is an incurable disease;
- that very fine leaders will help hook fish but probably increase the break-off rate, which doesn't matter that much;
- that a desire to move up and down the river because there are always more rises around the next corner often costs fish, but is a pleasant failing;
- that spotting, stalking and enticing visible fish outweighs blind fishing to the extent that the latter is soon forsaken;
- that landing nets, except in very demanding circumstances, are miserable instruments which get in the way;
- that fishing with others is always preferable to fishing alone, if only to verify one's own ideas and to seek out those of others; and
- that it is always necessary to fight the intoxication of temporary success.

Finally, those early safari days in southeast Australia taught me that I had probably bitten off more than I could chew. I found, while enjoying the fishing immensely at each stop, although I managed to complete a chapter in rough draft, keep up an illustrated fishing diary and take a respectable number of reasonable photographs, my major artwork production fell behind rapidly. Fortunately, in my early planning, I had allowed for numerous hotel stops along the way, and an eight-week catch-up gap between circumnavigations. Nonetheless I knew that, by the end of 1992, I would need to complete a number of paintings from photographs and that my photography and notes would need to be accordingly accurate.

Oh, there was one further consideration I had to make before departure (apart from mundane things like mail diversion and who would cut the lawns and feed the dog), and that was the all-important consideration of which fly rods to take with me!

In the end, the contents of my rod bag for the first trip included: the J. H. McGinn seven and a half foot experimental hexagon rod which would take anything from the #5/6 WF line I had on a Sage reel to (at least) the #7/8 WF line I had on a Hardy Princess Multiplier; an Orvis eight and a half foot #5-weight graphite rod with Battenkill reel and a #5 WF line; a Fenwick 857 graphite rod with which I normally used the Hardy Princess Multiplier and which had always been my favourite outfit in New Zealand; a J. H. McGinn Bombala eight and a half foot split cane rod which took the Sage reel and line admirably; and at the last minute, I included a Sage seven and a half foot graphite rod with a Hardy Gold Featherweight reel for #3/4 fine fishing.

So it was, at first light on Sunday 2 February 1992, that I turned away from my front door in Canberra with my six pieces of luggage and headed for the airport, keyed up to start a very exciting year. A prospect made even more exciting by the 23 months of research, correspondence, planning and practice which I knew had already gone into it.

My first mistake was to misread my airline ticket and arrive at Canberra airport 45 minutes early. Normally a mistake (on the conservative side) which ought to pass without comment. But, when that 45 minutes meant getting out of bed at 4.30 a.m. instead of 5.15 a.m., Gini was not amused and remarked that the next time I was so keen to go fishing perhaps she could stay in bed.

The airport procedures, trans-Tasman flight and progress south from Christchurch that day proceeded without hitch. I managed to pass my usual extra litre of Laphroaig through New Zealand Customs by declaring it essential for sustenance during highland fly-fishing, and by sunset was enjoying dinner at Ashburton, 80 kilometres south of Christchurch where I stopped on my drive south to Hawea. Over the years, I have normally chosen Ashburton in similar circumstances because of its convenient distance south on the way to Otago country after a late afternoon arrival from Sydney, and because it is the home of a very special tackle shop, Stirling Sports, where next morning I topped up with Stonefly Nymphs, Twilight Beauties and Dad's Favourites.

Just before I fell into a deep sleep that night I realised that the day (and 3,000 kilometres) had passed by without a single official comment—not even a raised eyebrow—about my 63 kilos of baggage. How long could it last? I mused as my eyelids shut.

I drove into Lake Hawea village at lunchtime the next day and was welcomed by the proprietors of the Glenruth Motel where I had stayed, on and off, during my previous six New Zealand visits.

My initial concern, however, was not with my accommodation nor with its owners, but with the state of my favourite (and delicate) river, the Hawea. This beautiful little short-run trout haven, which connects Lake Hawea from its dam wall to the mighty Clutha River, is entirely at the mercy of the New Zealand Electricity Authority who control the outflow from the lake. On six previous visits I had, on four occasions, fished the Hawea when the control valves were all but closed, allowing the river to remain in gentle and perfect condition. On the other two visits, the valves were open, the flow practically unimpeded and the river an unfishable torrent. What is more, over the years, I have found it impossible to ascertain when the valves might be opened or closed.

So on this visit I drove quickly to the dam wall, heart in mouth, to see what would be. At first glance I started to smile; I thought the river looked good, not too high, not too fast. But when I looked more closely and saw the outflow pipes from the dam wall frothing great quantities of water I had to admit that my initial impressions were probably illusions. The taps were not fully open, but open enough to make the river a little too fast for good fishing and (through hours of flogging the water) I found it fast enough to upset regular fish beats and to spoil the sport (and, if one thought about it, the tourist trade).

Mind you I tried! I put in ten hours thoroughly covering my favourite spots and pools, and also any corner that looked good, any inviting backwater—everything—and with detailed application. I saw one single fish and was broken off by another fishing blind into an impossibly deep swirl. I finally admitted defeat. I also admitted some sadness for my favourite river and, as gale-force northwest winds built up, I pondered a change of plans.

Tony and Sue Wolstenholme arrived to stay at the motel that evening (you may remember Nick, their son, at Lake Eucumbene?) Tony and Sue had just completed the Milford Sound walking track and were on their way to Christchurch before returning to Canberra. We had dinner and then I left them

in order to fish the evening rise which was non-existent. Something *bad* must have happened to the Hawea, I concluded, although I managed to hook one in a favourite pool downstream from the dam wall.

The next morning I fished with great determination and application until lunchtime without a result—something *bad* had happened to the Hawea: I noticed that the chenille head of the Stonefly Nymph I was using had turned electric blue in the water! I tested a similar nymph later, in my motel bathroom basin, and it also changed colour. So no answer lay in that direction; obviously the dye had washed out. But I kept wondering if that beautiful little river was suffering from over-fishing—or even pollution? I thought: We are all capable of making some mistakes, but extreme mistakes affecting our environment *must* be corrected otherwise we may not be around to make any more mistakes.

Anyway, as the northwest gale continued that afternoon, I retired to my motel room looking out over the lake to write and to sketch, when the telephone rang. It was Brian Thomson down at Ranfurly on the Taieri River. He said that the weather and fishing in his area were both admirable and that things were even better in the Mataura area where our friend, Phil Waldron, was doing wonders with a Red Spinner.

My mind was made up. I advanced my motel booking at Ranfurly, left a message for Gini with the Park Royal Hotel in Wellington about my plans (Gini had followed me to New Zealand and was looking at historic places before joining me later), told Brian I would be with him the next morning and started to pack my gear again.

Oh! The burnt toast?

When I arrived at Lake Hawea it was lunchtime, and a rumbling stomach persuaded me that I should cut slices of salami and put some bread in the toaster for a small snack.

With the bread inserted in the correct slots of a fairly impressive push-button machine, and having established that the power was on, I turned my attention to the rigging of my fishing gear (after its 63-kilo, 3,200-kilometre pilgrimage). Rods were lovingly extracted from metal tubes, new traces were connected to flylines, reels were fastened to rod butts, fishing vests were filled beyond capacity, foul-weather gear was placed conveniently, cameras were loaded, double-A batteries were installed in everything capable of passing a wiggly-amp, knives were sharpened and toe-nails were cut (socks and waders can suffer horribly if they're not).

All this took time, and time, as I discovered when black smoke poured into the living-room area, was something I didn't have. The blasted toaster wasn't automatic. One had to push a 'pop-up' button to release the toast and turn that piece of agricultural machinery off.

By the time I understood this comparative simplicity, smoke was billowing from my motel unit, staff armed with fire extinguishers were running up the drive, wildlife had scattered in all directions, an alarm was ringing somewhere and I imagined I could hear the bell on the Hawea Flat Volunteer Brigade fire unit wheezing itself into life as its museum-piece mother vehicle raced towards my hapless motel room, hell-bent on heroic preservation and rescue!

Of course, by the time all these remarkable relief columns arrived, I was totally in control. The toaster was off, the offending piece of carbon had been removed, all the windows and doors had been opened to clear the air (and a great number of my dry flies which had been placed on the living room table for my later selection) and I could greet my rescuers with aplomb and a somewhat fumbling apology. Other than hurt feelings, there was no great damage, and life returned to comparative normal.

Then, alas and alack! Next morning, as Tony and Sue were about to depart and we were saying our farewells, I was foolish enough to embark on another *gastronomique-de-toast!* Once again I was distracted, chatting away at the front door, until smoke billowing from my kitchenette altered my sense of purpose and, rudely, made me leave Sue and Tony in mid-sentence while I played fireman again.

Surely now, one would conclude that, except for the totally hapless, such mistakes could never be repeated. Not a bit of it, old chap.

My final farewell to the Wolstenholmes (having sorted out the second toast-saga) was a photographic session with the glorious background of Lake Hawea framing Tony, Sue and me (my Nikon on automatic) when, as the camera's magic eye stopped pulsing and I knew the photo was a masterpiece, I observed more smoke pouring from the kitchen. The management's response this time was to present me with a basket of fruit and a note to the effect that fruit is really much more healthy than toast.

The irony of all this (and something that King Alfred of the burnt cakes should consider if he were alive today) was that, eventually on emptying my garbage (including the three slices of carbon) into the motel master garbage bin, what did I see down in the (nowadays) recyclable slop? From the eight other units at the Glenruth Motel, at least another 30 slices of carbon!

But I don't think all this has a great deal to do with fly-fishing, and it wasn't a very successful start to my wanderings. Nonetheless, by the law of averages, my success with the trout family could only improve, and maybe that motel will buy nine pop-up toasters.

"Yellow Muddler Minnow"

Chris Cole

1992.

11
The Mataura, Ranfurly and the Taieri—Not to Mention the Infamous Lake Onslow

The drive south and east from Lake Hawea to Ranfurly, through Cromwell and Alexandra, took a couple of hours. The weather was mild, my expectations were high and I enjoyed driving, at first through the hills following the mighty Clutha River, and then across the plains of central Otago. I arrived at Ranfurly around midday, booked into the motel, sorted out my gear and repaired to the Thomsons for lunch and a chat about the fishing.

Brian and Christine were fairly busy running their shop and I still had plenty of writing and painting to do, so we agreed that I would return to the motel to scribble and daub, and rejoin them for dinner, after which Brian and I would examine a couple of the local dams, leaving the Taieri River for later.

All went according to plan; after a delicious dinner and a good bottle of claret, we were out in time for the evening rise. The only trouble was that a cold southerly was blowing, there was no discernible hatch and certainly no rise. We decided on an early night and made plans to drive south the next day to the Gore area and the Mataura River. The plan was to leave at lunchtime, allowing me the morning for writing and painting, and to arrive at Ron Jackson's house in time to set up for the evening rise. But it didn't quite turn out that way. My neighbours in the next motel unit were a very pleasant American couple who just happened to be fanatical fly-fishermen and wanted to swap ideas. Then Brian arrived and joined the discussion. As

a result, I didn't get much work done before it was time pack the car and drive south.

In the late afternoon we arrived at Ron Jackson's house (you may remember Ron and his eccentric housekeeper from Chapter 4) and immediately set out for the Mataura River in the Cattle Flat area to the east of Lumsden. On arrival we found to our great disappointment the cold southerly wind again, no hatch, no significant rise and plain evidence of heavy fishing pressure. Brian hooked one but was broken off and nothing further eventuated. We returned to Ron's house to be met by Ron and Phil Waldron and a four-pounder Phil had captured in the Mavora Lakes area earlier in the day. Despite our own lack of success it was wonderful to meet up with a team of great old buddies again.

We spent the whole of the next day on the Mataura, in the Cattle Flat area until evening and then further downstream for the rise. The evidence of fishing pressure was very marked: many campsites, footprints, cars, fishermen and holiday-makers all resulting in very spooky fish. But fish were certainly there. Ron caught a three-pounder first up, Phil was broken off by a good one, as was Brian, and I spotted and cast to six fish before lunchtime without getting one to take. It was also evident that the fish were chasing each other in pairs, a sure sign of early spawning, making them even more difficult to entice.

After lunch I fished a long, flat, shallow stretch, wading thigh-deep upstream, casting across to the far bank where Phil was in among the bushes spotting for me. Almost immediately we found a pair of large spawning-run chasers. I managed to get a size-16 Red Spinner over them and one of them took very aggressively. In fact he took the fly with such ferocity that my four-pound tippet lasted only a matter of seconds. I changed up to six pounds, replaced the Red Spinner and headed upstream towards the far bank where Phil had located yet another fish very close to the bank. I put my fly over him, which he inspected and refused; I tried three more times and he flatly refused to move, so I changed to a size-14 Copper and Hare Nymph. My first cast was blown wide of the mark by the southerly, but the second was right on target. He turned, chased the nymph and took it like an angel. A cross-the-river battle followed until I slid him up over the pebbles just in front of where I had parked the car—dinner for that night.

After the meal we returned to the Mataura, further downstream in the hope of avoiding the crowd. Having found a good stretch, Brian was the only one to score because he wisely managed to match the hatch using a Spent Spinner while the rest of us, using ordinary Red Spinners, were ignored. It really is amazing just how fussy fish can be, and how remarkable their eyesight is to be able to pick what they want in the half light when the object is much less than a quarter-inch in size, and part hidden in a fast current.

The next day, in very warm summer conditions, we chose the Oreti River; again in the hope of avoiding angling pressures. The Oreti is a wide, multichannelled New Zealand-blue stream, running fast over grey pebbles. Hard walking and difficult spotting are only relieved by observing fish cruising in quiet backwaters. Phil, with his remarkable eyesight, caught two while Brian, who was with him, did not score. Ron and I went the other way, downstream, and spotted and cast to half a dozen fish in backwaters without result. At one stage Ron climbed a willow out over one backwater and tried to dap a fly down to a couple of cruisers. What with the creaking of the branch, the curses and the leaves dropping onto the water, the result was predictable, but he scored a commendable ten points for effort anyway. On the way back to the car I had a go at four extremely big fish working in a very deep swirl below a cliff, with Ron spotting for me from above. It was simply impossible to get a fly down anywhere near them, even with my most heavily weighted nymphs. A sinking line or lead-core might have worked, but I have my doubts. Fish that live to become that size have usually worked out a safe place in which to operate forever.

We had lunch by the car and started to head for home when Brian said: 'Christ! I've forgotten my sunglasses!' He was particularly worried because they were an expensive French pair given to him by Christine; but his worry turned to annoyance when he realised we were all laughing at him. The glasses were still parked on the bridge of his rather sunburnt nose!

That evening we went back to our downstream position on the Mataura. As the light began to fade I saw a few rises in the fast water but managed to curb my enthusiasm and forced myself to concentrate on matching the hatch. At last I saw real evidence of a caddis hatch, and changed my Spent Spinner for a size-16 Light Blue Dun. Out on the edge of a fast run there was a dimple. I cast to it and there was an almighty swirl but no weight. Seconds later there was another big splash as the fish followed the fly down the current, but again no weight. Finally, as I thought that drag might spook him, I carefully lifted the fly from the water and cast again, eight metres upstream. This time there was no doubt; the fish took the fly like a very determined express train and with almost the same amount of power.

I had chosen the right fly and the fight was on.

He didn't jump so I couldn't estimate size visually; anyway it was getting too dark. He was a deep-down slugger and I knew from his fight that he was either a big fish or a very fit one, or both. His initial run had me out close to the backing and seven times in those 15 minutes of wonderful action I had him close in by the bank, only to have him race off midstream into the current again.

Finally I won the day and slid him in over the pebbles. He was one of the best conditioned browns I have seen, with broad shoulders and a very deep body. He was also magnificently and richly coloured with bright yellow flanks and vivid orange spots. I weighed him at four and a half pounds and gently released him back into the river. Fish like that deserve another day.

On return to the house we found that Ron's eccentric housekeeper had struck again. Brian discovered a thistle head in his sleeping bag, I found another wrapped in my pyjamas, one of Phil's sheets was missing and we couldn't find the whisky bottle. She had snuck in a day late to do the house cleaning, not expected, and with intelligence of our absence up the river. We eventually found the whisky bottle hidden in the onion cupboard and drank it (the whisky, not the cupboard), telephoned her with warnings of an imminent visit to wreak awful revenge and went out to start Phil's car with dreadful intent. As Phil started to back out from the garage, we all thought that his exhaust system had become unattached—a dreadful cacophony of banging tin and scraping metal. On inspection, however, we found the exhaust intact and a number empty beer cans tied with string to the chassis. She had struck again!

We laughed so much that we decided that drinking whisky was preferable to seeking vengeance and proceeded accordingly.

Next morning Brian and I drove back to Ranfurly, leaving Phil to fish the Mataura for a couple more days before joining us, and Ron with one of my watercolour fly paintings inscribed with my thanks to him over the years but saying, particularly, that there was no thanks to his housekeeper.

On return to the Ranfurly Motel I had to spend the rest of the day writing and painting, catching up after those three days of all fun and no work with Ron and Phil. I was convinced by then that artistic leanings certainly get in the way of fishing and that I was probably a nut case for trying to combine them both. Anyway, I mused, if I were not already certifiably insane, I would be by the end of the year.

I had dinner with Brian and Christine that evening and gave away the evening rise on the Taieri as a change came through and the rain poured down.

Domestics were in order the next morning, a Monday (10 February) with the shops open again. I washed a huge pile of very grubby clothes, sent postcards to the family, changed some travellers cheques and did the shopping; I also stocked up with booze and confirmed my next airline flights. I then brought my writing and diaries up to date and felt justifiably self-righteous by lunchtime, when I went down the Taieri to do some serious painting. That is when I started the watercolour of the Waipiata Bridge.

Later on, back at the motel, I found that my American neighbours had left, and their unit had been taken over by a journalist and a photographer, writing and illustrating an article on Ranfurly for a monthly New Zealand publication. We struck up a conversation and, when they realised what I was up to in 1992, they persuaded me to do an interview and photographic session with them, fishing on the Taieri the next day. They said the 'international flavour' would add to their article and I silently acknowledged that it would do my work no harm also. I needed no further persuasion when the journalist said that he might also make a lead and cover story out of the article for the monthly New

Zealand Airlines magazine (which, he told me, had world-wide distribution).

So next day, mid morning, we drove down to the Taieri with cameras, fishing gear, tape-recorders and notebooks, to put on a performance that would scare any well-meaning trout. The cameraman, Ralph Talmont, worked for an hour; close-ups of tying on flies, replacing tippets, greasing leaders and the like; distant shots of casting and retrieving (unfortunately I didn't rise a fish); then close-ups again in midstream when Ralph calmly removed his shoes, socks and trousers to join me! He took his shots with a magnificent Nikon F4 and a mass of lenses, and kindly agreed to use my Nikon at the same time, changing lenses and cameras faster than I could cast. It was a wonderful morning watching a true professional at work.

At that stage a fellow from Denmark, a member of the Denmark Fly Fishing Club, joined us; he said he'd walked the river since dawn and had seen nothing, confirming my own lack of fish during the photo session. Not to be outdone, however, and while waiting for Selwyn Parker, the journalist, I wandered upstream a little. On rounding a bend, looking upstream from a shallow beach towards deep water against the other bank, I saw a very obvious rise. It was about 11.30 a.m. by then and there was a significant damselfly hatch on the water, in perhaps the most beautiful summer conditions of the trip so far.

I flicked a Royal Wulff above the rise, and there was a dimple but no weight. I did it again, there was a bigger dimple, I waited for (what seemed like) ten seconds and was firmly connected to a two and a half pound brownie. Again it was a subsurface fighter, but a good fish which I returned to the river.

Selwyn Parker was back by the car when I returned and we had a hilarious hour's interview as I strolled around talking and he sat on a tree stump scribbling away in one of those journalist's notebooks. I must admit he was very thorough. He wanted to know, not only my own story and all about my travels, but every detail of fly-fishing— an impossible task to complete in an hour. But he managed to take in the history of Australian fishing, trout types and the insects they feed on (I had to spell *Ephemeroptera*), tackle, clothing, tactics, why fishing is more than just catching fish, tall stories and a lot of other jargon and information. If he can reproduce this accurately and correctly in condensed form, I shall be very proud of him.

Afterwards I fished for about an hour, rose two, missed one and spooked one, then returned to the

The Waipiata Bridge over the Taieri River near Ranfurly.

motel for a 3 p.m. luncheon (practice for Argentina?).

The work on my Waipiata Bridge painting led to a couple of snorts around five, then I joined Brian to contemplate the evening rise activity in some of the best weather I have ever experienced in New Zealand, or elsewhere for that matter. There is nothing like the tired and faded blue of mountains surrounding a heat-shimmering plain, with lush green willows bordering deep, dark trout water, to make me very excited.

The evening rise upstream of the Waipiata Bridge was good, but Brian and I only managed to prick a few fish; we didn't hook them and decided we probably hadn't been using the right flies. Afterwards we called at the Waipiata pub, only to see the tail lights of the publican's car moving off into the distance as he had, quite legally, shut up shop at 10 p.m. We resolved that Brian would have to come to some arrangement with him in future, to make special provision for hard working fly-fishermen.

The next morning, in still and clear conditions, I drove to Cogan's Bridge, about ten kilometres upstream on the Taieri from Ranfurly, with the car loaded with lightweight gear. Until then I had been using mainly the Orvis tackle and, occasionally, the Fenwick. This time I wanted to make the event (if there was to be one) very memorable.

In fact I was using a three-weight line and a two-pound tippet; both beyond the realms of foolishness in New Zealand.

However, the conditions were glorious: a manganese blue sky wisped with high cirrus, a promise of a change to come; dead still conditions with a heat haze; slow-moving, crystal clear peat-stream water, and a hatch of caddis and damselflies which brought joy to my heart. Certainly, I thought, conditions that deserved a lightweight approach.

I don't think I have ever encountered such good—nay superb—conditions in which to fish in New Zealand.

But the fish totally refused to rise! Oh, I did

see two dimples but, in that copybook atmosphere, their absence was most surprising. Anyway, I fished to the two dimples without success and continued, fishing blind with the dry fly until reason seeped into my heat-torpid thinking and I changed to a size-16 Emerging Copper and Hare Nymph.

As I tightened the tie, I glanced upstream to see another dimple at the bottom of a run in fairly deep water. I was on the high bankside with the run coming towards me, fishing upstream into it (for a right-hander). Across the river was the pebbled beach side.

My first cast was short and I cast again, longer this time.

The nymph sank momentarily, then WHIZ! Out went the line like a rocket! Fortunately, I remembered the strength (or lack of it) of the connection between me and the fish; apart from moving the rod tip upwards a couple of feet, I let things take their own course. The reel made that wonderful sound as line disappeared into the depths and adrenalin started to pump.

Then I saw the fish and immediately thanked my lucky stars that I had played it real cool. He looked huge—they all do through the water in such circumstances—and I began to worry how, if I had the luck to play him out, I could ever get near him.

The author rigging up beside the Taieri. (*Ralph Talmont*).

I was on a vertical bank, ten feet above the water and had at least 100 paces, up or down stream, before there was a place shallow enough for me to cross to the pebbled beach side to land him.

For the first ten minutes the fish took charge anyway, and all I could do was to move up and down the bank, trying to keep the line relatively short and myself out of any real trouble. For the next five minutes the fish became very cagey, keeping to the deep side of the river, trying to get involved with weeds and logs. I was fully occupied keeping him

The beautiful Taieri River near Ranfurly.

clear and could pay no attention to my own navigation. Then, at last, he became sullen and moved slowly downstream in the centre of the river. Some 150 paces downstream from the hookup point (as I measured later) I thought the river looked no longer deeper than my waist, and plunged in to cross to the other side where I though I might have a chance of landing, what had by then become my friend.

Two things happened.

I disappeared up to my armpits in very cold water, and my friend, who didn't share my sentiments, whizzed off downstream at the rate of knots. However, I made the pebbled bank and found that, luckily, I was still firmly connected.

Five minutes later the fish was nearly expended; he started surface flopping and finally allowed himself to be carefully slid in over the pebbles. The two-pound tippet was still intact and the nymph was stuck firmly into my friend's mouth cartilage—indeed I had to break the tippet (an astonishingly easy task) to release the rod. Then I weighed him in at just on five and a half pounds and removed the nymph.

It was one of the most exciting and enjoyable browns I have ever caught, and he was in top condition too.

Sometimes—just sometimes—weather, fish, tackle and environment all come together to produce something that, for me anyway, is worth all the other blank days of foul weather, hooks in trees or ears, and fish that refuse to rise.

Phil Waldron arrived that afternoon when I was kneedeep in pens, pads and paint brushes. We had dinner with Brian and Christine and made plans to spend the next day at the infamous Lake Onslow, before taking on the evening rise on the Taieri. We reckoned, at that stage, that because of some shocking weather coming our way (from Australia they said), I had only one full day's fishing left in New Zealand before flying out to Auckland and then South America. In fact, Australia had had floods, rain and people lost in the Snowy Mountains; quite catastrophic stuff—in the middle of summer too.

At least, I thought, I was ahead of the weather and travelling in the right direction.

The next morning my alarm burst into music at 5 a.m. I stumbled my way through the processes of teeth-cleaning, shaving and showering and arrived at the Thomsons around six to find they had forgotten their alarm and were still sound asleep. I packed my gear into Brian's 4WD, making as much noise as possible so that my hosts eventually saw the light of day and we left at seven for the trip to Lake Onslow.

As it happened that day, the weather was magically even better than its predecessor. A very soft early morning turned into fog as we climbed uphill out of the Taieri Valley towards the lake. Brown-top grass, on the verges of the track, turned purple in the ethereal light and, despite the late hour of the evening before (or was it an early hour of that morning?), it felt very good to be alive. What's more, I had that sixth sense again.

Total bliss was only disturbed by a puncture and the need to change a tyre on the way in, and by the occasional rabbit hopping across the road; although the latter really added to the magic of those moments.

Had the fog not hidden the cliff face, where Brian parked the car on our arrival at the lake, I would have gone 'white knuckled' again. But there we were, rigged up, feeling our way through the mist to the water—crystal clear with its mirror surface only broken by the odd ring of rising trout.

Within the first half hour, Phil caught one three-pounder and was broken off by a leviathan; Brian pricked and missed two, and I hooked one fish only to have the hook pull out. It didn't seem to matter too much what dry fly we used, they were apparently taking anything insect-like off the top. I was fishing a Kakahi Queen, Brian the Black Gnat, and Phil the Royal Wulff.

Then the sun started to burn through the fog, and I have seldom seen such beauty. The surrounding hills became more than suspicion, colours (other than grey and white) suggested themselves in washed-out yellows and blues, warmth became itself, and the secrecy unveiled showing us where we were. By this stage, Phil and I were walking together with Brian a little behind. The fog lifted completely and the heat of the day was apparent; remarkably, there was still no breeze, and the lake surface stayed glassy.

About 20 metres out we spotted a good rise. I stipped line and started false casting, once, twice. Then, much closer, another fish made a big swirl. I changed direction mid-cast and plonked the fly a metre ahead in the direction I guessed he was travelling.

Perfect!

A mighty swirl and my Kahaki Queen was engulfed, and the fight began. At first observation I said to Phil that I thought he was probably about a two and a half or three pounder. But, by the time Brian caught up with us some ten minutes later (beckoned by my shouts of triumph), I was not so sure. Five minutes later, when I was still playing him gently (using a three-pound tippet), I realised that this was a pretty fit fish. Indeed, when I eventually slid him in, I found him to be four and a quarter pounds of top-conditioned jack brown. It was a wonderful feeling in conditions one can only dream about. I subsequently wrote to Blackman and Banks to tell them of Lake Onslow at better times.

After lunch back beside the car, we lazily meandered in the direction of the Taieri. I started to doze and was awakened by Brian taking a steep bump rather hard, in fact the back seat lifted out of its holdings and smashed back with considerable force—something I was to rue later.

At the first crossing of the Taieri we met my Danish friend (fly-fishing in New Zealand for five months) and a farmer casting the fly, so we moved downstream to a point where, still in unusually calm and warm conditions, we saw a number of fish rising. The brakes were applied, we stopped and made a dash for rods and flies. That was when I discovered the effects of the backseat dislodgement: the seat had come down hard on the tip of my very precious Orvis rod!

It was stupid of me in the extreme to have left it loose in the back of the car without putting it in a tube, but I wonder how many of us have not caught a rod in somewhat similar and mistaken circumstances? Very fortunately, however, the break was very close to the tip-guide. Later application of heat to remove the end, and re-gluing of the guide to the tip, resulted in a rod shortened by less than an inch and with no discernible difference in action.

In this case, luck was doubly on my side. Not only was the rod completely repairable, but I couldn't fish immediately to those rises and was forced to change my role totally to that of the photographer. I used a complete 36-shot spool of film, photographing Brian casting to, hooking up, playing and landing a three-pound brownie from the Taieri. Sometimes it all just falls into place.

Back at Ranfurly we found that Phil's wife, Marg, was due to drive up from Dunedin to join us the next day. Moreover, Gini was also in Dunedin by then and due to join me the day afterwards for the trip north to Christchurch. A little gentle thinking, a couple of telephone calls and Gini hitched a lift with Marg to Ranfurly.

I spent that entire day working, then the girls arrived from Dunedin in the late afternoon. Thus it was that, on St. Valentine's Day, 1992, the families of the Thomsons and the Waldrons, together with their overseas mates, the Holes, all met up at Ranfurly for a dinner at the Patearoa pub that

should go down the annals of *Historic Feasts I Have Known!*

We took leave of our New Zealand friends the next morning. Thomson said we ought to make plans for another get-together in 12 months. I agreed, but said that next time I would bring two changes of clothes and my fishing gear only; nothing else. I added that then I would stay for a month!

Gini and I drove over the Dansey Pass to the Waitaki area, on through Otematata and Omarama, and eventually stopped for the night at Lake Tekapo. This was an unfortunate decision. Six bus loads of tourists arrived at the motel later in the afternoon. The drivers parked their buses obstructing the view of the lake, and a full-size rock band started playing in the dining room at sunset and kept thumping until the wee small hours.

The drive to Christchurch the next morning was suitably sombre. In the afternoon, Gini dropped me at Christchurch airport for my flight to Auckland and, later in the evening, she flew to Sydney and returned to Canberra.

I spent three nights in Auckland before boarding my flight to Buenos Aires on Wednesday, 19 February. It was a time for finishing the draft of my two New Zealand chapters, completing a major painting, catching up with the mail and other mundane domestic chores such as getting one's hair cut. And the latter turned out to be a task of no small undertaking. It was raining at the time so, as I borrowed a hotel umbrella from the concierge, I asked directions to a men's barber. These were supplied, but by the time I located the establishment my brolly was threadbare, I was dripping wet and I found that the establishment in question was a very special unisex affair where I was greeted by the statement: 'Can't fit you in, *Darhling*, until late this afternoon!' . . . all said with a flick of a very limp wrist.

In horror, I returned to my hotel, gave the broken brolly to the concierge with some unflattering comments about his brollies and his advice, and consequently was given better directions. This time I went to a large department store across the street which had a dedicated, old-fashioned men's hairdressing department. It made those under 50 feel slightly uncomfortable, and those over 50 totally relaxed in a six-chair mid-Victorian wonderland where one could choose from barbers who not only knew how to cut hair, but could be chosen by their conversation topics: politics, general knowledge, the good-old-days, history, and sport (including horse racing and fly-fishing!). When I departed, it had stopped raining and the sun was shining brightly.

Lake Onslow (in good weather).

The New Zealand visit had been largely successful and certainly a huge amount of fun. It is always sad to leave one's friends and to move on, but I had things to do and a great deal more of the world to see.

Brian about to make contact!

12
Patagonia (or Heaven on a Stick)

The very word Patagonia brings to mind intrepid travelling, fly-fishing authors like Farson, Haig-Brown and, importantly with regard to Argentina, Ernest Schwiebert and William Leitch. In the same thought process, it also reminds me of Paul Theroux' absorbing tale of that epic train journey from Medford, in northeast America, to Esquel (or was it further south?) in Argentina. A beautifully told story of a remarkable railroad adventure from the heartland of American conservatism into the celluloid 'end-world' of Butch Cassidy and the Sundance Kid.

Theroux, however, had an aversion to the language of writers whose inspiration came from the window of an aeroplane; hence, I guess, one of his reasons for choosing the steel-lined route. He wrote:

> The literature of travel has become measly, the standard opening that farcical nose-against-the-porthole view from the plane's tilted fuselage. The joke-opening, that straining for effect, is now so familiar it is nearly impossible to parody. How does it go? 'Below us lay the tropical green, the flooded valley, the patchwork quilt of farms, and as we penetrated the cloud I could see dirt roads threading their way into the hills and cars so small they looked like toys. We circled the airport and, as we came in low for the landing, I saw the stately palms, the harvest, the rooftops of the shabby houses, the square fields stitched together with crude fences, the people like ants, the colourful . . .'

And his next paragraph was even more cutting!

But I wondered, as the Jumbo jet climbed out of Auckland, if it would ever be possible to cross the South Pacific in the unhurried awareness of the train traveller's environment.

Maybe a sea voyage?

I had covered enough nautical miles in my navy days to enjoy the comfort of the jet, ponder on Theroux and come to the conclusion that I was travelling the best way under the circumstances, but that I should promise myself not to describe anything outside the porthole as we descended into Buenos Aires—or anywhere else for that matter.

On the other hand, I thought, there were certain unique points about a 10,000-kilometre great circle flight across the bottom of the South Pacific. A dateline to cross, two Wednesdays, time zones to think about, how far south would we go, and at what line of longitude would we make that southernmost point? I determined to ask the air hostess (do they call themselves 'flight attendants' or 'pursers' these days?)—if she was attractive—to prise this information from the flight deck.

Time zones and datelines are largely misunderstood by the population of this planet. I have found that it is only maritime navigators, aeroplane people and the like who really have a grasp of this mathematical simplicity. They understand that, unless one wants to be relative (to a sunrise or sunset for example—even a bus timetable), if one wants to communicate (a dreadful but unfortunately necessary word) with others in different time zones around this world, one should revert to the common denominator of GMT (Greenwich Mean Time).

I can recall in my seagoing days when we used to cross the dateline, going east to west, having left Pearl Harbor on our way back to Sydney for example, we would *lose* a day in the vicinity of Fiji.

But it was all relative. We would check the ship's books to see if there were any sailors whose birthdays fell on the *lost* day. If there were (and I don't recall a time when there were not), instead of jumping from, say, midnight Monday/Tuesday to midnight Monday/Wednesday, we would delay the switch until a quarter past midnight, and in those 15 secretly found minutes, wake up the birthday boys, wish them an astonishingly happy birthday and jump, miraculously, to Wednesday.

As I say, it is all relative and has absolutely nothing to do with faded curtains, a communist plot or cows going dry.

At the turn of the century—the nineteenth going into the twentieth—there was a sea captain (after my own heart) who just happened to be crossing the Pacific very near both the Equator and the dateline on 31 December 1899. With considerable forethought, an enviable sense of humour and great panache, he positioned his vessel accurately on those two imaginary great circles and recorded in his decklog:

> 2359/0001;1899/1900: One quarter of my vessel lies in the Northern Hemisphere on Sunday in the 19th century; one quarter in the Southern Hemisphere on Tuesday in the 20th century; one quarter is in the same Hemisphere on Sunday in the previous century, and the port after section lies in the Northern Hemisphere but two days hence in the 20th century, if one views it from Sunday. Miraculously my ship is still in one piece.

Those who understand these things would deduce that he was in the right spot at the right time, and travelling eastwards. Or, if travelling westabout, had turned his ship through 180 degrees just to further confuse anyone reading his decklog.

As I say, he was a man after my own heart and I bet he never travelled to Patagonia by train.

I did ascertain our most southerly point on that trip. Indeed I was lucky enough to be invited onto the flightdeck at that point, on a still, clear and starry night at 58 degrees South, 120 degrees West. We landed at Buenos Aires International Airport mid-afternoon on the second Wednesday, 19 February, and I must admit to some porthole gazing as we crossed the South American continent. The only observation I'll make, however, is to say how much the scene reminded me of parts of inland South Australia.

I cleared customs and immigration with unbelievable ease, picked up my luggage, and was clear of the airport 20 minutes after arrival, only to be stopped and searched by the *Federalis* some ten minutes later. There were no explanations and, fortunately, no problems, but it was a disconcerting experience. Afterwards, as I drove on towards the city, the landscape struck me as being very flat and dry, shimmering in 38-degree heat; it was a welcome relief to arrive in the relative comfort of the air-conditioned hotel.

I had two nights there, washing and sleeping out my jetlag, and catching up with my missing mail before I left for Patagonia and San Carlos de Bariloche; but I must make some mention of the hotel before leaving it.

The 60-year old Alvear Palace is an expression of a bygone era. A mixture of South American and Spanish baroque, huge ornate columns rise from marble floors to support sculptured gilt ceilings. It plays host to a roof garden and ballroom, an enclosed breakfast verandah which doubles as a social afternoon-tea hideout, an oyster bar and grill, and an ambience—even an aroma—which reflects a genteel shabbiness that, no matter what attempt is made at updating, is impossible to conceal. I wandered upstairs to look at the roof garden and ballroom but, on crossing the once plush carpet, found the decaying velvet drapes closed. Tables and chairs in the ballroom and its gallery were stacked high and covered in dust, dumb waiters and other machinery were cobweb-encrusted, and discarded streamers strewn over the floor bore evidence of last night's (last year's? last decades's?) ball. I rather expected to find skeletons in the cloak-check booths: one draped in white tie, decorations and tails, the other in long white taffeta with a tiara. It was, nonetheless, my imagination, but this was supported I might add by the sight of an ancient retainer busily polishing the brass banisters leading to the balcony above the ballroom as, no doubt, he had done for decades while all else around him was slowly crumbling and silently crying out for maintenance. Although the Alvear Palace may be a face-lifted Raffles of the 1950s, it is a wonderful place in which to stay.

But fishing was my business and I had to move on. At least this time I knew I would be returning to the same hotel in eight days and could leave a little luggage behind in order to reduce the excess (on leaving Auckland, they wanted me to pay $US120 excess, but I managed to talk them out of it).

In the battered red Hi-lux with its cracked windscreen, the drive from Bariloche to Estancia Huechahue, 15 kilometres east of Junin de Los Andes, took a little over two hours. At first the road followed the Rio Limay to its hydroelectric dam, then it turned north to pick up and follow the Rio Collon Cura until that river branched into the Rio Chimechuin and the Rio Aluminé. I followed the latter, crossing it at La Rinconada and pulled up at the *casco* (homestead) around 5 p.m.

It was a spectacular trip, even judged by the

standards of the journeys I had made so far. With the snow-capped Andes visibly rising to heights over 12,000 feet to the west, vivid blue, fast-flowing rivers (whose clarity made Gordons look like mud) to follow, and a stark bright landscape of buttes and mesas surrounded by pampa supporting at least six different varieties of tussocks, it was unbelievably beautiful. The mountains and the waters reminded me of New Zealand but, at that high altitude in the Andes, the colours were clearer, sharper, and almost overpoweringly bright. During my eight days in Patagonia I came to worship this scenery and tried to capture it, but it largely eluded me.

I was introduced to my hostess, Jane Wood, on arrival at Estancia Huechahue and she immediately won my eternal gratitude by suggesting that, after I had unpacked, she would take me down to the river for an hour or so's fishing before dinner. I've never unpacked so fast.

The Aluminé was only five minutes' drive away and very soon I was up to my ankles in its fast-flowing cold clarity; surrounded by Patagonia and bathed in the last sunlight of a perfect summer day.

They had told me that most of my fishing in Patagonia would be wet-fly fishing and, paying lip-service to this advice, I tied on a nymph (Copper and Hare I think) and cast to some likely looking places while examining my surrounds. Around half past seven a pronounced caddis hatch started and, as I changed to a size-16 Light Blue Dun, I heard the first 'plop'.

Zeroing in, I cast and was immediately connected to a fat rainbow which fought like the very Devil. My first Argentine fish, caught on my first day, and on the dry fly too. I felt as though heaven had been offered to me on a stick.

The rise lasted a further 20 minutes, during which I caught and released another rainbow of about one and a half pounds.

I found that catch-and-release and barbless hooks were the commendable unofficial policies for most Patagonian waters bordering the *estancias* (stations). Lakes and waters bordering public land, parks and reserves, despite licences and regulations, were apparently open slather due to a lack of policing. Whilst all Patagonian rivers (like Australian rivers) are public property, in order to balance the public lack of care, and maintain a good fishery, the *estancia* owners keep locked gates and do not allow uninvited access to the rivers across their lands. This, together with the catch-and-release and barbless hook policies in the parts of the rivers passing through their properties, has indeed balanced the bellyman and an acceptable *status quo* has been maintained.

It would seem that, once again, dedicated private management of fisheries (even if unofficial) is an effective guarantee of their continued conservation.

The 14,000-acre Estancia Huechahue has a remarkable history.

George Wood arrived in the Argentine from England in the 1890s, as a baby. He spent his life in the agricultural business, running company farms throughout Argentina, and purchased Estancia Huechahue in 1931 for his eldest son, Geoffrey. But, when Geoffrey was killed serving in the RAF during the Second World War, the *estancia* was taken over by his brother, Jim. Jim and his wife lived their lives in the original *casco* (on the left as one enters the front gate), the newer, two-storey house not being built until 1955 when Jim had it constructed for his foreman with the thought also that it might be used by his children in the years to come.

The 1955 house is built entirely from local materials found on the *estancia*: hand-made bricks, and a timber called *Rauli* (of the beech family) which starts its life a polished yellow ochre colour and darkens with age.

Geoffrey did a great deal of the initial work on the *estancia* and Jim followed. The outhouses were built, the land fenced, levelled in parts and cultivated; dams were built, power and water systems installed and, in the 1960s, 6,000 Corriedale sheep were running on the property. It was also in those earlier times that the mass of magnificent trees were planted around the *cascos*: an apple orchard, pines, poplars, oaks, beeches and towering California redwoods blend with a natural bush setting and sloping lawns to provide a quiet and comfortable haven.

During the Peron regime in the 1970s, the foreman died and his house remained unoccupied and unmaintained for a decade. Then, in 1980, Jim's son, Walter, took residence with his wife, Jane, and began a large scale improvement program. Both were civil engineers by profession and this learning is evident when one first encounters the place.

In the early 1980s, sheep were abandoned in favour of cattle and the *estancia* took on 300 breeding Hereford cows. At the same time, with a view to capitalising on their interest in horses, fishing and hunting, Walter and Jane built a three-bedroom guest lodge up the slope from their house, in materials which matched all the other buildings including the *casco*. In 1990 a most attractive paying-guest program followed. Trail-riding among the monkey-puzzle trees, bamboo and soaring peaks and

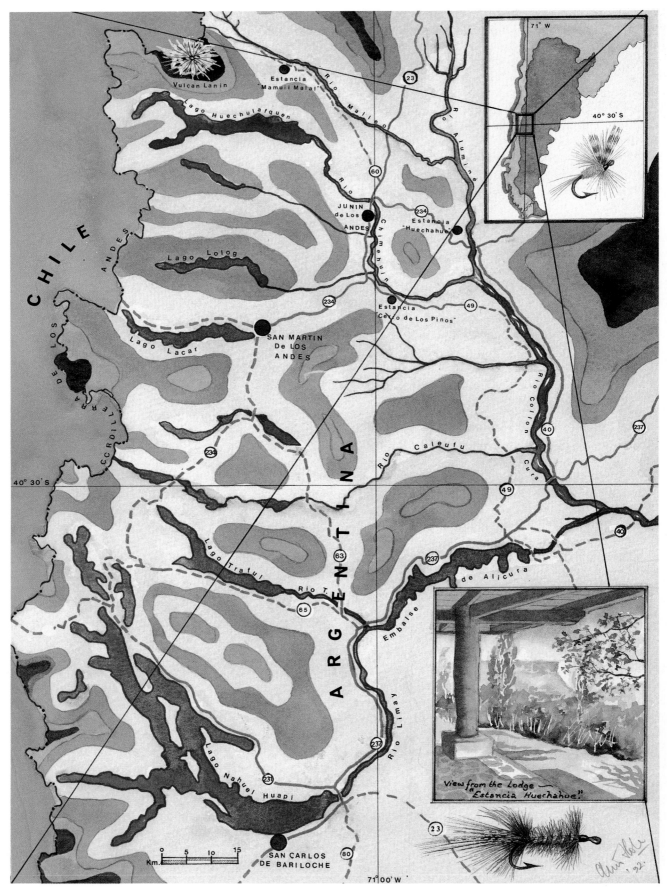

Mudmap of Patagonia's northern fly-fishing zone in Argentina.

Jane Wood and the author at Estancia Huechahue.

Hooked up while rafting the Collon Cura.

volcanoes of the Andes; fly-fishing in streams simply teeming with wild browns and rainbows, and winter hunting for geese, wild boar and red deer, was complemented by an almost unequalled relaxed and luxurious lifestyle at the lodge.

Then in 1990, disaster struck. Walter was tragically killed in a farm-machinery accident leaving Jane, with her two very small boys, supported by her mother-in-law in the old *casco* and the *estancia* staff, to run it all.

If the enjoyment of my visit—apparently shared by the other guests I met—is any yardstick, all I can conclude is that she has more than made a success of it . . . and the farming side as well.

At breakfast on the morning after my arrival I was introduced to my fishing guide, Santiago. What followed was two more days of heaven on a stick.

From morning until dusk on those magical days we rafted the Rio Collon Cura, fly-fishing for rainbows and browns with such success that I lost count of how many we caught and released each day. At about nine each morning we took the raft,

The author returning his three pound rainbow to the Collon Cura.

Outside Estancia Cerro de Los Pinos fishing lodge . . .

. . . and inside.

a pump-up rubber Zodiac affair, to the river in the back of the Hi-lux, together with our gear and lunch. By ten we would have assembled the raft, stowed our equipment and be midstream with Santi expertly handling the oars and me, a little less expertly, handling my rod as I wobbled on the rubber bottom.

I found that Santi possessed a wealth of experience. His German grandfather had bequeathed a passion for fly-fishing to him so that, as a very young boy, he was versed in the fly rod and all its unwritten laws. Years of subsequent experience on his favourite Patagonian rivers produced a guide, probably without peer, with a good command of English and a wicked sense of humour.

The only flaw in those first days (if indeed it could be called a flaw) was that, as is the case in a number of other countries where salmonids have been introduced to fast-flowing rivers, the wet fly was used in the early days and, probably because it is still so successful, continues to be used in preference to the dry today. On those first few days on the Collon Cura, I really had to seek out backwaters and swirls, or places where fish were visibly rising, to get away from the across-and-down principle which, although constantly successful, is not nearly so exacting or exciting as dry-fly or nymph fishing to me.

I won't try to describe all the fish action in those first two wonderful days; it would take ages. Two matters, however, stand out and ought to be related. They were, in order, lunch, and my most exciting fish.

Around 2 o'clock each afternoon we would beach the raft under a willow on a rocky island or by the bank of the river. Out would come the freezer box to reveal a cold quiche, salami, tomatoes, two or three cheeses, salad, bread, fruit, mineral water and a bottle of excellent Argentine claret from Mendoza.

Just imagine, lying back in that scenery: faded pink cliffs, cobalt sky, willows and poplars, eagles overhead and an ultramarine, crystal-clear, fast-flowing river at your feet; a magnificent lunch, and the knowledge that not only had you hooked a mass of fish in the morning, but the afternoon was still to come!

And my most exciting fish?

As well as casting from the raft, when we found a suitable pool or run which was better fished from an island or a bank, Santi would beach the raft and I would start casting from dry land. Late on the second day we stopped at such an island and Santi, looking thoughtful, said: 'I bet I can guarantee you a good fish in this run.'

We were fishing wet again and I had tied on a size-eight Green Woolly Bugger. I started moving slowly down the pool, casting into its deep, green swirling depths. No action. Further and further down the pool I went with Santi looking glummer and glummer with each step I took. Finally, with probably two or three steps to make before I reached the end of the pool, Santi came up and sheepishly said: 'I think I shutta my big mouth'.

'Hang on, Santi,' I said, 'we've still got about three casts to go.' Whereupon I cast far out beside a willow branch in the water, and WHAM! A rainbow took like a rocket, exploding spray and water as he cartwheeled his three pounds into the air.

They are all good fighters in the Collon Cura, but this fellow was exceptional. I was using a three-pound tippet and was worried that with the strength of this fish it might not hold. So out to the backing twice I went, and had 15 minutes of action before I slid him up over the rocks, weighed him, had the obligatory photo taken and released him.

That heavenly stick was showing again!

Oh, I forgot to add, Santi was a pretty good photographer too. Everytime I hooked a fish he would have my Nikon and Minolta around his neck in a trice, and film would disappear as fast as my fly line.

Then, at the end of each rafting day, the Hi-lux would miraculously appear on the river bank to take us back to the lodge where malt whisky and a shower would make that celestial stick positively vibrate. I would then complete my day's diary and walk down to the *casco* for dinner with Jane and the other guests around, 10 p.m.

But it had to come to an end, and I knew that I would need to get some writing and sketching done. On Monday and Tuesday, 24 and 25 February, I spent two days at the lodge doing just that. It was not all, however, work making Jack a dull boy. On the first evening Jane arrived on the doorstep to suggest that we, her two children and Sean, their tutor (a South African), should repair to the Aluminé for fishing and a barbeque. You couldn't see me move for dust.

It was a perfect, still, hot night with hatch after hatch of insects. Sean and a Canadian chum were in the river before the rest of us and managed eight apiece on the wet fly. I immediately tied on a Blue Dun and went upstream into a perfect glassy tail which became deeper and bigger as I moved up into it. The surface was foaming with rising trout and I took two good rainbows in the first five minutes. Sean joined me but remained fishless with the dry, and I, too, went through a ten-minute period when they simply refused to take my dun. I then woke up to the fact that there was a new hatch and changed to a size-12 Black Gnat to hook one good brown and be broken by another monster before the barbeque was ready.

It was a starry, clear night, the beef was magnificent and washed down with a shared demijohn of rough Argentine red. Sean, who also moonlighted at weekends playing guitar and singing at a San Martin bistro, brought out his guitar and started singing:
'Summertime, and the livin' is easy,
'Fish are jumpin' and the . . .'
The celestial stick went into orbit!

Having brought my work up to date, I packed an overnight bag and, at 9 a.m. on Wednesday 26 February, the ever-reliable Santi arrived on the scene again. We loaded the Hi-lux and departed for two days of fishing the Rio Chimehuin and the Rio Malleo. But by then the weather had changed somewhat, as it so often does. Although clear and bright, it was blowing a strong nor' wester—howling might be a better description.

The Chimehuin is a smaller river than the Aluminé, and much smaller than the combination of the two when they join to become the Collon Cura. The Chimehuin retains, however, considerable strength and the super clarity of those Patagonian trout havens.

We drove through Junin de Los Andes on the way to the river and stopped so I could phone Australia, buy some whisky, visit the local fly-fishing shop and talk to the local Fisheries man, a strong supporter of the controlled entry and catch-and-release policy maintained by the landowners. In Patagonia this was reiterated time and time again. I'm of the opinion that there ought to be an international exchange program for fisheries officers and officials. It could only result in improved conservation and trout conditions world-wide.

We arrived at Pedro Larminat's Estancia Cerro de Los Pinos, 20 kilometres south of Junin de Los Andes on the Chimehuin, in the late morning. I unpacked and settled into the three-bedroom, fully staffed (Martha and her mother) dedicated fishing lodge and explored the area briefly. The *estancia* was big and very well maintained; it ran both fine-wool merino sheep and hereford cattle. The lodge, and all the other buildings and outhouses, were constructed in local stone and *Rauli* (again) and surrounded by lawns, gardens, poplars and monkey-puzzle trees. Pedro also employed a fishing and lodge

manager, an ex-policeman who looked after guests and river policy with admirable efficiency. I felt quite privileged, 30 minutes later, when Santi took me to the river for a short session before lunch.

At that point, however, the wind continued to blow straight downstream at 25 knots with stronger gusts, so I stepped up to my eight and a half foot, seven-weight Fenwick, and started casting a small Yellow Montana Nymph. It was hard work getting the fly up into the wind; in the end I found it best to put my back to the wind, face downstream, and backcast the fly up and across so that it would dead drift under the willows on the far bank. This accounted for two pan-sized rainbows when, between a gap in the willows, I saw a very obvious, very healthy rise. Changing to a size-14 Royal Humpy, I fluked a backcast into the right spot, there was a boil of water and I was firmly connected to a rainbow of about two pounds. I felt particularly pleased to have succeeded with the dry fly in fairly difficult circumstances.

At lunchtime we returned to the lodge where I met a group of fellow fishing companions: three Americans (two were brothers) and a Canadian, all vice-presidents in IBM, who had fished Patagonia together every second year over ten years. We swapped a lot of lies and had great fun together. I found the Canadian, John Thompson, used to be on the board of directors at Havergal Girls' College in Toronto, a school my daughter had visited in 1987 on an international school exchange visit.

After lunch Santi took me to Harry and Betty Thompson's farm, on the very banks of the Chimehuin, for the afternoon and evening sessions. I discovered that Harry was an expatriate Englishman, a Mosquito pilot during the Second World War, a 707 captain (now retired) for Aerolineas Argentinas and a very keen trout fisherman. I also found out that Betty's father was an Australian from Bega. After our fishing session, we returned to the house for drinks, and Harry gave a demonstration of casting and skipping a large, palmered Spider Fly on the Chimehuin from beside his front door—where, Santi told me, his grandfather used to cast in his twilight years from a chair with a gin and tonic in hand.

The fishing that late afternoon was still in very windy conditions. I managed a number of fish on the wet fly before persuading Santi that I thought I should try a dry, upstream, as I was close enough to gain some protection from the willows.

It worked. I took two good rising rainbows, one on a Caddis, and one on a Twilight Beauty when a mass of duns started floating downstream. Dinner

Fishing the Malleo in the shadow of Vulcan Lanin. Surely this must be 'Heaven on a stick'!

The author fishing the Chimehuin at sunset.

Fishing the fabulous feeder under the Shadow of Vulcan Lanin.

Cattle mustering at Estancia Mamuil Malal.

at the lodge was at 10 that evening: Argentine beefsteak, Mendoza claret and good company. I recorded in my personal diary: 'What a wonderful place, wonderful people, and wonderful fishing.'

The next day, my last fishing day in Patagonia, dawned clear, cloudless and warm, without a breath of wind. Santi had saved the very best for last: a day on the Malleo, dry-fly fishing in the shadow of Vulcan Lanin. We left the lodge at nine in the morning, having said goodbye to and exchanged addresses with my North American friends (they were leaving for two days rafting the Aluminé before returning home). It was a two-hour drive over fairly rough country before we reached Estancia Mamuil Malal, an outstanding and beautiful *estancia* owned by the Grahn family who, I found, were familiar with some Australian friends of mine through riding and polo interests.

Having picked up the keys to the locked gates, we moved down to the banks of the Malleo. In all my years of fishing some very attractive places, I don't think I've ever seen anything quite so beautiful. Crystal-clear, bright, fast-flowing dry-fly water with its surface broken occasionally by rising fish; surrounded by willows, monkey-puzzle trees

and bush, and overlooked some ten kilometres away by the overpowering snowcapped cone of Vulcan Lanin where glacial ice exploded in the heat of the day as it reached another 7,000 feet into the cobalt blue; this was Paradise indeed.

When we first parked, we saw a couple of dry-fly fishermen working the far bank, so moved upstream half a kilometre or so to hit the jackpot! We stopped by a feeder stream for the Malleo which was simply teeming with wild trout untouched by human exploitation.

I caught and released over 30 fish from the little feeder that day. From narrow, clear water with its sandy and pebbly bottom, I plucked them from impossible gaps between willows, I took them from groups of five or six clearly visible through the water, I hooked them on the second, third, and (sometimes) fourth slash at the fly, I spotted them, I stalked them and occasionally I lost them as they disappeared under willows or broke me off. I left four or five dry flies in the willows, I forgot my hat and suntan lotion in my enjoyment, and eventually I almost wept with the sheer pleasure of it all. With only two exceptions (when I fished a Copper and Hare Nymph), all those fish—about half browns and half rainbows—were taken on the Adams (size 14 to 18). To add to the pleasure, I was using a three-weight Sage rod and line and a three-pound tippet. Moreover, my biggest fish was a wild four and a half pound rainbow who fought like Satan himself and took 20 minutes to land!

We broke for lunch at 2 p.m. and lay in the shade of the monkey-puzzle trees for an hour, applied suntan lotion all too late and ate tortilla washed down with Mendoza claret. That night, after returning to the lodge, and having had drinks with Pedro the owner, then dinner at 10.30 p.m., I wrote in my diary as I worked until 3.30 a.m. in order to catch up: 'had the *best* day's fishing since the old screwpile jetty at Granite Island in the 1940s!'

With a feeling of total contentment we drove back to Estancia Huechahue the next morning, via San Martin de Los Andes where I did some shopping and sent a mass of postcards. Twenty four hours at the *estancia* followed when I tried to catch up with my writing and painting, but it was very difficult to concentrate.

On leap-year's day I said goodbye to a part of the world I had come to love dearly. Sean gave me addresses and instructions for his hometown of Cape Town and drove me to Bariloche airport for my afternoon flight back to Buenos Aires.

At the airport we bumped into my Northern American friends again. I thought at the time it was Hemingwayesque that six sunburnt fly-fishermen—three Americans, a South African, a Canadian and an Australian—could be sitting there after some incredible fishing experiences, drinking ice-cold beer in an airport bar, high in the Andes on a late-summer afternoon, waiting for their flight to Buenos Aires while they ogled four gold-lamé-miniskirted dolly birds who were only there to promote the Bariloche casino!

And fish?

I caught (and released) well over 70 in four day's and two night's fishing; my biggest being the four and a half pounder from the Malleo area.

Ain't half bad for a rookie visit to Patagonia!

I said it was heaven on a stick. But I was very wrong.

Patagonia is Valhalla on a 40-foot pole!

On return to Buenos Aires I had only one night at the Alvear Palace Hotel and it was a visit that made me think that my earlier impressions were probably a little jaundiced. I had arrived then after a long international flight, the temperature was in the high thirties, and my hotel room was small and stuffy with an old-fashioned air-conditioner, built through the wall, which wheezed and clanked all night. On the second visit, I was given a top-floor suite (for some unknown reason—perhaps those who hook over 70 fish in four days have some special entitlement?); it had its own doorbell, a living area in which one could probably cast a three-weight, a view to Montevideo, an electronic spa bath and telephones everywhere. It provided a wonderful rest before I left the next morning for my flights to Rio de Janeiro and from Rio to Cape Town.

My South American adventure had, however, one more chapter to play out. On arrival in Rio I noticed that, not only did I have a five-hour wait before I had to leave for Cape Town, but it was Annual Carnival week in Rio—the genuine Mardi Gras! I hired an air conditioned taxi for two and a half hours and put my watch, Nikon and signet ring in my briefcase which I locked in the taxi's boot. With my little Minolta and empty pockets, I took on the Carnival and the Copacabaña using three rolls of film photographing a kaleidoscope of colour covering a vast acreage of bums, tits and pooftahs!

No one moved in Rio that evening, they *samba'd* everywhere! It was a remarkable climax to an exceptional visit to South America which was only topped by a Rio airline official finding my luggage had been wrongly routed to Johannesburg from Buenos Aires, instead of to Cape Town. They caught it in time and thoughtfully saved me some real headaches on arrival in South Africa.

I still haven't worked out what the Carnival of Rio has to do with fly-fishing; moreover, I can't remember any fly-fisherman I know of being sidetracked into that Mardi Gras, although they have often ended up in equally unusual places.

But, as I've said, fly-fishing is more than . . . etc.

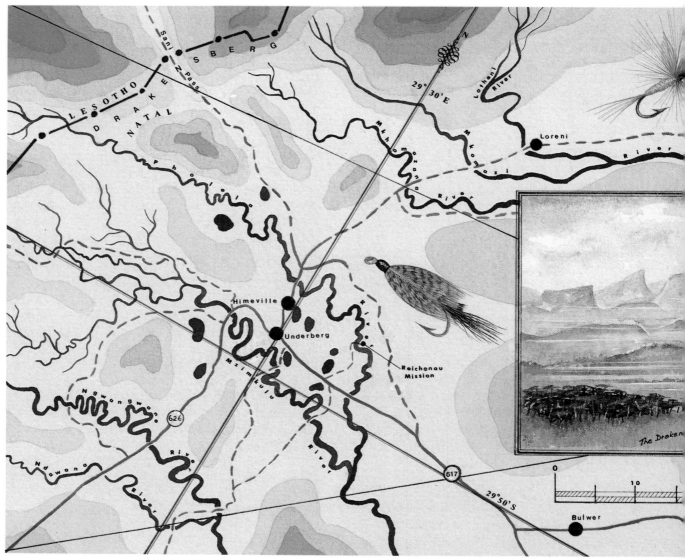

Mudmap of the Drakensberg fly-fishing area in Natal, RSA.

13
Fly-fishing in the Drakensberg

Cape Town, unfortunately but not surprisingly, found me feeling somewhat depressed. One simply can't catch over 70 fish in four days in breathtaking scenery, visit the Carnival of Rio, then travel some 8,000 kilometres in 24 hours without experiencing a consequent let-down. Anyway I can't, and I'd be obliged to anyone who has done the same thing, remained on a high

and can prove me wrong, if they would tell me their secret recipe for sustenance.

On arrival in Cape Town, having nearly lost my luggage, with the pre-booked car nowhere to be seen and feeling decidedly 'post Rio', 'post-Patagonia', 'post airline air-conditioning' and, generally, totally 'post', I somehow made it into town together with my 63 kilos of luggage. I arrived at my hotel, had

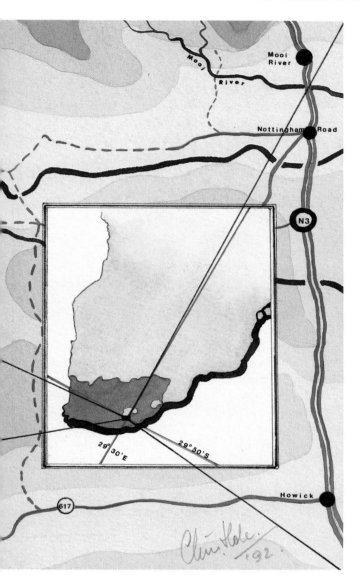

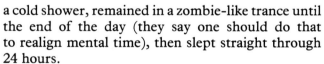

Two views from Table Mountain in Cape Town.

a cold shower, remained in a zombie-like trance until the end of the day (they say one should do that to realign mental time), then slept straight through 24 hours.

Mail and faxes piled up at my door but, in my somnolent state, I didn't give a damn. I didn't even dream about fishing!

It was a pity because Cape Town has so much to offer, and when I did rejoin the land of the living, as well as completing the chapter on Patagonia and catching up with some of the backlog of mail and artwork, I squeezed in a cablecar trip to Table Mountain, a visit to the beaches and a tour of the markets and the harbourside pubs and restaurants. I wished that I had longer there, but that was not to be. In any case I didn't exactly welcome the general feeling of being back in the confined concrete of a big city again after the wilds of Patagonia. I was eager to return to trout country and to remove myself from South African politics which were hammered into my senses every time I switched on the radio or television. After four days in Cape Town, I flew to Durban on Friday, 6 March, and was immediately struck by the size and spread of this city with the wind, spray and surf of the Indian Ocean to its east, and acres of sugar cane disappearing into the hinterland to the west.

Fred Pilkington met me at the airport (my 63 kilos had made it again—but only because the check-in official at Cape Town was a lover of jazz music and fishing).

Fred is a remarkable man. A civil engineer by profession (his mark remains on many buildings and structures in Durban); a Spitfire pilot with the RAF in the Far East during the Second World War and an exceptional fly-fishman, he was introduced to me by the Tichbornes of New Zealand. One of Fred's sons had married a New Zealand girl and the Tichbornes and Pilkingtons had met before and at the wedding in New Zealand. A common interest in fly-fishing and Nancy's art cemented a lasting friendship. My early contacts with South Africa were thus with Fred on the advice of Bryan and Nancy Tichborne.

Fred and his wife, Peggy, made me feel very much at home in their house overlooking the Indian Ocean. They gave me a guided tour of the town, and a recce of the route out to the Drakensberg; above all they gave me a big, open family room in which to sleep—heaven after air-conditioned aeroplanes and hotels.

So I drove to Underberg the next day, totally refreshed and ready to go. The 200-kilometre drive took a little over two and a half hours through an impressive, rolling countryside which became more and more steep and inspiring as I climbed to the first plateau of the Drakensberg. I thought to myself, as my ears popped with the altitude and the car sped past conifers and maize: Of all sportsmen, only trout fishermen can guarantee themselves constantly beautiful surroundings in which to operate, and time to take it all in. Others, like yachtsmen and skiers, have their share of scenery but they are often too busy to notice on the one hand, and blinded by bad weather on the other. I guess, however, that mountain riders and trekkers see it all too.

I arrived at Underberg, 5,000 feet above sea level, around 11.30 that Saturday morning to find the little town a hive of activity in the midday heat as the locals, often with parcels piled high on their heads, rushed to buy their weekend stocks (mainly alcohol)

before the shops closed at lunchtime. I joined in, buying fishing flies, a licence, some postcards and maps; then thought: When in Rome . . . and added a bottle of whisky and some good South African wine to my shopping basket.

On registering at the local hotel, I was given for my accommodation, a *Rondavel*, a circular, white stucco, conical thatched-roof native hut with a separate bathroom. It had no fridge or TV (thank heaven), no shower but a bath big enough to satisfy a six and a half foot Scuba diver, and a view over rolling lawns to the steep, blue-shadowed escarpment of the Drakensberg which was unbeatable. Having hastily unpacked and set up my rods, paints and other equipment, I repaired to the hotel bar in search of ice-cold beer and fishing information. While I found the beer in abundant supply, I was told that the representative of the Underberg and Himeville Trout Fishing Club (UHTFC) was present in the club office only from eight to ten each morning and that I'd have to wait until the next day for advice and 'rod allocation'.

Inland fishing is licensed in Natal (where salmonid ova were first introduced in the 1890s). All land bordering rivers is titled with riparian rights and access for fishing is controlled, where private property is involved, by landowners through clubs, and where Crown property is involved, by the Natal Parks Board. Landowners operate with the clubs for allocation of access which is granted to club members who pay annual susbscriptions, and to visitors at a fee of R20 ($A10) per rod per day. The clubs control the number of rods and their allocation to the various rivers at any one time. All revenue, except payment for licences, is club-controlled and guaranteed to be reinvested in the administration, upkeep, improvement and conservation of the sport. Licence revenue, however, disappears into consolidated government revenue. Catch-and-release is actively promoted, realistic bag limits are imposed, and both club members and casual visitors are encouraged to report catches to the clubs so that records can be maintained.

When I visited the UHTFC the next morning I was made aware of these very sensible rules, met the charming club secretary/manager, Bob Crass (author of a number of fishing books), and was allocated my rod/beat for that day. In the meantime on that Saturday of my arrival, before this introduction, I had lunch at the hotel and went exploring in the car (with camera and rods ready just in case). Somehow I stumbled upon a particularly attractive homestead at Ericsberg Farm. The owners and their guests were enjoying the end

A beautiful Drakensberg trout stream.

of a leisurely lunch party and insisted on the 'wandering Australian journalist' joining them for cheese and wine. It was indicative of the outstanding hospitality and kindness I was to receive throughout Natal during my all-too-short stay. When at last I managed to tear myself away, the owners insisted that I fish their section of the Mzimkhulu River below the house and return for drinks afterwards.

As it came to pass, however, on the way to the river I bogged the rental car, broke off the front number plate and had to walk back, explain my ineptitude to the owner and have my car towed out by the farm tractor.

It was late afternoon when I eventually reached the river, and I saw one or two definite rises. Up until then, all the advice given to me in South Africa had been to use wet flies downstream (does Patagonia, fast water, and colonial days ring a bell?) In fact Fred had said to me in Durban when we were discussing fishing: 'The Mrs Simpson is a good fly, and I often use very small hooks, they seem to work better, even as small as size four to eight!' I began to mumble something about sharkhooks but closed my mouth to listen to the locals.

Anyway, when I saw the rises I stuck to my preference and my floating line; I tied on a size-14 Adams and started taking rainbows off the top with great regularity which continued until dark. They weren't big fish, nothing over 13 inches, so I won't describe the action, it was pretty much regulation upstream stuff, but they fought hard and I had a ball. I left the river on dark, thanked my hosts for their outstanding hospitality (I didn't stay for a drink, by then I thought they'd done more than enough for me) and returned to the Underberg Hotel, about five kilometres to the southeast on the R617. Having showered and changed, I drove five kilometres north to Himeville, the other major town in this trout fishing area, for dinner in the local pub, then back to my *Rondavel* and bed—not a bad start to the visit, even without an official rod allocation. The rental car, however, was looking rather muddy and tired after only 30 hours use.

The next morning I met Bob Crass as I have already described. Once again, I mused, Australian fisheries officials might have something to learn about salmonid management from an overseas country.

As the weather was very hot that day I delayed using my rod allocation until the cool of the late

My 'Studio' at the Hudson-Bennett's . . .

. . . and the view from my work chair!

Drayton Farm . . .

. . . and the view from the lunch table.

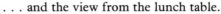

afternoon, planning to write and paint for the morning and afternoon. Once again, however, my plans spun 180 degrees out of phase before I had so much as put pen to paper. Shortly before lunch I was called to the hotel office to answer a phonecall from a Mrs Lola Hudson-Bennett. She and her husband, Dr Meyrick Hudson-Bennett, had been told of my ventures by Peggy Pilkington and they invited me to come over for lunch. I made feeble murmurs about writing and painting but was agreeably overruled and dropped everything to drive to their house on the northern outskirts of Himeville.

Meyrick is a retired Durban doctor. Once a great sportsman and polo player, he remains a keen fly-fishman, as is Lola who also takes a great interest in local life, is an amateur artist and a professional floral artist of world class. I was not only warmly welcomed into their cool and very comfortable house with its rolling lawns and beautiful garden overlooking the climbing peaks of the Drakensberg, but instructed to move my gear from the hotel into their guest suite the next day. I thought at the time (and still believe it to be true) that South Africa, particularly Natal, stood out on my safaris as the country of generous and outstanding hospitality.

For my studio I was allocated a worktable, benches and chairs outside on a pink brick patio under the constant shadow of a massive plane tree. It looked down the green sloping lawns, over roses and grevillea, pear, prunus and apple trees to farm fields gradually rising to the escarpment of the Drakensberg—mountains which changed colour with the hours of the day—as doves cooed in the branches above my head and the house dogs lay at my feet.

My private Valhalla had travelled with me.

After lunch that first Sunday, I returned to the

Reichenau Mission on the banks of the Pholela River.

hotel and managed three hours at my desk before fishing my allocated beat on the Ngwangwane River in the comparative cool of the late afternoon. Again I waited for the evening hatch which was a beauty, but was mainly small midges, often known as 'Fisherman's Curse'. I went down to a size-18 Adams and managed to entice two small rainbows before the rise stopped as though turned off by a light switch. I reported progress to Bob the next morning and both he and the club treasurer, John Campbell (of Australian and Duntroon origins), were surprised yet delighted with my upstream dry-fly success.

By now I was becoming an adopted member of the local fly-fishing community. Contact was made with another property owner, Michael Youngleson and his wife, Gaye, at Drayton Farm near Nottingham Road some 90 kilometres to the northeast. Michael had six kilometres of Mooi River frontage, reputedly the best brown-trout water in Natal and, with common links through a one-time

UK High Commissioner (Sir John Leahey) in Canberra, I was invited to Drayton Farm the next day for lunch and fishing.

Next morning, having left the hotel, moved in with the Hudson-Bennetts and had a rim-seal puncture repaired, I drove through remarkable scenery in the Drakensberg. As Sean told me in Argentina, the scenery is similar to Patagonia; high mountains, strata of changing material and colour in the buttes and escarpments, and moderately swift trout water. In Natal, however, the colours were lusher and greener, the high country less stark, and the rivers not nearly so clear.

I arrived at Drayton Farm (with yet another puncture) in time for a delicious lunch of gravdlaks, cold lamb salad and beer. Luckily I'd had the first tyre repaired before the trip and Gaye took the second to the local garage for repairs while Michael and I went fishing.

I found that Michael had fished a great deal of the world, including Chile and Patagonia; what's more, he had a magnificent 21-pound steelhead from British Columbia mounted in his study. His river, the Mooi, is a beautiful brown-trout river, meandering through the undulations of that Drakensberg countryside. Indeed it meanders so much that, like the Taieri in New Zealand, we could park the car at one spot, take a 15-minute walk over a saddle, and fish the winding river upstream carefully for four hours, to arrive back at the car at last light.

It was a hot afternoon with little activity, although in the first two hours I managed to connect with three browns, all down deep, one on a weighted Copper and Hare Nymph and the other two using a size-ten Mrs Simpson. All seemed to take short or throw the hook. Michael suffered similar difficulties. But as the sun dipped below the mountain line, I hooked and lost another brown while Michael managed to grass one of around half a pound. I repeated Michael's feat a few minutes later, but that was it for the day. I think Michael was disappointed, and he assured me that things were usually much better at that time of the year. Nonetheless, I wasn't dismayed. It had been a wonderful afternoon in storybook scenery, and I'd hooked five even though I'd landed only one. Additionally, I'd been entertained by charming people in their very elegant homestead and, what's more, on the way back to the house we saw a number of buck silhouetted on the fading skyline. After drinks I rang Meyrick and Lola to say I was leaving at 7.30 p.m. and should be home for dinner in two hours. But I took the wrong direction on the N3 and didn't get back for whisky and cottage pie until nearly eleven.

And when I emerged the next morning to sort out the mess in my rather grubby, punctured, broken and 'lost' rental car, I found the houseboy had sorted out my gear, cleaned and dried my fishing boots, scrubbed the car inside and out and clipped the front number plate back into its correct position. I thought that was being very spoilt until I arose early on the next two mornings to work in the cool shade of the plane tree, to find that tea was delivered to me on a silver service at seven-thirty as the dogs sat at my feet, the birds chorused in the garden and the moles played havoc with Meyrick's immaculate lawn.

The trout may not be as consistently big in Natal nor as plentiful as in some other places in this world, but one would have to go an astonishingly long way to beat the hospitality and beauty of the Drakensberg.

My final fishing session in Natal was in the late afternoon of Wednesday 11 March, when I returned to the Mzimkhulu, this time at the Lower Rocks beat. As a parting gesture, Bob Crass had allowed me a gratis allocation and let me buy a club tie and badge although these were normally only available to full members and not to casual visitors. It was another indication of Natal hospitality which I returned in some small and insufficient way by presenting him, and all my hosts, with watercolours of trout flies.

That final evening on the Mzumkhulu was another relative blank. Conditions were extremely warm and a hot dry wind was blowing. The surface water temperature, I concluded, was way above the accepted trout comfort zone and, although there was a significant hatch of spinners after the sun went down, only one or two foolish six-inch fish (one of which I hooked on the Copper and Hare Nymph) ventured into the surface layers, while the remainder stayed deep, content to wait for cooler conditions no matter how long the wait might be.

My fishing score in South Africa was not impressive, probably mainly because of warm water conditions; but neither was it brilliant in the trout fisherman's mecca, New Zealand (for other reasons). On the other hand, I had not been foolish enough to embark on my travels expecting a Patagonian bonanza at each stop. Heaven forbid! Each area has its ups and downs and, if every place continually turned on a 'Malleo day', the excitement of fly-fishing for wild trout would soon fade; much of that excitement lies in expectation, and certainties would spoil this.

I made my farewells to my hosts and friends in the Drakensberg after lunch the next day, then drove the highly experienced and abused rental car to Durban where I spent a final night with Fred and Peggy Pilkington before flying out to Harare in Zimbabwe on (of all days) Friday 13 March.

By that point in my adventures, I was beginning to feel that I had gone about ten rounds with Mohammed Ali. I acknowledged that I had taken on too much too quickly, although it had all been a wonderful and successful experience in some of the most breathtaking scenery in the world.

On tally, I reckoned that, in 40 days and 40 nights, I had:

- covered some 35,000 kilometres;
- visited six countries;
- caught over 90 good fish in less than 21 days' fishing;
- stayed in 17 motels, hotels, lodges and houses;
- operated mainly above 5,000 feet above sea level and in temperatures in excess of 28°C;

- visited the Carnival of Rio;
- taken over 400 photographs;
- written four chapters of my book;
- painted three major (and a number of minor) watercolours; and
- maintained three diaries (two illustrated) and demolished five litres of duty free malt whisky.

I was looking forward to Zimbabwe, but I was also looking forward to getting home.

Finally, a word on life in South Africa (as I saw it).

While I have never been one to mix politics with sport, the turbulent political situation in South Africa then could not be avoided, even by disappearing into the mountains to fly-fish, write and paint. The painful and slow process of emerging from apartheid into some sort of democracy was vibrantly apparent, no matter where one was situated. Six million whites, and upwards of 25 million blacks, from a number of vastly differing ethnic groups, were ingredients that combined to make the break-out from the cocoon of apartheid extremely volatile, especially as 85 per cent of the black population was largely illiterate and without any formal education. I was told then that an immediate jump to total democracy—one man, one vote—would accordingly be catastrophic, and that President De Klerk's plan for an interim federation based on ethnic, rather than direct geographical, parliamentary groupings had the best chance of ultimately bringing full democracy to South Africa, using a slow transition period to allow for education and acceptance. Indeed, many I spoke to saw De Klerk as the leader of the South African people into the light of democracy from a long, dark and painful tunnel. At the time, all were anxiously awaiting the outcome of the Referendum planned for 17 March 1992 .

I found also that not all the problems in South Africa were necessarily politically based. Much violence, theft and damage was apparently caused by feuds, and a jealousy of those who had worked hard to improve their lot. Both reasons could, arguably, be traced back to politics, but I preferred to think of them separately. Example cases were all around me in Natal.

Several years before my visit, Fred and Peggy's houseboy and gardener had been shot and killed apparently because he was next in line in a family involved in a 'McCoys and Martins' styled family feud, reminiscent of Kentucky in the 1920s, although the boy was not personally involved in any way. It followed that his death would have to be revenged, and so on, *ad infinitum* (?)

I was told also that the owner of the excellent sports store and fly-fishing shop in Underberg had been burgled twice and his shop burnt to the ground once in recent years because he was quite legally and painstakingly doing well, and held expensive and attractive stock while others were less enterprising.

And, most horrifyingly, Lola's housegirl and cook, Cecilia, had, because of her hard-won status in the hinterland of Durban some years before her employment with the Hudson-Bennetts, been 'Necklaced' (a burning car tyre, filled with petrol, placed around her head and shoulders) by a marauding mob! Miraculously she had managed to remove the necklace and escape the mob before she collapsed. But she bears the horrifying scars.

Indeed, for all of these and other unfortunate reasons—both political and non-political— security measures were extreme and obvious in most homes; bars and multiple locks on doors and windows, trained dogs and staff, ever-burning nightlights, alarm systems and a high ownership of firearms among householders were standard procedures.

It was a sad indictment of a beautiful country I had come to enjoy immensely. As I left I prayed that a peaceful way would be found for South Africans to emerge from these troubles.

Incidentally, I forgot to mention that, during my visit to South Africa, back in Australia and New Zealand, the World Series Cricket was being fought out between England, New Zealand, the West Indies, Zimbabwe, Sri Lanka, India, Pakistan, South Africa and Australia. When I arrived in Cape Town, the very first words anyone said to me in South Africa, were spoken by the man on the Immigration Desk at the airport who took my passport, looked me up and down and, with a deadpan expression, said in a loud voice: 'We beat you!'

We both burst out laughing and he waved me and my 63 kilos of luggage through and clear of the arrivals area without further comment.

14
A Change of Pace in Zimbabwe

It had to happen. It simply had to happen.

When I faced the check-in at Durban airport for my flights to Johannesburg and Harare, together with my 63 kilos of luggage, I knew I had reached the end of the freeloading road. The girl at the desk may not have been one of James Bond's female adversaries from SMERSH, but that's what I silently called her. Large but short; cropped hair, steely-eyed and the epitome of efficiency and officialdom, she didn't smile, nor, indeed, show any facial expression during our entire 15-minute transaction. Rubber stamps surrounded her, rubber stamps were the very backbone of her trade.

She efficiently checked my ticket, noted the computerised prebooked seat and activated a machine that spat out my boarding pass as stamps (various) thumped the table. Then, with calculator in hand, she weighed and checked my luggage, came to an abrupt halt and barked in strong guttural tones: 'Yoo hef tzoo moch lockij!'

I immediately embarked on my by then rehearsed *spiel* about fishing, writing and painting my way around the world to produce a book that might give her wonderful country more publicity and tourists. I even added that I'd already covered 35,000 kilometres on six different airlines, all of which had recognised my quest and had kindly allowed my baggage through without extra charge.

'Surely', I said, 'your airline, who've already been so good to me, wouldn't ruin a wonderful record?'

Long pause, then: 'I vill hef to consilt di sooporwisor!'

The result was that, with 64 kilos (they measured one more!), 34 above the normal allowance, they would charge me for only 20. But when I found that the excess charge per kilo roughly equalled that of retail smoked salmon, I asked as a last resort to speak to the supervisor.

I should have had more sense; if my 'girlfriend' was Bond's adversary, the supervisor I silently called 'Attila the Hun'. I was the only one who smiled during that interview too, and I knew from the outset that it was a lost cause.

Admittedly they let me off with 14 extra kilos for which I should have been very grateful, but it was rather like completing 85 per cent of a hopscotch game without treading on a line, to suddenly be caught, foot-on-line, on the home stretch. As I buckled my seat belt just prior to takeoff, however, it suddenly dawned on me: It was Friday the thirteenth! Accordingly, I ordered champagne and set about drinking out my excess luggage bill in free booze in the five hours to Harare.

But more troubles were ahead. On arrival at Harare airport I found that the airline baggage handlers had managed to punch a hole in my good suitcase, and break the securing latch from my airline briefcase. Paying for excess luggage was one thing and necessarily forgivable, but that damage, occurring on Black Friday on top of too much champagne, made me feel positively unhappy for the very first time in 36,000 kilometres.

On arrival at my Harare hotel I found several notes waiting for me, including one from Gib Lanpher and his wife inviting me to dinner that night. Gib had been the number two at the American Embassy in Canberra in 1989–'91; he is a keen and competent fly-fisherman and we used to fish together frequently in the Brindabellas. His note reminded me that he was now the United States Ambassador in Harare and, at dinner, he said that he would be joining me for a day's fishing at Troutbeck later in the week.

The other note of consequence was from Eric Jones and this was followed, an hour or so later, by a visit from Eric himself. He, with his knowledge of the country and its waters, a passion for fly-fishing, and direct involvement in the Troutbeck

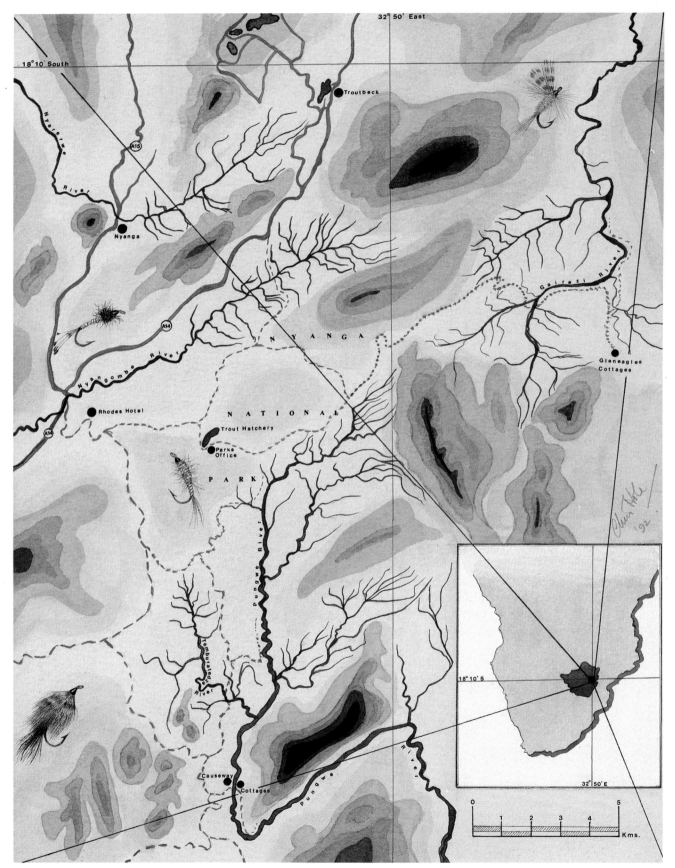

Mudmap of the Nyanga National Park in Zimbabwe.

Inn where we planned to stay, was to be my guide, mentor and fishing companion for the next week.

Eric is a very remarkable man. A Yorkshireman by birth, he came to the then Rhodesia in the 1940s and joined the British South African (Company) Police force in 1946. In Rhodesia they were known as the 'Police of Southern Rhodesia' and Eric is one of the few remaining holders of a Southern Rhodesia driving licence. He served with the force for 20 years, which included the brutal 1950s and '60s during the country's civil war, and retired as a superintendent in Harare in 1966. On retirement, and after a brief sojourn to England, Eric resumed life in Zimbabwe, taking on the job of assisting with the financial management of the Zimbabwe-Sun hotel group, the largest hotel group in the country. He has been a keen and very capable fly-fisherman since the 1950s and introduced me to his favourite streams and lakes in Nyanga National Park, some three hours' drive east and south of Harare.

Incidentally, he was introduced to me by Zimbabwe-Sun hotels and, in particular, their Troutbeck Inn, when I first researched and booked accommodation in Nyanga 12 months prior to my visit. A policeman's policeman with a heart of gold and a kindly sense of humour, I could not have chosen a better companion for my visit.

The next morning I packed my gear, Eric collected me and we drove to the rental car company head office to collect the 4WD ordered six months previously and confirmed by Eric shortly before my arrival. But they couldn't provide the 4WD and the best they could offer was a beaten-up pickup truck with a cracked windscreen, a right indicator light which lit up when the footbrake was applied and which, indeed, made the battered red Hi-lux, with its cracked windshield, in Patagonia look like a Rolls Royce. The company, moreover, had the effrontery to put their logo on the doors and, when this miserable conveyance blew a radiator three days

later in Nyanga, wanted me to take it to a local garage for repair.

I made it plain at that stage that if they didn't provide me with a decent car and remove the junk heap within four hours, I would be forced to dedicate an entire chapter of my book to their inefficiency! The new car arrived with half an hour to spare! But when they wanted me to pay for the petrol, time, mileage and insurance for its delivery voyage from Harare, I really hit the roof.

The three-hour drive south and eastwards from Harare to Nyanga National Park, Troutbeck and the inn was wonderful. For the first hour we passed through flat grassland and maize farms; eucalypts, conifers, wattle, acacias and spruces lined the route, and I hardly noticed that we had climbed to 5,000 feet. In the second hour the hills were more obvious but still gentle. Granite undulations, with trees growing more sparsely, and the appearance of bracken and thorn trees were the indications of change. In the final hour, climbing to nearly 7,000 feet, we really entered the mountains. The scenery was very beautiful. Huge granite outcrops and towering mountains and escarpments stood sentinel to deep and misty valleys. The distant peaks were a faded blue which became deeper in the middle ground, changing to granite-grey, interspersed with pink and red clay, in the foreground. Big clumps of conifers and bracken lined the road and occasional apple orchards broke the sequence.

We arrived at Troutbeck and the inn at lunchtime. The inn is built in a storybook setting with sweeping lawns and flower beds leading to a well-stocked lake surrounded by fir trees, a golf course and riding trails. The main buildings are built as two terraced storeys, with the upper storey at ground level on top of a rise and the lower level recessed into it. It was the dream, in 1947, of a Major Herbert McIlwaine (who taught Eric to fly fish in 1954),

Troutbeck Inn, Nyanga National Park, Zimbabwe . . .

. . . and the view from my 'studio'.

but has undergone considerable changes over the years. There is a remarkable set of photographs at the entrance to the dining room showing the history of this famous hostelry.

It is 'touristy' but somehow not so and, in an indefinable way, mildly Victorian. In addition to the fishing, golf and riding, there are tennis courts, squash courts, a bowling green, swimming pool and a billiards saloon. In all, I found it very attractive and very comfortable.

Exploring after lunch I found that there was a chapel in the grounds when a large, attractive and brightly coloured wedding party paused on the lawns in front of my room for photographs. I grabbed my Nikon and, with the bride's permission, 'the touring fly-fishing Australian journalist' took half a roll of film, much to the annoyance of the professional photographers. I haven't yet worked out the connection with fly-fishing, but then I couldn't in Rio either.

Eric and I fished the lake for the remainder of the day, taking a number of rainbow 'stockies', all of which were in the three-quarters to one and a half pound category. Although they were stockies which took easily and didn't fight very hard, it was a lot of fun. Once again, however, I observed that my companions were using sinking lines and large wet flies. I achieved most of my successes in that lake using weighted Stick Caddis Nymphs of size 12 or 14 and, early one morning, further amazed some of the locals by taking a number of trout, using a size 16-Blue Dun on the surface. One or two friendly fellows I talked to simply couldn't believe that a trout could see anything smaller than a size ten.

Trout fishing in Zimbabwe National Parks is a government controlled sport using a costed licence system. We spent $Z24 ($A7) each for a week's licence in the knowledge that, while such revenue disappears into government coffers, the park officers take an active interest in the preservation and upkeep of their areas, including the trout fishing. Also I was told that those businesses and organisations which attract foreign currency into the country (and places such as Troutbeck and its fishery do just that) may keep 15 per cent of their earnings in foreign currency to further their causes, the other 85 per cent being converted into Zimbabwe dollars by law.

For the next two days Eric and I fished the Pungwe River in the National Park. It is a very beautiful, clear, rocky stream which changes, as it tumbles through the Nyanga mountains, from waterfalls to runs, from ripples to long deep pools, and from deeps to quiet backwaters. Access is quite difficult and, even when on the river, I often found passage along its banks impossible in parts. Nonetheless, to look at this beautiful water and its wild surrounds was enough to gladden the heart of any fly-fisherman.

But we caught hardly a fish.

Oh, we hooked a couple of par-marked five-inchers, but I couldn't believe our lack of success in such glorious trout water. I don't think we missed many either; the water was so clear one could see everything through it without even having to use polaroids. Eric was naturally as disappointed as I was. All he could offer was that the drought might have been partly at fault and that the rivers could have been subject to heavy fishing pressure. Driving back to Troutbeck on the second afternoon, stopping to fill the radiator with a bucketful of water every ten minutes, we discussed the problem and Eric said the wild trout population might increase markedly if they closed some rivers for a couple of years. On questioning him I found him to be sensibly quite serious; he thought that Parks could possibly do just that. I thought to myself: Imagine New South Wales Fisheries even considering the closure of Bobundara Creek, for example, to improve the quality of trout fishing? No way! Those in power could lose too many votes.

On Tuesday 17 March I took the day off from fishing (apart from 'stockie-bashing' in the early morning and late evening) and caught up with some of my writing and painting. Eric visited the local hatchery in order to get permission for us to fish the wild Gairezi River the next day; he also fished one or two dams with some success.

That evening the Lanphers arrived from Harare, as did Eric's friend, Peter Turnbull-Kemp, whom Eric had kindly invited to Troutbeck to meet me and to talk fishing. As Eric said: 'Peter is one of the keenest and most knowledgeable men in Zimbabwe when it comes to trout.' Before, during and after dinner we discussed plans for the next day, and then talked fishing well into the night, ordering large cut lunches (to double as breakfasts) for our 6 a.m. departure.

I discovered that Peter was a companion of Eric's during their police days together; he then worked extensively for the National Parks and developed a vast knowledge of those places and their flora and fauna. He had published a book about the leopard, worked for television, and had an unsurpassed knowledge of trout in the local area.

He told me that trout were first introduced to Zimbabwe from South African ova in 1904/5 and that, on one memorable occasion, the train carrying

Clouds over the Eastern Highlands.

the trout ova had broken down in the Transvaal on the way to Rhodesia. Apparently the railway guard was a caring and diligent fellow (like most of his breed at the time), who took the only course open to him to save the ova. He immediately released them into a nearby river, where trout continue to thrive.

It was then, just before we retired for the night, that Peter threw some light on the reason for the lack of trout in the rivers. He was convinced the problem was caused by eels and, the more I saw of the area, the more I came to agree with him.

Coffee was served at five-thirty the next morning and, by six, we had loaded Gib's Landcruiser and were on our way to the National Park's office to pick up the key to the gate that would allow us access to the Gairezi River, and to purchase special additional licences for that hidden stream. There followed a two-hour crawl over a 'white knuckle' highway equivalent at least to the one of the original name down to the Clear Stream in New Zealand. Heavily eroded, boulder-filled red clay marked the track in, drops from the roadside were often around 1,000 to 1,500 vertical feet; on the way in, low cloud and mist hid most of the dangers, but on the way out they were highly visible as staggering escarpments dropping to

infinity through the bracken or climbing into the cobalt blue through granite outcrops above.

After crossing a *drift* (ford) over one feeder stream, we eventually arrived at the foot of a valley and forded the Gairezi.

It was truly beautiful. Surrounded by the astonishing heights from which we had descended, this bubbling, crystal-clear trout water gushed down the valley, bordered by rocks, heavy reeds and bracken, conifers, thorn trees and ferns. Wildebeest were visible on the way in, the birdlife was prolific and Peter kept talking about leopards—to put me in the mood, I thought—although there were none around. But he had also offered to swap seats with me in the Landcruiser, as he had the 'white knuckle' side to consider on the way home, whereas it had been hidden from me by the mist when I had that side on the way in.

If the track in to this Shangri-la had been difficult, walking(?) the edge of the river was even more so. It was a case of stumbling over boulders, avoiding vertical drops through 'Vietnam jungle', going round impassable cliffs and pushing through long grass and vegetation which could hide almost anything (including leopards).

But fish it we did.

Fishing the beautiful Gairezi River in Nyanga National Park.

The pools, once one had reached them, were very beautiful and very exciting. I must have cast most of the flies in my boxes up into those storybook runs for hours, perpetually sure that they housed monsters which I knew I would hook. I tried my best nymphs, some dry flies (although nothing ever rose), extraordinary weighted nymphs, and even swallowed my pride at one stage and tied on some massive and gaudy wet flies.

But nothing. Absolutely nothing!

Between the others, I think five or six fish were taken, all on a Walker's Killer (or something), but all of these were five-to-eight-inch, par-marked minnows that I would have discounted. Naturally Peter was disappointed, and it was at that stage that we resumed the discussion about eels. I also noticed that the caught fish were all very silvery outside and pink on the inside, and that there were numerous, small freshwater crabs evident in the water and its surrounds.

Somehow it didn't all add up to me, but I acknowledged a lack of local expertise and a memory that recalled consistent bad days in other places at other times. I was certainly prepared to give the area the benefit of any doubt, and in any case I was totally won over by its scenery and isolation. Maybe it *was* the fault of eels, but I saw no visible evidence.

We returned to Troutbeck in the late afternoon and, after another very successful session of 'stockie-bashing' in the lake, I was extremely grateful for a hot bath to ease the grind on my cartilege-reduced footballer's knees before drinks and dinner.

Peter left us after dinner that night, and Gib and his family returned to Harare the next morning. I spent my last day at Troutbeck writing and painting (and arranging the charging of a flat battery in my new rental car), while Eric fished the lake from a rowing boat with great success.

My final Zimbabwe fishing session (as I then thought) on my first round-the-world venture was in the lake before dinner that evening, dressed in waders (for the first time in Zimbabwe) so that I could patrol the reed areas where I had seen some good fish rising the night before. I caught two, persuading them to take a small Hare's Ear Nymph near the top, and it was quite exciting trying to get them into the shore through the reeds. When I subsequently counted the respectable fish that I had taken in my Southern Hemispherian safari, I discovered that the total was 99. I then set the alarm for five-thirty the next morning, determined to make my century before leaving for Harare and home.

After a good night's sleep, I threw my clothes on when the alarm went and raced to the lakeside, nearly oblivious of all else. It was a cloudless, clear early morning; the moon was just sinking below the fir trees, there was enough light to see, but the surface fog over the lake was so thick that it was impossible to see more than ten paces. I was determined that my final fish would be spotted and not caught fishing blind, so I waited to see something nymphing or rising; I had a small Hare's Ear Nymph on my trace. While I was waiting, Eric came down to fish from the other bank.

Then I saw it; a nymphing swirl, only seven or eight paces directly in front of me!

First cast; about right; the fly landed around a metre in front of the fish (if I had picked his direction correctly).

I twitched a slow figure-of-eight retrieve.

A swirl, and I had him! He fought quite hard for a 'stockie' but I dared not call out to Eric until I had landed him; I'd made that mistake and lost fish before. In any event, I think Eric probably heard him splashing on the surface. Eventually I brought him into the grassy edge and was about to slide him over the bank when the hook pulled out! The fish, however, didn't know he was my hundredth, and appeared even less concerned about himself because he let me scoop him up and throw him onto the bank!

I grabbed him and yelled out to Eric: 'Hundred up!' My companion had seen it all and was already clapping.

A little while later I spotted another fish which simply refused to take an interest in any of my flies. Eric had joined me by then and suggested breakfast. I replied that I would return to my room to shower, shave and pack, but that Eric ought to have a go at the fish while I was packing, and we would meet over our final kidneys and bacon in the dining room. All went to plan, but when Eric joined me over coffee he had a broad grin all over his old policeman's face and said: 'You remember that last fish you pointed out to me?'

I nodded.

'Well I caught him first cast', he said, 'on a Hamil's Killer too. And do you know? He had a strange tattoo on his flank...a number I think... it looked like "A HUNDRED AND ONE"!'

I reluctantly departed from Troutbeck and my hospitable fellow anglers at eight-fifteen that morning and wobbled the rental car back to Harare (its front wheels were totally out of balance and alignment; what's more, the radio was apparently only there for show). Arriving a little before lunch, I checked into the hotel and returned the car. While

Beside the Gairezi River (*l. to r.*) Gib Lanpher, Eric Jones and Peter Turnbull-Kemp.

the company agreed with my calculations of a reduced rate for their service (or more truly, the lack thereof), only a weak and forced apology and a 10 per cent discount was forthcoming. I even had to pay for my taxi back to the hotel. That rental company had joined the luggage-destroying airlines, wire coat-hangers, laundered shirts with all the buttons done up, butter and jam in those dice-sized peel-back packets, socks that come back from the laundry as individuals when they were delivered in pairs, and airport departure lounges on my list of things to be avoided at all cost.

I spent 40 hours in Harare, completing my writing, sketching and diaries, before flying to Johannesburg early on the morning of Sunday 22 March, and from thence to Australia, arriving home in the late afternoon the next day.

So an exciting and unusual period came to a close. In all, I had travelled in excess of 1,000 kilometres a day for 50 days. Six countries, seven airlines and two (one dubious) car companies had looked after my movements. I had caught 100 good fish in 27 days' fishing (returning almost all of them), with the biggest fish (in New Zealand) being five and a half pounds, and the most in any one day (30 plus) being caught in the Malleo area of Patagonia. I had stayed in 17 hotels, motels, lodges and homes; I had operated mainly above 5,000 feet above sea level and in temperatures of 25 degrees Centigrade or more, and had taken over 500 photographs. I'd also visited the Carnival of Rio, and a wedding in Nyanga, and met some extraordinarily kind and hospitable people in areas of unsurpassed beauty.

But it is always a nice feeling to return home.

I sometimes envy, but really pity, those nomads who keep travelling forever. At the time of my visits to each of those trout meccas, I thought I could stay forever. That, fortunately in a way, was not to be. I admitted to myself, however, as we flew across the vast expanse of the Indian Ocean, that eight weeks to follow in the parochialism of Australia's national capital (I found that most capitals tend towards the same fault), would probably have me begging to return to Estancia Huechahue, the Malleo, Santiago, the Woods' hospitality, and the incredible shadow of Vulcan Lanin—and those fish.

That's the way it should be.

Finally I pondered on just what I had learnt on my first trip. I certainly needed to reduce my luggage; I could cut down on my rods and carry two to a tube, I didn't really need a net, I could probably reduce my fishing gear by 25 per cent and my clothing by close to the same amount; also my stationery and art gear would need further examination. I calculated I could probably get the total down to 40-plus kilos, a much better weight with which to approach airline check-in counters.

Next, although my Northern Hemispherian program allowed me more time, I knew that I would have to recast within that program to allow one full day writing and sketching after each two days' enjoying myself fishing; and that I would really need every bit of the programmed average of five days between countries (chapters).

Finally, I found that my travels had made me very much more aware of other countries, other people and other problems. Hence my reference to parochialism at home. Undoubtedly travel broadens one's view, and hopefully creates greater tolerance. The day that Gib, Eric, Peter and I travelled that fascinating 'white knuckle' highway to fish the beautiful Gairezi River in Zimbabwe was a day of many other meanings too. Firstly we heard the news of the landslide referendum result giving President De Klerk his mandate to pursue democracy in South Africa (the actual referendum question which was put to whites only and which received a two thirds 'yes' vote was: 'Do you support the continuation of the reform process which the State President began on 2 February, 1992, and which is aimed at a new Constitution through negotiation?') The result made my companions in that wilderness very relieved (particularly Gib), because they knew that any suggestion of a return to apartheid in their neighbouring country could only result in further unrest—even anarchy—which could quickly spread over the border.

PART IV

THE NORTHERN HEMISPHERIAN SAFARI

15
The Famous Chalkstreams of Hampshire

In a book such as this, the very mention of Hampshire should immediately evoke a response: the Itchen and the Test. But, because of my naval background, it means more to me than just those world-famous chalkstreams. Within that beautiful English county, I joined the Royal Yacht *Britannia* at H-Moorings at Whale Island in Portsmouth just before Christmas 1962; I undertook my Navigation Subspecialist training and Advanced Subspecialist Training in 1964 and 1969 near Southwick village at HMS *Dryad* (Eisenhower's headquarters for the D-day landings during the Second World War); I have dined and drunk in hostelries from Winchester to Waterlooville, Wickham to Fareham, Portsmouth to Hambledon, and from Bishop's Waltham to Liphook; I have played golf in as many charming places, and watched and played cricket at the famous Bat and Ball. Indeed, the county of Hampshire is perhaps my favourite in all England.

I pondered on this in May as I left Australia for the second time in 1992 for the Northern Hemisphere and my first planned fishing stop on those venerable chalkstreams. Ambrose Streatfeild of Winchester (you will remember him at Brindabella in Chapter 2) was to be my host and guide, and I pay tribute, here, to his first-class organising ability. We had corresponded for months since our last meeting at Brindabella and, by the time I arrived in England, I was totally confident that he would introduce me to those holies of all trout holies with panache and success. It also occurred to me at the time that, although I had a not-unexpected number of naval fly-fishing friends, I had also named a few gentlemen from

the RAF. There was Ambrose in Chapter 2 and now, again, in Hampshire; Harry Thompson the Mosquito pilot from Patagonia in Chapter 12; and Fred Pilkington from Durban, the Far-East Spitfire pilot mentioned in Chapter 13. I wondered, as I flew out of Canberra on that autumn morning, whether there could be some connection between a pilot's fast responses and a fly-fisherman's quick delicacy, and came to the conclusion that it was highly probable.

This time I travelled via Singapore, carting with me 60 kilos of luggage once again. I found I simply *couldn't* reduce my kit, despite the best intentions; I was to be away longer than in February and March, I had much further to travel and a greater range of climates to cover. But I did manage to reduce my rods to five (in three tubes), with a new, experimental McGinn hexagon promised for delivery to me along the way . . . it never did turn up and I found, on return, that John was even more heavily involved in the salt-water market.

In the end, and after much thought, I took with me: my nine and a half foot Hardy #9/10 with Sunbeam reel and a spare spool for salmon and Arctic char; the Fenwick outfit for medium to heavy fishing and for bonefish; the Orvis outfit for probably the majority of my trout fishing, backed up by my McGinn split-cane #6 and Sage reel as a pleasant alternative; and finally, the lightweight #3/4 Sage with Hardy Gold Featherweight reel for mad excitement.

I stopped in Singapore for two days to break the trip; also, I remembered that I had once found a prewar, unused Hardy Palakona there (in the old

'Change Alley'), and had bought it for $100. Unfortunately luck was not to be with me this time. I travelled on to London, arriving early on Friday 22 May to spend three days there (with a visit to 61 Pall Mall of course) before driving to Winchester to join Ambrose. My son, Sam (of sailfish infamy in Fiji), who had been tutoring at a school in Hertfordshire since January and whom I hadn't seen since then, met me at my London hotel and stayed until I left for Winchester. It was a wonderful start to my second circumnavigation, enhanced by a feeling of relaxation which was missing at the start of the first trip, resulting no doubt from the experience and practice gained in February and March. Moreover, the rest of my family were planning to follow at various times and we had agreed on some pretty exotic rendezvous.

I wondered how many diversions, like the Rio Carnival, the Zimbabwe wedding, gold-lamé-miniskirted dolly birds, leopards and others would surface on this second exciting trip and concluded it was better not to think about them. Undoubtedly unplanned, and hopefully amusing, incidents would occur, enhanced by their very elements of surprise and spontaneity.

On Monday 25 May I collected my rental car in London and drove Sam and one of his school friends to Marlborough, before turning southeast to cross from Wiltshire into Hampshire and to Winchester where I met Ambrose. The summer weather had been particularly warm since my arrival in England and the drive that afternoon, through the heat haze covering the English countryside was an absolute pleasure. I kept thinking of past visits, the all-enveloping sense of history, and the song about the man who 'went to mow a meadow'.

After I settled in at my digs in Winchester, Ambrose gave me a tour around the Pilgrims' School and Winchester College, then took me to supper with friends in a wonderful old house overlooking the River Itchen—absolute bliss.

The next morning heralded the beginning of my Northern Hemisphere fishing; and what better way to start than a day on the Test with a good friend? Ambrose collected me at ten and we drove to Romsey to fish the Mead Mill beat of the Test where Ambrose's club holds rights to a kilometre of carrier stream on both banks, and about the same distance on the east bank of the main river. I was told the west bank in that area was owned by the Plessey Company, and the water downstream, through the town of Romsey, by the town for its people.

This was my first detailed experience of the very strict rights and laws of inland fishing in England,

although I was familiar with them through my readings. It was a good introduction because with the town stretch opened to the residents, and the club waters running through open fields, the whole matter seemed more relaxed than examples I found later, particularly on the Itchen where very select, manicured short beats were totally controlled by the owners of the rights, strictly policed and limited, for example, to two rods per day, six days per week, normally taken by the same two people on that set day, week in and week out during the season. Albeit, later in my travels other Englishmen assured me of wild fishing of great quality on the Itchen, and Ian Hay of the Rod Box confirmed this. Moreover, I later found further examples of even more exclusive and more tightly controlled fishing in other countries. Nonetheless, if inland fishing regulation in New South Wales is at the uncontrolled end of the scale, the control over the chalkstreams of Hampshire must be a good example of the other extreme. I think that regulation somewhere in between is more attractive; regulation that gives better access to wild unmanicured water while enforcing rules which will preserve the resource and its environment for the future. But if the need for preservation necessitates the extremes of Hampshire and other overseas countries, then so be it; in my opinion it is preferable to exhausting the resource.

During that first morning on the Test, Ambrose took me on a tour of the water. We spotted a number of fish and I cast to one or two without luck. Ambrose was disappointed that, after all our planning, the mayfly hatch had come unseasonably early and we were looking at the tail end of it. But after a delicious picnic lunch, we spotted a number of rising fish as the afternoon wore on. Up to my hips in the cold water of the Test, I cast to two fish feeding regularly in a series of runnels between weed beds; I had six attempts at this pair and they won hands down each time although I pricked them both a number of times.

Ambrose was the first to score, landing a good brownie on a Mayfly about 50 paces upstream from where I was being beaten by the impossible pair. After releasing his fish, he called out for me to join him as he had spotted, he said, a big one in among the reeds on the far bank. Would I like to have a go? It was a real challenge, the sort of thing any Pommie would offer a Digger given half the chance.

Up to my hips in the cold Test again, I moved slowly through the weeds towards the other bank, ten paces or so downstream from my quarry who continued to feed regularly. I knew I would have only one chance and the cast would have to be just

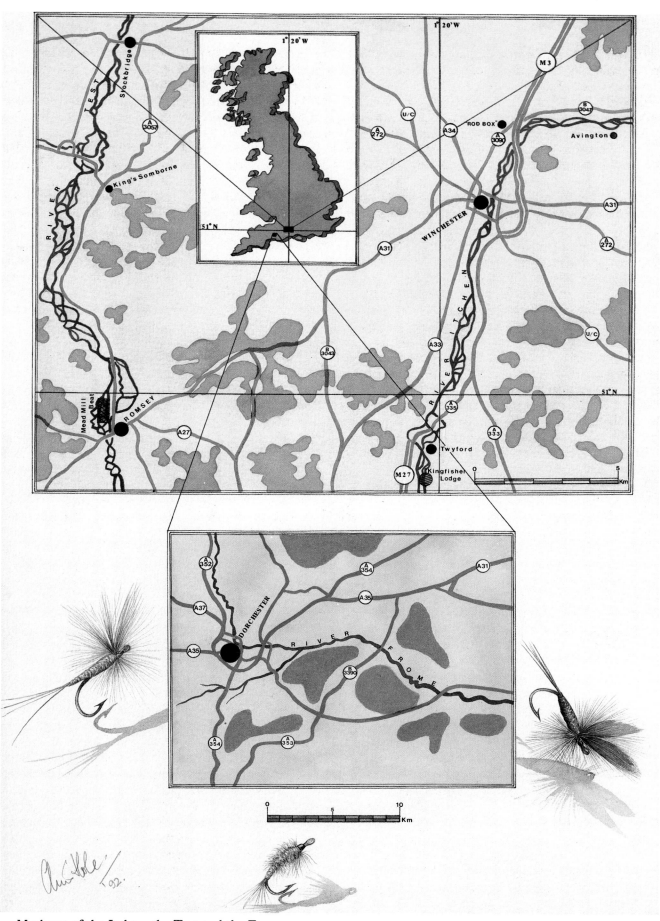

Mudmap of the Itchen, the Test and the Frome.

right; too long and I would spook him, too short or too wide and I would catch in the reeds and it would be all over. Out went the little Blue Dun and, as I allowed the fly to drop on the water, I thought it would be too short. But it landed apparently right on the limit of the fish's peripheral vision. He turned quickly, followed, slashed at the fly and I was connected. What followed was a cartoon comedy: the Dance of the Weeds! He would dive for cover, I would painstakingly extract him. I would unknowingly step into a deep spot, he would take advantage of my confusion and break for cover again. So it went on until, eventually, I slid him into the clear side of the river below Ambrose and won the day. My first Test brown trout (of about one and a half pounds), taken on the Blue Dun!

Later, and a little further upstream in a deep curving corner pool below a willow, we observed a good rise followed by an explosion of water and a shimmer of silver and gold as a brownie of around two pounds took to the air. It was Ambrose's turn to get wet and into battle he went! As he was casting to the fish we saw two soft rises below, and one good slash above his target area. He was soon connected to a good brown on the Mayfly; it was a fish of a little over a pound and probably not that first one.

I followed Ambrose into the pool, changing to a little Copper and Hare Nymph to attack the very soft rises further downstream. The fish were obviously taking something just under the surface, and on my second retrieve there was weight on the line. It fought quite hard and felt heavy, but not like a trout. 'Grayling, I think,' said Ambrose. Sure enough, when we eventually netted, there was a beautiful one and a half pound grayling in the net, its magnificent, huge, violet dorsal fin flapping in identification—my first-ever grayling.

I took another brown trout from the pool and then Ambrose suggested that we ought to give them a rest until the evening, and spend an hour or so in Romsey to look over the Abbey and have a cup of tea. It was a very welcome stop for me, not only because my sneakers were full of grit and starting to pinch, and a cup of tea would be most refreshing, but a visit to the lovely old Romsey Abbey, its almost audible sense of history and Lord Louis Mountbatten's grave left me feeling humbled but ready for the next round with *Salmo trutta*.

Back on the Test, Ambrose sighted an early salmon, an eight-pound grilse, as it started its way upstream, jumping like an airborne torpedo into the sunset. The evening rise was plentiful but, at first, I couldn't seem to find the right fly; everything I chose to cover the fish was ignored or, worse still, caused fright. Eventually I tried a New Zealand dun pattern (it looked a little like the local sedges), a Twilight Beauty, which was immediately slashed at by a number of fish, all of which seemed to rise short (or was I waiting too long to tighten?) Remembering that grayling have to be struck quickly, on the next cast, as soon as there was a boil of water, I struck. Very effectively I was connected to one, a feat that I repeated three more times before leaving the river, by which time I had learnt to differentiate between this take and that of a brown trout.

We drove slowly home, munching fish and chips washed down with cans of ale. Ambrose was upset that the fish and chips were wrapped in butcher's paper and not newspaper. He remarked that newspaper and fish and chips went together like bacon and eggs and that only the blasted Common Market and Brussels would prohibit the use of newsprint!

It was a wonderful day's fishing on a world-famous river and I felt very thankful to have been allowed to enjoy it.

The following day I was kindly taken to what seemed to me the ultimate in privileged, manicured boutique fishing; a session on the River Itchen at Kingfisher Lodge near Twyford. It was one of those areas of severely restricted and controlled fishing for stocked fish among landscaped and beautiful gardens. My host, John Phillips, and the other rod who shared the day with me could not have been more charming, hospitable and helpful. The water was crystal clear and the brown trout numerous, quite large and often very difficult to entice. I managed, nonetheless, by changing to a New Zealand Kahaki Queen once again to simulate a local dun, to take two brownies up to two pounds in copybook fashion.

We had champagne and then lunch under a blue and white umbrella on the freshly mown lawns bordering the water; the fish were jumping, the birds were singing and the banks of the river were lined with the vivid colours, beauty and scent of flowers in an English summer. It was all gorgeous stuff but, to me anyway, a long way removed from the wild trout fishing in places like the South Island of New Zealand and the Malleo River in Patagonia. To each his own, however, and once again (thanks to Ambrose and my hosts) I had kindly been given a glimpse of something very special. And, of course it *was* special . . . as it was always meant to be. Evolved over centuries of time and within layers of social strata where salmonids were the sportfish of kings (and poachers) and coarse fish food for the hoi polloi, it remains a Holy Grail of the trout world (yes, there is more than one!) It is remarkable that this (and other overseas examples) remain in a world of ever-increasing human pressure. Certainly relief-valves are offered in stocked dams and vast public waters (often at considerable daily expense), but the *raison d'être* for exclusive fishing in England does not seem quite the same as that of many other overseas countries where the rules are equally tight for preservation but with an obvious economic undertone: simply that income accrued per fish taken (and released?) for sport is around 10 to 15 times that per fish taken commercially. Whatever the future holds for that very cradle of trout fishing in England, it is going to be difficult— almost impossible—to maintain a top quality and wild salmonid fishery in the face of ever increasing human and population pressures (including the examples posed by recent and continuous droughts) without degrading the quality of the resource through stocking and other 'remedial' measures.

On Thursday, 29 May, my craving for wild, open-country fishing was answered. Ambrose, in his inimitable and thoroughly researched style, knew I would be looking for such a contrast and arranged for Andrew Mackean to be my host for a day's fishing for wild brownies on the Frome near Dorchester. We drove down in the morning and had one short session on a lower beat, when I managed to rise one fish and miss him, before the clouds rolled in and it started to rain gently. That fishery was one of the best I visited in England. Andrew's club has several miles of Frome frontage through fields and undulating meadows; regulations are not numerous yet seemed correct and sensible if preservation of wild stock is to be maintained. Club fees, to me, seemed remarkably good (the annual subscription being the same price as the daily charge by some lodges!); the sport is excellent, in keeping with the number, size and condition of the fish, and any thoughts I may have harboured about top English fly-fishing being a privilege of the tweedy set were soon dispelled.

By the time we had drunk a pint of beer at the local pub (the smallest in England) and shared some sandwiches, the skies had begun to clear and a prolific mayfly hatch had started. This continued for the remainder of the afternoon. Andrew and I were sharing a rod and he took the first fish, a brown of about one pound, within minutes of reaching the river. He impressed on me that, although the rises were obvious, the fish were very shy, requiring a stealthy approach, accurate casting and fast striking. By obeying his directions, soon afterwards I landed a small brown from a difficult lie. After that, however, although I cast reasonably well and managed to get a good number of fish to rise to my fly, except on two occasions I simply couldn't seem to hook the fish. Andrew missed a number in similar circumstances but did manage to hook at least six more. It was exciting yet frustrating fishing, and the two fish I did hook both broke off. The second of those, tight in by the bank in less than a foot of water, was a one-cast-only attempt, balancing the line over reeds with only the leader and the fly on the water. It worked but he broke me. Andrew, being a kind host, said he was the fish of the day. Perhaps? But it was certainly a good fish, as those that beat us always are.

We finished the day in time to drive to Stockbridge around 9 p.m. for steak and oyster pie washed down with pints of beer, then drove home in the happy knowledge that, although the Frome had won, I had enjoyed every minute of it. It is the sort of river to which I would always want to return.

On Friday 29, now in cooler and occasionally damp weather, I spent the morning shopping and catching up with a backlog of tasks before joining Ambrose for lunch at the historic and wonderfully comfortable Wykeham Arms in the centre of Winchester. Lunch was a pint of beer and a generous helping of utterly delicious fish pie. I was beginning to find that, despite the travel and exercise, the overwhelming hospitality during my safaris was playing havoc with my waistline; my fisherman's belt had moved out a notch in four months and was looking for more.

After lunch we drove back to the Mead Mill beat on the Test. We fished the carrier stream where I had caught a number of grayling on the Tuesday visit but, like the Frome, despite the presence and rises of good fish, we just couldn't hook them. Moving up to the main river, we covered the beat where the two fish had beaten me six times on that first day. By concentrating hard and fishing with as much delicacy, care and accuracy as I could muster, I took those two fish on nymphs and was broken by another big one in an impossible lie. Care and attention breeds success, and success normally breeds more success: I followed with two more brownies, up to two pounds, one taken on an Emerging Nymph and the other on a Black Gnat. Ambrose also took a good one before we wandered downstream to meet Brian Clarke, well known angler, angling author and fishing correspondent for the London *Times*.

The Mead Mill beat on the Test in summer . . .

It was a delight to meet him and I found him most helpful with tips to assist my adventures. Once again it was Ambrose who planned this introduction and I was extremely grateful for it.

We talked and fished together until dark when Brian departed (on the way to Newfoundland to write an article about whales), and Ambrose and I left for Winchester and Chinese dinner. At the

'Boutique' fishing—the Itchen at Twyford.

restaurant we bumped into Ian Hay of the famous tackle shop, the Rod Box. I had an introduction to Ian from the wife of the houseguest at the Outpost II in Australia who had written the story of the Kangaroo Nymph in my fishing diary (Chapter 6). Her father had been a regular Rod Box customer and the rod that caught the Kangaroo had, indeed, come from that wonderful shop. We made a date to call the next morning, when Ian took a copy of the story, gave me some good advice for my travels and joined us for a photographic session outside the shop. In the afternoon I worked and then watched the cricket at Pilgrims', where Ambrose was umpiring.

The next day, Sunday 31 May, I didn't fish. I worked hard with my pencils and paints so that I could make use of the following day, programmed

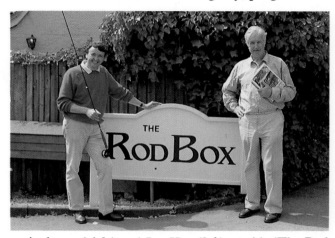

Ambrose (*right*) and Ian Hay (*left*) outside 'The Rod Box'.

as 'a spare for work', to fish the Frome again. I did break for lunch, however, when Ambrose took me to the Eislers' (where I'd had supper on the first evening in Winchester) for Sunday family lunch beside the Itchen near Avington. I managed to paint a collage of their house and a rainbow trout, which I gave to their young son, Edward, a mad keen and very competent fly-fisherman.

That evening Ambrose very kindly gave a small party in my honour. I realised I was being very spoilt but it further occurred to me that fly-fishermen, throughout the world, are an extraordinarily kind and hospitable breed; what is more, their sport seems to transcend many diplomatic and political hurdles. It reminded me a little of Louis Armstrong in the 1950s and 1960s, when he travelled the world on a magic carpet of New Orleans jazz and, despite cold wars and iron curtains, forged many international ties. He made an LP at the time, *Ambassador Satch* I think it was called.

My final full day in Hampshire had been set aside

A fly-fisherman's memories of Hampshire.

for catching up on my work. But, because I persuaded myself at Ambrose's supper that I had nearly caught up, and because it was probably my last day on those chalkstreams for a long time, Ambrose and I decided to have one final four-hour session on the Frome at Dorchester.

Maybe it was because I was greedy, but the day didn't really work. It rained overnight and continued as we drove to the Frome. The river was relatively dead before lunch, so we repaired (for the second time in a week for me and the first time in 30 years for Ambrose) to the smallest pub in England for lunch in the expectation that the afternoon would produce clearing weather and a mayfly hatch. As far as those expectations were concerned, we were rewarded. But, although the river was covered in hatching mayflies, the trout seemed little interested. Ambrose took one of just over a pound on a Royal Wulff, but I finished the day scoreless, unless a wire barb in my hand, hayfever and nettle stings can be added to sundries.

As I packed that night, before leaving for London the next morning, I pondered on the week and felt very happy about the successes and failures achieved (or not achieved). It had been a real test of fly-fishing which I loved, regardless of the outcome. What's more I had used, exclusively, my J. H. McGinn split-cane rod on those chalkstreams because, as Brian Clarke agreed, cane deserves special occasions and the Itchen and the Test, for me, were very special occasions.

The McGinn cane rod performed perfectly.

As a final treat, Ambrose organised a small luncheon at the Flyfishers' Club (established 18 December 1884) in London, where Tony Barton-Hall was our charming host. If I had fished the waters of the holies of holies, I was succoured at their inner sanctum in splendid style. What is more, after lunch I was given good time to examine their wonderful collection of museum pieces and memorabilia—a fitting finále to the wonderful chalkstreams of Hampshire.

16
Atlantic Salmon in Norwegian Rivers

The Norwegian Fly-fishers' Club was founded in 1988 by a German from Hamburg, Manfred Raguse, together with a group of close friends, all actively involved in the preservation and management of Atlantic salmon. They wanted to build an international organisation (probably only possible in the European salmonid fishing world) which could use its financial and political powers to defend the real values of salmon fishing both by securing extended leases on good rivers (in this case the Gaula and the Stjördal near Trondheim) where traditional fly-fishing could be practised, and by constructively contributing to discussion directed towards providing a better environment to help secure the future of salmon.

The club aim is: to conserve and manage salmon, and to provide very good fly-fishing water at a reasonable price.

So simple, so effective (if achieved); and an aim I wholeheartedly support for the control of *all* fishing for salmonids. In terms of providing good fly-fishing at reasonable cost, the Guala and the Stjördal are rated, respectively, as the second and seventh best salmon rivers in Norway, respectively 50 kilometres south and 50 kilometres east of Trondheim. The club's ten to 12 kilometres of beats on these rivers are excellent; the leases are extensive and are expected to be maintained; club patronage and support are very good despite the recession, and costs (as much as 60 per cent lower than other comparable European salmon waters) are accordingly expected to be kept at a reasonable level. Both rivers pass through truly beautiful surroundings and are said to produce some of the most reliable salmon fishing in Norway during the season which runs from 1 June to 31 August each year.

Before formation of the club, Manfred spent many years searching for the best fly waters in Norway. Additionally he became actively involved in the politics of conservation of the fishery, and took part in the many campaigns directed towards the elimination of netting (1979 was the last year of netting in the Gaula and drift netting was banned in the fiords from 1989). When I talked to him about these things, it became apparent that it was yet another example of the world-wide problem of resource allocation. Should commercial exploitation be allowed in order to maintain employment and to add to the economy, or should it be restricted—even curtailed—to allow the preservation of a resource and the maintenance of a different economy based on a different use of that resource? In the European area, particularly in regard to Atlantic salmon, I was left in little doubt that the revenue per fish derived from the latter was around ten to 20 times that achieved from the former and that employment could be redirected accordingly.

The club continues to pursue every avenue in order to preserve the salmon, and statistics are showing that, with the reduction in netting and other measures directed towards conservation, native salmon are on the increase in Norwegian waters and the sport is improving year after year. Moreover, a great deal of the commercial requirement is being provided by fish farming which is conducted without depletion of the resource and with little effect on the environment, other than the risk of cross-breeding when farm fish escape.

For nearly two years before I finally arrived in

Norway on 7 June 1992, Manfred and I had exchanged correspondence. This included the background I have mentioned, details and advice about tackle, transport, accommodation and clothing, and the occasional updating of this information. Manfred runs his 'shop' very efficiently, even to the extent that I once rang him from Australia and he answered me on his mobile telephone on the banks of the Gaula as he was about to net a 20-pounder for a house guest. And later he sent me a VHS video tape of that 1990 season.

I lightened my load before leaving London for Oslo and Trondheim by storing much of my kit at my London hotel. I was learning fast, and limited my suitcase to basic fishing clothing and foul-weather gear, waders and a wading staff, my overfilled vest (the contents changed to cope with salmon) and my art materials and papers. I also took my camera bag and the nine and a half foot Hardy and associated reels, spools and lines.

I arrived at Trondheim Airport, which is in fact at Stjördal, at 5:15 p.m. on a Sunday afternoon; Manfred met me and we drove to Øverkil House, the club's leased fishing lodge on the banks of the River Stjördal, 25 kilometres east of the airport. I found that, while the club leased its waters (and the lodge), the majority of the other, non-private water in Norway is administered by an official 'association'. This association manages its water, selling daily and weekly tickets to tourists, travellers and locals, but never to the extent of overcrowding, for example, the Gaula and the Stjördal; if too many applications are received, then there is a waiting list. A fair portion of water, however, is owned by landowners and farmers who either lease it (to the club, for example) or keep it for their own use. The entire system appeared manageable (in as much as these things can be managed to the satisfaction of most) if not equitable, although some antipathy between association and private management was evident.

Øverkil House is a wonderful 150-year-old Norwegian fishing lodge with eight upstairs bedrooms which share two bathrooms, a very comfortable main living and dining room, kitchen, laundry, cellar, various storerooms, and a front entrance covered in rod racks, weather gauges, line driers, scales, wader holders and a board full of notices allocating fishing beats and giving other vital fishing information. Although the house is old and in need of further repair, Manfred and the club have done much to restore this little haven; particularly giving considerable attention to the electrics and the plumbing.

In addition to Manfred, the staff included the fishing guides: Jan Palmer, a teacher and friend of Manfred's of long standing; Richard, a local from Trondheim; and Simon, a Yorkshireman and one-time ghillie from the Hebrides (my most welcome guide for the first three days); as well as Lucy from Devon, who was in charge of the cooking and the house, and who was also steeped in knowledge of the local flora.

My upstairs room looked out through the leaves and boughs of alders and silver birch trees, in full bloom for the short Norwegian summer, to the River Stjördal where the far bank climbed quickly to rustic farm houses, then upwards through groves of beech trees and fields of cowslips and buttercups to a forest of Norwegian spruce and Douglas fir.

We had dinner at seven-thirty each evening, which is roughly the start of the day in that land of the midnight sun. Fishing started an hour or so later and continued well into the next morning. There was a sort of soft half-twilight for an hour or so around midnight and, during my visit (when daytime temperatures often approached the thirties), the fishing was much better 'at night'.

In the beginning we fished only the Stjördal, the Gaula being too high and fast ahead of its initial salmon run. But the Stjördal offered 19 pools over four kilometres sometimes from one and sometimes both banks. Additionally we had over two and a half kilometres of the Forra, a tributary of the Stjördal, covering 11 pools. So there was ample water for the houseful of guests to fish in comfort, rotating beats every 12 hours.

I found it best to fish from after dinner until five or six the next morning, then sleep until lunchtime and, afterwards, work in my room overlooking the river (or sometimes in the garden) until dinnertime again. In all, it was a very pleasant lifestyle, if not at times exhausting, ideally suited to the fisherman who needs to spoil his day by writing and illustrating as well.

On that first day, a Sunday, the owner of our leases had 'his day on the water'. He took one 16-pound fish on spinning tackle that afternoon, and his companion, a man well over 70, landed a 31½-pound monster after a two hour battle—then slept for the remainder of the day.

My first cast in Norway, in the drifting rainbow mist of a waterfall, was on the Fossen Pool of the Forra using my Hardy which looked tiny alongside the 15-foot, double-handed, 11-weight outfits that my companions invited me to use. When I did, I have to admit that my first efforts were not attractive.

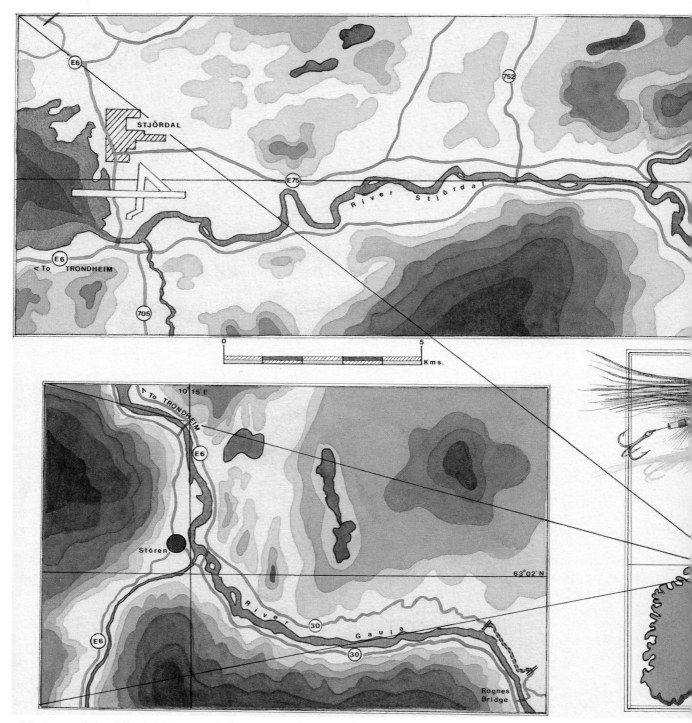

Mudmap of the Stjördal, Forra and Gaula rivers in Norway.

A shooting head, a heavy line, a 25-pound monofilament tippet, and a huge treblehook monster whistled around my head and, more often than not, landed quite close to me, not achieving that added strength and distance for which I was—probably too enthusiastically—striving. For the rest of that night, when not a fish was taken by the lodge, I reverted to my Hardy, promising myself that I would

practise and become adept with the big rod in the days to follow. A promise, incidentally, which I fulfilled very soon afterwards when I realised that the transition from a single- to a double-handed rod was simply an extension of a casting technique and not a requirement to overcome a new and frightening bogey.

Monday 8 June was another very hot day (as

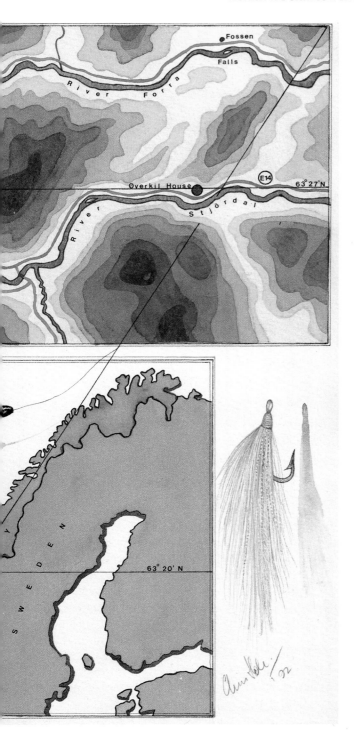

The 'old guy' and his big salmon beside the Stjördal.

Simon fishing the Fossen falls at 3 a.m.

indeed was every day I spent in Norway) when little was achieved other than casting practice, a thorough recce of all the beats and a liberal dose of sunburn. During the night, two of the lodge guests managed to entice fish: one big one was played for 20 minutes before the hook pulled out, and the other rose mightily to a fly even before it hit the water at the end of a long cast! But it was not hooked. In the

The falls above the Fossen Pool on the River Forra.

inevitable discussions following these events we (of the lodge) somewhat naively agreed that:

- 90 per cent of salmon fishing is luck;
- 10 per cent is a mixture of finites: the right fly, the right water, the right weather, the right season, and so on;
- the longer the fly is kept on the water, the better the chances of taking a fish;
- if a fly is not on the water it is impossible to catch a fish;
- one must never give up; and
- mean time between fish (MTBF) is seldom quantifiable but, on average, a very long time.

We were also unanimous in acknowledging the skill and excitement of stalking and casting to visible, large brown trout, but agreed that the hooking of one of the 20-pound monsters from the Stjördal would be a fishing experience beside which most others would pale in comparison. Indeed, most who *had* taken salmon gave it as the reason for their return to salmon waters time and time again although they might wait several weeks before taking another big fish.

In such a frame of mind I fished continuously, carefully and thoroughly from 9 p.m. on Tuesday 9 June until 5 a.m. without a single touch.

Sometime after midnight, Simon, who was with me, said: 'What day is it?' I replied that I wasn't sure because we seemed to have mislaid night-time. It took us several minutes to work out that it was Wednesday morning and, although we had no fish, we were thoroughly enjoying a glorious early morning in one of the most beautiful parts of the world.

I slept until lunchtime when I found that Yves, a French guest at the lodge who was the chef for our dinner the previous evening, had taken a small salmon the night before and another of about 12 pounds that day.

Three Americans arrived just after lunch, intent on three days' fishing. I talked to them and to Manfred for a while before working in my room until dinnertime. Manfred's discussions about salmon management (past and present) and the future of the sport in Europe were both thoughtful and enlightening. So it was that, after dinner, I went forth once again, to try to coax something from that river—alone this time, as I'd completed my apprenticeship in both local geography and in double-handed casting. I fished the upper beats of the Stjördal thoroughly and carefully from after dinner until an hour after midnight. I remained empty-handed, as did Yves who was fishing the other bank. I tried some pools further downstream, and even tried a selection of dry flies and gaudy salt-water flies. Still, nothing!

As luck would have it, I arose the next morning to find that Simon (who had fished with me until the previous night, without scoring) had taken a 15-pound salmon at 5 a.m. from the very pool I had fished four hours previously.

I wasn't annoyed—not a bit of it. I was happy for him; it was his first fish in a week and a half since joining the staff and he deserved it. No, annoyance and disgruntledness can only make it more difficult to take fish. Instead I became philosophical: perhaps the real joys of salmon fishing are due to the hard work and frustrations between brief glimpses of jolting excitement. Certainly I found, as I ventured out the next afternoon, my enthusiasm had not waned. On the contrary, I was beginning to get a feel for the area and an increased confidence. Although, once again, I did not see a fish, I felt as though I was close to a point of extraordinary excitement. After all, Hemingway's 'Old Man' had an 85-day blank period before he

Simon's fish from the Stjördal.

On the doorstep of Øverkil House: standing (*l. to r.*) the author, Herbert and his fish, one of the Americans, and Lucy; seated (*l. to r.*) Simon, Yves, and a second American.

Thoughts of Norway and the midnight sun—Øverkil House merges into the mist of Fossen Falls as I struggle with the 30-pounder.

hooked his monster in those cobalt Cuban currents.

Coincidentally, Manfred received a phone call from the Gaula area telling him that the first run of salmon had begun. Yves, who I found had fished the area for 12 years and fished with Manfred for a lot longer, very kindly offered to take me to that second best salmon river in Norway for an overnight attempt at the early-run monsters.

We took off after dinner in his 4WD Mercedes and, without interpreter, gesticulated our way the 100-odd kilometres from the Stjördal at Øverkil House to the Bridge Pool near Stören on the Gaula. Despite the lack of understanding of each other's language, it was one of the funniest trips I have taken, with much of the discussion in sign language interspersed with many a *très bon,* a *sehr gut* and a *no problems,* as arms, regardless of vehicle control, were flung out in the international expression of all understanding.

I was told that the club beat furthest upstream under Rognes Bridge, the Bridge Pool, was the best on the Gaula. We made a beeline for it with Yves pronouncing around the Gauloise cigarette hanging from his bottom lip: 'Bridge Pool, big *Laks* [Salmon], you get lucky, him number one!'

By that stage I was using a borrowed Hardy 13-foot fibreglass rod with a System Two reel and an intermediate-sink, shooting head, nine weight line. But Yves made me change to one of his 14-foot Sage graphite rods, which was much lighter and unquestionably better.

The Bridge Pool is 150 metres long, starting just below the bridge at Rognes, flowing fast, wide and deep downstream to the next maelstrom of rapids. It is fished from the right bank (facing downstream) which is rocky and tree-lined but wadeable to about four metres from the bank, allowing reasonable casting if care is taken to keep the backcast high. The opposite bank is a steep cliff totally unsuited to fly-fishing.

I started at the top of the beat, casting far out into the current, letting the fly swing downstream. Cast, swing, take three or four stumbling steps over the rocks. Cast, swing, step; cast, swing, step . . . Halfway down the pool with the fly swinging across from the main current: TUG! Pause . . . Then again: TUG . . . TUG! Gentle; very consistent; unquestionably a fish; wait for the almighty strike?

Nothing.

Wait. Still nothing.

Cast again; and again, and again. Cover the position, don't let it be an illusion—PLEASE.

Nothing!

Cast, swing, step. Cast, swing, step . . .

We returned to Øverkil House and bed at 6 a.m. It was the only incident in a long night fishing the Gaula. As Yves left me, he gave a Gallic shrug and said 'Laks better later', as he drove away into the hot morning light.

Although the Americans saw several fish trying to jump the falls at Fossen that night, no one took a fish and, when I emerged for food at lunchtime on Friday 12 June, a German guest (reputed to be a good fisherman) said to me as he stomped down the hallway: 'Am adwancing my aircraft bookings tomorrow. No Laks. Haf one veek Scotland, then I giff op salmon fishink! All luck, no skill!'

I still had four full days' fishing to go and remained silent as I returned to my room and to my pencils and paints for the afternoon. The routine resumed that evening with dinner cooked by my German friend, Herbert, on his then last night which happened to be Lucy's day off. Delicious pork, sauerkraut and beer would not normally be my choice before seven or eight hours' fishing over midnight, but it proved to be not only delicious and sustaining but kept me well anchored by gravity to the rocks on the bottom of the river that night with no possible chance of being swept away.

At 3 a.m. most of us were back in the kitchen at Øverkil House, talking about yet another blank day while we drank cups of hot coffee and nibbled Lucy's biscuits. But the night had some painfully ironic, Scandinavian twists of fate yet in store for me.

About half an hour later, Simon suggested that he and I should return to the falls on the Fossen Pool of the Forra to have a go at the jumping salmon by skipping large dry flies over the top of the white water. All else had failed and it seemed eminently sensible to change tactics. After an hour of fruitless casting, my companion suggested that I should cross the river to the other side of the falls where, from the rocks above the white water, I could dibble a fly with comparative ease. But before I had so much as recovered my line, Herbert the German, with a similar (but preplanned) strategy in mind, had arrived at and crossed the river (I was unaware it could be waded at that point). He took up station on the rocks and allowed his lightweight tube fly to move down the current until he checked it, leaving it skidding on the top of the white water. The rocks behind him resembled a crude granite armchair into which he settled comfortably, fly in position, ready to doze. I murmured to Simon that I would rather be caught netting than catch fish like that, and returned to the lodge and my bed (in high dungeon? No, only medium dungeon I think!)

Later that morning, after five hours' sleep, I entered the kitchen to be bombarded with the story of Herbert's 21½-pound salmon! Apparently, the strike had woken him in his armchair position (just after I had packed up my camera and left the area with Simon), and he eventually landed the fish after a great fight with the help of Yves (who had miraculously appeared on the scene from downstream).

I simply couldn't believe it. And, in a fit of self-centred pique, retired to my room to work out my feelings behind a paintbrush. I could imagine the discussion in the dining room, reliving every moment of that battle, and I knew that, sooner or later with well-meant sympathy, someone would chaff me and say: 'Your turn next, Chris; why don't you go down to the falls rocks and have a sleep with your line out?' I figured it was more tactful to remain in my room covered in French ultramarine than to clobber a fellow guest.

I eventually emerged sheepishly to congratulate Herbert, who had already reverted to his previous travel arrangements and was organising to have his fish mounted. He was, however, humble and magnanimous in his success; he said not a word about my own lack of it, and invited me to share a litre of single malt with him, the landowner and some Swedish friends. It was a kind gesture made by a good fisherman who had achieved success after days and days of frustration. Perhaps I *was* beginning to understand something about salmon fishing after all.

The routine resumed after dinner that night. I couldn't make up my mind which pools to fish, I had little confidence in any of them and, despite Herbert's luck, I was damned if I was going to go armchair fishing. In the end I fished my allocated beat upstream on the Stjördal until midnight and, from 2 o'clock on Sunday morning, moved inexplicably to the falls on the Fossen beat of the Forra.

All was quiet until around full sunrise at 5 a.m., by which time I had found some rocks below the armchair from which I could cast to visible fish if they chose to jump in the white water. I had brought both the big Sage with one of Herbert's flies attached, and my little Hardy which, in desperation, was sporting an Australian white and fluorescent-green Saltwater Smelt fly dressed on a two-0 hook.

At five-ten, real, live, huge Atlantic salmon started to roll, porpoise and jump five or six paces directly in front of me. Shaking like a leaf, I grabbed the big rod and put Herbert's fly among them. The fish rolled enthusiastically over the fly but refused to take it. By now, almost unaware of what I was doing in my frenzy, I discarded the Sage, picked up my Hardy and slammed the Saltwater Smelt fly down hard just inches from the snout of a leviathan.

He rolled, I paused and tightened; there was gentle weight, then there was heavy weight, and finally I was convinced I was connected to the Simplon Orient Express! Simultaneously, the fish sounded in ten metres of white water under the mist of the falls, and Simon poked his head over the rocks, clapping with delight, having witnessed the entire bizarre circus.

The fish was simply a solid, powerful weight. He held position stubbornly and shook his head violently. Who was this fool with a toy, single-handed rod who dared impair the progress of the spawning run of kings? At five twenty-five the fish rose about halfway to the surface and I prepared for a run, but he didn't like it and effortlessly returned to the comparative comfort of the deep, making a nonsense of the full compression on the Hardy Sunbeam, set to the 15-pound tippet on my trace! WHIZZZZZZZ!

Moments later, he dropped back from the falls, staying deep, while I hung on to my double-bent rod and prayed. He answered by moving out and away from me, then by rapidly coming up. I back-pedalled and recovered as fast as I could, keeping the tension, albeit somewhat less than when I held him (or he me?) in the deep. And that was probably my mistake; an almost imperceptible release of tension and, with a couple of shakes of his head, the hook was thrown and I had to admit defeat after a 40-minute battle etched on my brain forever.

The rod had stood the test, as had my knots and joints, but who knows what would have happened had we fought to the end? I staggered back to my bed after a straight nine hours' fishing, knowing I would sleep until Round Two (out of Three) at 3 a.m. on the Monday morning, with the score standing at 1: nil against me. But I figured my luck was extraordinarily overdue for a change.

By now I was behind in my writing, behind in my artwork, I'd taken insufficient photos and I had no clean clothes left in my suitcase.

But it didn't matter.

Nothing mattered now except the fish!

Maybe I *had* found the incurable magnetism of salmon fishing?

The alarm broke through a curtain of mushy fatigue at 3 o'clock in the morning of my last full

Yves with three good Gaula salmon.

day of that extraordinary and unforgettable visit to Norway. The processes of climbing into tired fishing clothing and driving to the Fossen falls were entirely automatic; by then I had fished for 80 hours in eight days and slept for fewer than 25.

Nothing mattered now except the fish. But there had been a change in the weather overnight; after three weeks of hot sun, the Stjördal area lay under overcast and drizzle as I drove towards the falls. Such conditions, I was told, were perfect for fishing but, maintaining their irrational independence, the salmon at the falls stopped jumping and seemed to disappear totally. Meanwhile, Yves had snuck down to the Gaula and caught three.

I put the fish from my mind, went back to the lodge for a shower and breakfast acknowledging, at last, the first *duck* in my round-the-world series. Strangely contented, I devoted the rest of my last day in Norway to writing and painting.

On that last night, in a moment of sheer desperation, I accepted a lift back to the Gaula with Manfred at 6.30 p.m., acknowledging I was now totally hooked on salmon-madness. Manfred drove the Mercedes stationwagon through Trondheim to Stören with speed and aplomb while chatting to people in Budapest and Finland on the car-phone—with me acting as his secretary, opening files to reveal the telephone numbers he wanted to call.

I remember that we fished the Gaula mainly in the Bridge Pool that night from about 9 p.m. until 6 a.m. I had one touch and Manfred hooked into a big one only to be broken off moments later. Meanwhile, we learned that back at the falls on the Forra, apparently the salmon were jumping again. One day I might get my act together.

I returned to Øverkil House at noon with a head full of cottonwool. After a shower, shave and lunch, I packed my gear and left Stjördal at 4 p.m. flying via Oslo to London at the end of yet another extraordinary and fascinating experience. Although it was, apart from the jumping fish in the falls, strictly blind fishing, across-and-down for whatever might lurk in the deep, it was *something* that had me incurably addicted. Manfred kindly offered to have me return as his guest for a couple of days if my program allowed and, had it been possible, I would have done so with great enthusiasm; his organisation is first-class, meets its aims, and if I could, I would return again and again.

The misty vision of 30 pounds of very aggressive Atlantic salmon connected to me via a nine and a half foot trout rod keeps reappearing in my dreams. And, although it was my first *duck*, I would not have missed it for anything.

"Hairwing Heggeli"

Chris Hole. 1992.

17

Summer Fly-fishing in Devon, and a Pause with my Family

The airline which flew me from Oslo to London at the end of my Stjördal episode managed to lose my rods in transit. With considerable—but probably unnecessary—urging on my part, they were delivered to my London hotel 15 hours later.

After three further days in London I repacked my (by now) protesting luggage, collected yet another rental car and set out for Lifton in Devon, very near the border with Cornwall. It was an easy drive west on the M4 Motorway to Bristol, and southwest on the M5 to Exeter, bypassing each major town, finally to leave the M5 and to take the A30 to Lifton, where I arrived around teatime on Friday, 19 June.

The motorways, although obviously crowded, moved quickly enough and, as it was the height of summer, the days remained long and balmy in the gentle heat haze which appeared to be permanently glued to the rolling hills. It was all very beautiful and, once again as a travelling fly-fisherman, I experienced the joy of existence, even though suffering from hayfever due to the extraordinarily high pollen count.

I had booked ahead into a well-known fishing hotel, the Arundell Arms, where I was made most welcome on arrival. Run by Anne Voss-Bark, the owner-manager and wife of Conrad, fly-fishing author and one-time angling correspondent for the London *Times*, the hotel is promoted as being a wonderful haven for rest, relaxation, fishing, shooting and country life. It certainly provided very comfortable facilities, gourmet dining, and many thoughtful extras aimed at making guests happy and content. I was told that the main building was once an old coaching inn built on a site dating back to Saxon times, and I found that the grounds included an ancient circular cockpit used in the days of cockfighting which had, more recently, been converted into a fishing and rod room. The entire area is located in a valley of five rivers which still supports considerable wildlife, despite increasing human and urban pressures and pollution. The hotel has been an established fishing retreat for more than half a century and boasts 20 miles of fishing on the River Tamar and four of its tributaries, primarily offering quite exciting lightweight fishing for small, brightly coloured wild brown trout, but with runs of sea-trout and salmon in quantities depending on the season and the environment.

I made early contact with the two hotel fishing bailiffs, David and Roy, in the cockpit; we discussed beats and access, flies, fishing routine and all those matters usually discussed before someone new to an area goes out to fish it. They were most helpful, providing sound advice laced with a good sense of humour, and took my big Hardy rod to resecure the runners after its encounter with the salmon in Norway. Between us, we established a routine for me that was similar to, but much more relaxing than Norway. After breakfast, I would visit the cockpit for the latest advice, replacement flies and allocation of beats. I would then fish until a late lunch, after which I would write and paint until

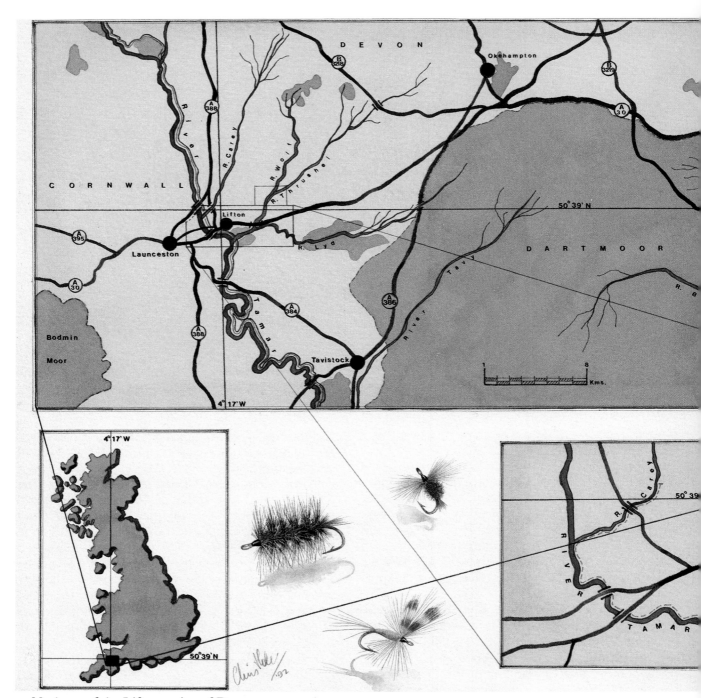

Mudmap of the Lifton region of Devon.

time for drinks and dinner. Quite often after dinner I would go out again to fish for sea-trout (but also in the hope of a salmon) until midnight. Each third day I would not fish at all, devoting the day to exploring, taking photographs and catching up with my paints and paper.

On the first two mornings I caught quite a large number of very small (up to ten inches), highly coloured, wild brown trout, using my lightweight Sage outfit with a two-pound tippet. Although the fish were small, the work was exacting and delicate, a challenge in itself which never seemed to fade; the twentieth rise to a fly was just as exciting as the first. It was undemanding and relaxing fishing in a beautiful countryside, although I was disappointed in the lack of clarity of the water (the area was suffering from a heavy road construction program, drought, and chemical problems).

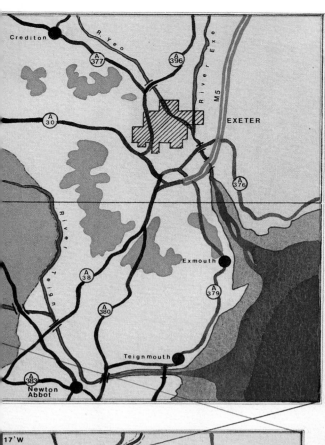

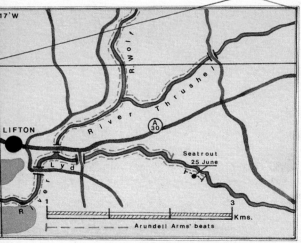

The Devon countryside in summer.

The cockpit at the Arundell Arms . . .

. . . and the interior . . .

On the second morning I noticed a fellow on the other bank from my beat on the River Tamar take a sea-trout of around two pounds fishing with bait. So I rigged up my Orvis gear (five weight outfit with five-pound tippet) to have a go myself. This was despite Roy and David suggesting that a sea-trout strike required a seven-pound tippet. Surely, I thought, if six- and seven-pound rainbow trout in the Hunter River in New Zealand can be handled

A couple of liars estimating fish sizes outside the cockpit at the Arundell Arms!

on six-pound tippets, there was no need to go stronger with these lighter fish? It was a bit like those in Norway insisting that the only way to play a fish with the certainty of success was with skull-dragging leaders and very large equipment. Thanks for the advice, chaps, but I would rather do it my way, even though I may lose some fish.

That evening, although I caught (and released) a one and a quarter pound brownie (big for the area) on a Muddler Minnow, and lost something much bigger when a size-20 Adams pulled out, I had nothing of consequence on the bank to prove my enjoyment or judgment.

The next morning, while again taking an intriguing mass of little brownies on two-pound tippets, I heard an almighty splash behind me. Thinking it was a bough falling into the water, or perhaps a cow coming down to drink (there were undoubtedly more cows per 100 paces of river than good fish and I balked at thinking about nitrate levels), I took my time before I turned to see what had caused the splash. There was nothing to be seen save ever-expanding circles. A salmon? A sea-trout at least? Who knows? But I decided to leave it for the time being and to return to that part of the river in the evening.

It was a warm, balmy night. I had long since given up wearing my neoprene waders; they were much too hot and heavy and, some days before, I had reverted to walking boots and old cotton trousers (no matter how wet they became). But despite a good coverage of the river that night (in this case the River Lyd near its confluence with the Tamar), I scored no more than my usual dose of small brownies which seemed content to take almost any fly that hit the water, including size-eight salmon doubles.

I didn't fish on Tuesday, 23 June. Having topped up the car with petrol, I had a haircut, spent some time photographing the areas I had been fishing and devoted the rest of the day to writing and painting. Although the haircut was mild compared with the New Zealand variety, I noticed that the somewhat effeminate barber (and a number of other locals for that matter) kept referring to me as: 'Young man'! Aged in my mid-fifties, at first I took this to be a compliment, but began to query my judgment when I was so addressed by locals in their twenties. I found it was a fairly normal West Country form of address rather as we in Australia (unfortunately in my opinion) call everyone 'mate' regardless of whether the addressee is a true mate, a wife, lover, brother, friend, or—more often than not—a potential enemy.

Wednesday 24 June was, as my plans were then, the last day that I had allocated myself exclusively for fishing. Thursday was to be a working day, and the day after that I had to depart for Taplow for two weeks with Gini and Sam. I wanted to remain flexible, however. If David and Roy thought it better to fish on Thursday, then I would swap; and if they thought it better to fish on both days then I would naturally give in to their advice.

I started with another happy and relaxed morning of lightweight dry-fly fishing for small brownies on some very attractive new beats on the River Lyd. About mid-morning, a voice greeted me from the bank and I joined the local Water Bailiff to present my licence (all in order) and to discuss fishing for the best part of an hour. He confirmed some views that were beginning to form in my mind about excessive fishing pressures in England, the fishery becoming denuded of wild stock and supported by pellet-fed 'stockies', pollution and the need to control it, and other associated matters. He struck me as being a particularly thoughtful and competent character with the very best of intentions covering the preservation and improvement of his fishery for the future.

Then, after lunch when I returned to my room, my day was somewhat spoilt when I found the local council repairing the minute right-of-way outside my window. This 'major operation' to re-tar less than three square metres of track took most of the afternoon, a pneumatic leveller, a steam packer, a roller and their assorted drivers; six workmen, two supervisors and one supervisor's supervisor. I was left wondering about the waste in terms of cost, equipment and manpower which, otherwise, could have been added to the effort of building the bypass so badly needed around the little village of Lifton.

Anyway, I worked through the noise and smell until dinnertime and, afterwards, returned to my beat on the Lyd in the hope of a sea-trout.

Two things happened that evening. At dinner, prior to my fishing, Anne Voss-Bark suggested that on the following (and my final) night I should fish a different beat of the Lyd which was said to be very productive. After dinner I caught no fish at all, while Roy and a customer, fishing Anne's recommended beat, caught two good sea-trout. Next morning I thoroughly examined the productive beat, ready for my final night's encounter, and took two reels of film to record the area just in case of success, and also because it was so beautifully photogenic. For the remainder of the day I worked and (once again) packed my suitcases ready for departure the next morning.

Arriving on my beat around 10 p.m., I walked to its upstream limit, keeping well back from the river. Roughly opposite the advised sea-trout position, I moved cautiously in towards the river bank, keeping low and using maximum cover from the bank foliage. The River Lyd, at that point above a weir and above murky inlets, was pretty clear and I was keen not to spook anything. Once in position, I prepared my gear and settled down to wait for darkness (10.30 p.m. by my reckoning). I had been offered several pieces of good advice: big Muddler Minnows skipped over the surface, wet streamers allowed to sink then retrieved in jerks, and flies like the Peter Ross similarly fished. For some reason (which remains obscure) I tied on a size-eight, very long-shank Woolly Worm, one of three which had remained in my fly box since Patagonia.

I was determined to wait until ten-thirty before disturbing the misty summer tranquillity of that evening by cutting the heavy air with a fly line; that was until I heard the unmistakable stripping of a Hardy reel on the other bank. The next door neighbour, who came down nightly to take a sea-trout or two on the fly, was at it again.

It was ten twenty-three and, if he was about to start, then so was I. I cast across and up, or directly across, letting the fly sink momentarily then, as it began to swing in the slow current, I would figure-of-eight retrieve. On the third cast I took a little brownie, which was returned; then rising circles seemed to appear miraculously all over the river, but there were no big sea-trout splashes. I cast to a small rise beside a tree on the far bank; as I retrieved there was a TUG . . . TUG, TUG . . . something was following . . . then a determined but not overpowering take, and I was connected to my first sea-trout from Devon. He fought very hard, emptying much of the reel in his early runs during those first few moments. I was more than impressed. Then, as fishermen do, I began to think about the problems ahead; once again, I was on a steep bank with no net, I knew I would have to play the fish out before drowning him close in front of me in order to tail or mouth him from the water. So I settled down to the task. After less than two minutes intensive battle, however, the fish simply went limp and gave in. Somewhat surprised, I lay on my belly, pulled him into the bank and released him. He was a one and a half pounder, and the next two I hooked—also on the Woolly Worm (one the same size which I released, and one of two pounds which I kept)—behaved exactly the same way. I was left wondering whether it was the drought, interbreeding with 'stockies', river pollution, or one of a number of other explanations which crowded through my mind, that might account for this weak performance.

Apart from this worry (similar in substance to anything that detracts from expected performance), it was a hugely enjoyable evening and a fitting finale to fishing in that part of the world.

I said my goodbyes the next morning, exchanged addresses and notes with David and Roy, and left a watercolour fly painting with the hotel before motoring north to London. Anne Voss-Bark was particularly kind, providing me with assistance with publishers, and informing me that Conrad's next book, a history of fly-fishing, would be released in London the following week.

I retraced my miles on the A30, the M5 and the M4 and arrived in London at 2 p.m. on Friday, 26 June 1992, to meet Gini, whom I had left in Canberra six weeks earlier and who had since travelled through America (on the way having beer and shrimps with a lady friend who had just turned 100!) to join me on my quest for the Holy Grail of Izaak Walton. We overloaded the car with her luggage on top of mine and drove to Taplow, near Maidenhead, only 40 minutes from west London. There we took up residence for two weeks in a cottage on the Thames in Cliveden Estate so I could

Sea-trout territory on the River Lyd.

complete my first round of writing and painting before taking on the Arctic Circle in earnest.

Those who can recall the 1960s will be familiar with Cliveden if they are not already aware of this magical and imposing monument to English aristocracy, architectural and landscaping design and *joie die vivre*, with its firmly established and dramatic history outside that singular decade. The 1960s, of course, relit Cliveden's limelight when it was chosen by the principal players in the Christine Keeler affair—Profumo, Dr Stephen Ward, 'that Russian', Mandy Rice-Davies, Christine *et al.*—as one of their more spectacular stages.

Whether Gini, Sam and I, or our occasional lunch guests, actually stayed in the cottage at centre stage or not doesn't really matter. What is important is that the cottage—'New Cottage', Cliveden Estate, belonging to the National Trust—was one of the most beautiful places of all those in which I resided in my world travels in 1992. It was small and humble yet pretty and comfortable; the Thames, with all its overhanging greenery, was ten paces from our front doorstep; there was a landing stage, dinghy and oars; log fires which we never used because of the hot summer; peace and tranquillity, and an ambiance I can only describe by saying that I was convinced each evening that Mr Toad would send a servant to invite us to his Hall for dinner, and that we would probably stumble over Mr Jeremy Fisher on the way there.

I had booked the cottage nearly two years beforehand, again part of the early planning, and could not have been more satisfied with the outcome. All the arrangements were made through the National Trust, who were particularly helpful in providing this haven in immaculate condition and at very reasonable cost. Whilst the National Trust administers the estate, Cliveden itself is leased as a five-star hotel with sporting facilities, including a boathouse on the Thames near our cottage, which housed three vintage river craft painted Royal Yacht blue and decked in polished mahogany, which were available for charter. We just happened to lease our cottage during the Henley Royal Regatta, and part of that long-thought-out preplanning had included the hiring of one of these geriatric but exceedingly beautiful Thames craft, complete with skipper (I would take on the Pacific, Atlantic, and even the Straits of Magellan—but not the Thames at Henley) and English picnic lunch for the final Sunday at Henley. It was a non-fishing day of absolutely crazy enjoyment. Collectively, the whole Cliveden scene (which, stretching the imagination, probably

'New Cottage', Cliveden Estate.

included leopards and gold-lamé-miniskirted dolly birds) had hit a score out of ten which equalled the Taieri in New Zealand and the Malleo in Patagonia.

Henley Royal Regatta 1992.

18
Iceland: 'You should have been there on Monday!' And I was!

Included in the niceties of New Cottage at Cliveden was a miniature landing stage in front of the house, complete with two-man fibreglass dinghy. The boat was padlocked to its landing for security, and the keys to the padlock, and the shed where the oars were kept, were hung on labelled pegs in a cupboard inside the cottage. My family and I occasionally paddled about the Thames in front of the cottage in the evenings, taking photographs of the ducks, casting the odd fly at rises and drinking gin and tonic. A pleasant interlude.

But the dinghy had a much more important task to perform, or so I thought.

I had ascertained that to land private fishing tackle in Iceland, it was first necessary to have all the bits and pieces which could possibly be contaminated in other countries—waders, rods, reels, boots, lines, knives and the like—fully disinfected, and a certificate to that effect signed by a veterinary officer within seven days prior to departure for Iceland. A most sensible safeguard that can only be applauded. Further investigation revealed that decontamination could be achieved by immersing the tackle in a 2 per cent formaldehyde solution for ten minutes.

Therefore, while at New Cottage I rang the local vet concerning this matter. He immediately suggested that he should bring the formaldehyde to the cottage to carry out the operation because, he said, the clinic was far too small. On the face of it, an apparently simple solution involving only the bathroom at the cottage. But, on further consideration, I pondered: (a) that the vet wanted a peek at Cliveden and possibly the arena of Christine Keeler's affairs? Unlikely, because he could do that at any time without having to clean fishing tackle in formaldehyde. (b) He wanted a cup of tea or a gin and tonic after his task? The tea he could get at the clinic, and it was highly unlikely that a vet would drink gin and tonic at noon. Or, (c) formaldehyde was extremely toxic and had such a revolting smell that he would rather remove it from his clinic? Almost a dead certainty.

So I pulled the dinghy up from the landing stage onto the front lawn, provided a bucket to carry and mix the water, put my waders, reels, boots, knives and other tackle on board, and stood by to receive the vet.

It should have worked like well-oiled clockwork. But, when the vet arrived and we reviewed the situation, we concluded that it would take us ages to fill the dinghy with fresh water; moreover we had no immediate source of rinsing water after decontamination, and no easy access to sewerage disposal for the 'leftovers'—we certainly were not going to put them on the garden or into the Thames. So, up to the bathroom we went, and completed the task reasonably efficiently with little residue odour and—very probably—a resultant super-clean sewerage system. Gini spent that night in London with friends.

During my planning of the Icelandic episode, it soon became apparent that I was to visit a salmonid fishery at the very top of world class in terms of fishing, management, water purity, scenery, exclusiveness and many other factors including, unfortunately, price. For these very reasons I included Iceland in my travels, limiting the actual fishing days because of the cost. Reykjavik also provided a logical geographic stepping-stone to the Northwest Territories of Canada and to Baffin Island. I was excited about the visit, what's more Gini was coming with me and we were both eagerly looking forward to it.

To avoid excess luggage charges on this, the first in a series of out-of-the-way flights in small aeroplanes crossing 65 degrees North latitude, I reduced my kit as much as possible. Spare fishing tackle (we always carry too much), maps, outdated papers and files, unwanted clothing and an increasing pile of newspaper and magazine articles were boxed up and sent home by sea mail.

With considerable regret we left New Cottage after breakfast on 10 July, drove to Heathrow, returned the rental car which had served us so well and boarded the Icelandic flight to Reykjavik. An entirely new experience awaited us 70 miles south of the Arctic Circle.

The trip to Keflavik Airport and on to Reykjavik was not entirely uneventful. I had mistakenly put my two fishing knives in my hand luggage and these were seized at the departure immigration point with polite efficiency and a promise of delivery (with all other personal luggage) on arrival in Iceland. I would never have had the courage to hijack an international airliner, least of all with an Everlast filleting knife, but sadly it was the last I ever saw of my fishing knives!

Then, at Keflavik Airport, having completed a number of forms in triplicate about the missing knives, as we passed through arrival procedures, I joined a substantial queue of ruddy-faced individuals holding rods and other fishing tackle—in itself, encouraging. Happy in the knowledge that I already held a vet's clearance, and in the belief that my processing would therefore be a formality, I was dismayed to find I had to pay the same fee (per rod) as those who had not had their tackle precleaned, and who were quite happy to wait ten minutes while the Icelandic officials did it for them, without having to pay the vet's additional fee in the first place. To add insult to injury, the local decontaminant was an iodine solution and not smelly old formaldehyde.

We live and learn, but I'm sure I could have been better advised about the regulations.

The day did not improve; we picked up another rental car and somehow became lost in Reykjavik looking for the hotel—the map proved to be outdated. We eventually found the place, settled in comfortably, and went downtown for one of the best seafood dinners I have ever eaten; the price—

being roughly four times that to which I had become accustomed (even by then)—matching the quality.

After another daylit night like Norway, we left Reykjavik the next morning driving generally north towards Borgarnes, meandering along the banks of the fiords as we went. It was our first proper look at Iceland; I don't take in a great deal when my knives go missing, I get lost, and I pay too much for a wonderfully satisfied stomach. More relaxed that morning, we found a majestically stark country, a little like New Zealand but more darkly dramatic, whose pronounced volcanic origins provide the dominant colour which, in summer, is tempered by the greens of grasslands mantled by snow-capped blue-greys. Other than a further colour contrast etched by white concrete and iron dwellings with brightly coloured roofs, there was little else on the immediate canvas. There were no trees and the resulting moonscape was somehow both beautiful and sinister. Nordurá Lodge, where we were to stay, was 30 minutes drive from Borgarnes, on the banks of the Nordurá River, right in the middle of some of the most imposing of this Icelandic scenery. We arrived there in time for lunch and were greeted by Jon Borgthorsson, the executive director of the Angling Club of Reykjavik, with whom I had been planning our visit during the previous 18 months.

Set on top of high basalt cliffs looking down to the beautiful Nordurá, this oiled timber and weatherboard lodge of the Angling Club of Reykjavik is one of the best remote fishing lodges I have ever encountered. The club, which was established in the 1930s, and which has negotiated leases for fishing on the Nordurá and leaseback arrangements for the lodges they have constructed and extended over the years, is particularly well administered and runs the pick of the fishing in a country which could well be called the pick of fishing countries in the world. The lodge contains 13 double bedrooms with all facilities, and four more which share a bathroom. Thus a total of 34 guests can be accommodated, which is more than double the 12-rod allocation on three major beats covering over 25 kilometres on both banks of the Nordurá. Thus, when the house is roughly half full or more, actual fishermen come to share rods or bring non-fishing partners for whom walking or riding through the splendid scenery is a joy in itself.

As well as very adequate staff quarters, the lodge provides a large sitting room overlooking the river, a sauna, rod and drying rooms, a cleaning room for fish, and a large cold room. The dining room can support the maximum guest capacity at one long table which is probably the start point of the fishing

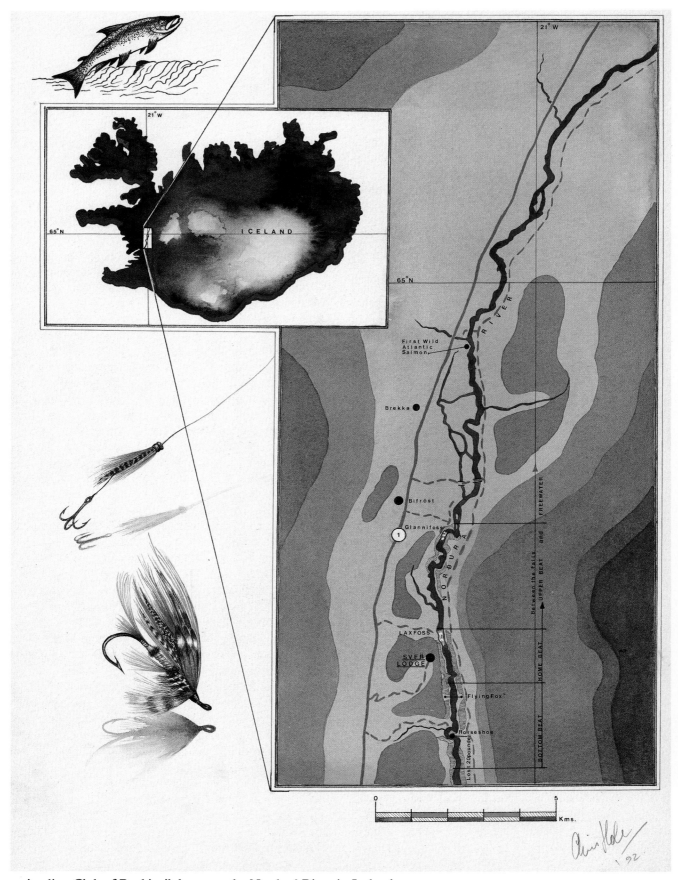

Angling Club of Reykjavik beats on the Nordurá River in Iceland.

Laxfoss on the Nordurá River in Iceland.

day when breakfast is served at 6 a.m. The first fishing session is from 7 a.m. to 1 p.m., lunch is served around the long table from 2 to 3 p.m., the second session, when beats are changed, runs from 4 to 10 p.m. and dinner starts at 11 p.m. or later. The beats change again next morning and after each six-hour session; so, after three sessions, if the angler takes a second full day and a half (and most take a total of three days' fishing), he has seen some of each beat before he repeats himself. This makes it ideal for the newcomer (on a three-day visit) who can take a guide for the first three sessions before going solo for another three, covering the beats he has already fished and been advised about. Conversely, those familiar with the area have two goes at each beat in a three-day session, seeking out their favourite spots.

As we arrived on a Saturday, and I was not due to start fishing until 4 p.m. the next day, I had a full 24 hours to examine the area quite thoroughly, talk to other fishermen, take photographs and get settled. I wish I could make myself do this at every new place, it obviously pays big dividends but it is very hard when only self-discipline (and not regulation) is there to enforce it, and the river is full of jumping fish.

When, at last, I came to fish the Nordurá, starting that Sunday afternoon at 4 o'clock, in warm, clear weather, I was unaware at the time that I had before me three days of something very close to Paradise.

Before describing those days, however, I shall endeavour to sketch briefly some of the background to Icelandic sport fishing for salmon because it is so closely linked to the success of the industry as I saw it.

Until 1991, commercial harvesting of salmon was a moderately large and important business. In particular it involved mainly landowning farmers who either netted salmon in the main estuaries (primarily early in the season when the bigger fish run to spawn and when the price of salmon is highest), or sold the rights to do so. In the case

Gini 'enjoying' the invigorating weather at Nordurá Lodge.

of the Nordurá, netting in the fiord area near Borgarnes effectively choked the early salmon spawning run of big fish, not only for that river, but for three other important rivers running into the same fiord.

In Iceland there are several angling clubs, the largest and most important being the Angling Club of Reykjavik (SVFR) with 2,200 members. There is also an Association of Angling Clubs, loosely aimed at consensus in the preservation of the sport, and a further Association of Angling Rights Owners. In addition, there are several articles of legislation governing fishing policy. In 1991, initially for a one-year trial period, the clubs and associations negotiated a deal with the netting rights owners to buy out those rights in order to stop netting and to preserve and then enhance sport fishing (which, in any case, was producing a price per kilo for salmon which far outweighed that which could be achieved commercially). Subsequently similar buy-outs were negotiated for 1992, 1993 and 1994. The value of purchase was negotiated around the average commercial price per kilo of wholesale salmon, with allowance for indexation over the years, and the cost spread throughout the users in proportion to their expected usage. It was a brilliant scheme resulting in great preservation of and an increase in the sport (and therefore revenue), while the old commercial netters—the farmers and landowners—gained a no-risk source of income, without effort or maintenance, while pursuing their other prime farming interests. A small commercial salmon industry remains and is maintained by limited specialised fish farming, sufficient to fulfil the commercial need.

There being no such thing as a free lunch, however, the cost of buy-out eventually had to be passed down to the user, the sport fisherman, who was already paying for his share of land and river rights (his purchase of 'a rod' on a beat) and for his accommodation and meals, and for a small club (lodge or owner) profit margin. The biggest factor, undoubtedly, is the cost of leasing land and rights. The associations and clubs negotiate leases from landowners, normally at the close of each season in September. Leases are often negotiated for several years in addition to the next season. Costs are then passed on to the fisherman for his rod and, subsequently, accurate records of catches in specific areas are kept, which form the basis for the next lease negotiation, the more productive areas bringing the higher lease prices.

Additionally, salmon fishing in Iceland is regulated by legislation and by club and association rules. The season lasts from 20 May to 20 September, but only three months may be used in this period (normally 1 June to 31 August); and, by law, fishing may only be undertaken between the hours of 7 a.m. and 10 p.m. and then only for a maximum of 12 hours during that period. Moreover, the clubs and associations work out and allocate the maximum number of rods that are allowed to operate on any stretch of the various rivers.

Clubs and owners, armed with all this information and accounting, lease their holdings, make their estimates and add the costs of netting buy-back, food, accommodation and profit margin, then sell rods to club members and outsiders in order to meet costs and leave the small profit margin.

The entire organisation is tight, super-efficient, totally pure and extremely environmentally friendly, but very expensive. Moreover, it is run entirely privately and is greatly admired by locals and overseas visitors alike. But that represents the very top end of sport fishing in Iceland.

At the other end of the scale, the average local or visiting angler may indulge in excellent fishing (particularly for trout) using farm holiday accommodation or camping areas, all at very reasonable prices while having the advantage of those all important (and partly paid for) factors of purity, good management, conservation and wonderful scenery, and with no problems of pollution or overcrowding. In essence, I believe Iceland provides arguably the best fly-fishing in the world; it is only a pity that, for most, it is so remote—a factor which undoubtedly adds to its attractiveness.

Ingo was my guide for the first three of my six sessions of six hours each. For the first session we were given the furthest downstream beat together with one rod shared by two fascinating Germans from Munich, and two rods fished by Frenchmen, part of a large and regular group who spent a great deal of their time and effort ensuring they had the best spots. Positions on each beat were meant to be exchanged at the three-hour mark but, over the ensuing days, this system became somewhat subsumed by Gallic confusion, resulting in the sub-allocation of river banks on given beats for the entire six hours, changing banks on the next occasion of fishing the same beat. This didn't worry me much. I thought all of the water was magnificent, but it would have been unfair to the angler who had only one 18-hour visit on three beats, when he would fish only one bank of each and not both.

Ingo and I crossed the river by flying fox and I started casting my big Hardy in what he described as the most difficult part of the Nordurá. Big, slippery rocks, fast-flowing water of unbelievable clarity and jumping salmon were my memories of that first session when I caught no fish but twice went 'swimming' involuntarily in the icy waters. The beats were all different; the downstream one running through a steep-sided volcanic canyon culminating, downstream, in a horseshoe bend with white water over most of its length save one or two mirrored pools. The next upstream, cleared the canyon at a deep, sharp, white-water bend to broaden and slow in front of the lodge; the immediate rock faces remained quite steep and colourful but more vegetation was evident, and stark volcanic strata cliffs rose in the background to the east. That central beat stopped, upstream, at Laxfoss (the Salmon Falls), probably the most famous falls in the area and a scene (shared from our bedroom window) of breathtaking beauty. For me it was also the most productive beat. The final beat, upstream again, ran from Laxfoss to the next falls, Glannifoss, and above, through continuing steep country at first, then flattening into a wide valley where the river became more like a gravel-bottom trout stream, meandering slowly north to disappear finally into the mountains again. All of it simply wonderful fly-fishing country.

Ingo was a good guide, an excellent fisherman and a very pleasant companion on the river, even if he tended to cover the ground over the rocks on the first occasion like an express mountain goat— a little too fast for me. His (most successful) advice was to use a very small tube fly (about half an inch long) and a size-14 treble hook.

After only a few hours sleep, bleary-eyed fishermen were awakened the next morning at six to be greeted by a really super day. The warmth was already apparent at that early hour (even taking account of the lack of night); there was not a breath of wind nor a cloud in the washed blue sky which hung, as though drying, from the surrounding mountain peaks. I had the uppermost beat that morning and Ingo took me way up the valley to the 'trout water', where I fished non-stop in that hot light, seeing not another soul all morning. My guide was a little worried about things being too bright and clear but I made it evident that this was 'trout stuff' to me and said: 'Let's go fine and small.' He wouldn't agree to go lower than ten-pound Maxima (although I would have preferred seven), but the size-14 Blue Charm tubefly looked perfect. The first run was a glassy glide over pebbles, with a bank on the left facing downstream, and with me on a gently sloping gravel bank on the right.

Centrally there was a rocky outcrop around which the water swirled and over which it glided into a deep green run, continuing some 200 paces downstream. I started above the outcrop, casting across, letting the fly swing down as I slowly retrieved with a short, slow stripping motion, remembering to keep a low profile. After the fourth or fifth cast, when I was wondering if I shouldn't be fishing upstream with a dry fly, a beautiful silver shape jumped clear and splashed back into the water only yards from me. Instantly I became a believer! And two casts later, was connected to an extraordinary weight which just kept shaking the line: jolt . . . jolt . . . jolt! About ten minutes later, after a very satisfying battle, I landed my very first wild Atlantic salmon of six and a half pounds. I hasten to add that, because of the old netting policy, the majority of fish in the Nordurá were then grilse, but the number of older and bigger fish returning to the river was expected to increase.

After fishing the length of that pool I tried one other without success. On returning to the starting point on the first pool, however, I hooked a second, smaller fish on the third cast as the fly was drawn over the rocky outcrop into the deep swirl. At 8.30 a.m. I was all fired up, super-confident and ready to fish until I dropped in the total certainty that it was going to be a great day.

We left that pool and drove in Ingo's 4WD Niva downstream along the higher left bank of the river, slowly polaroiding as we went. Salmon are quite visible under such conditions, obviously so when they jump, but also when they hold in a lie in the water. In such clarity their broad backs and swaying fins can be seen for some distance from above when their colour appears to be a pale shade of earth green against the contrasting gravel, rocks and moss.

Five minutes along the track, Ingo stopped above some rocks where a stormwater overflow pipe ran into the river. Through polaroids we counted four or five fish and knew that others would be around. Backtracking upstream then crossing a shallow bank in the 4WD, we drove along the gravel to a position some 150 paces upstream from the fish. In I went and started casting across, close to the other bank. Cast, swing, step . . . cast, swing, step . . . cast, swing, step. I eventually approached the target area and could see the wash around the submerged rocks at the outlet. I don't believe I've ever been more certain that there were fish there and that I would catch some.

Such an attitude is very healthy.

And the first time my fly swung over the wash there was a big swirl; I was connected to a small

henfish (about four pounds) which fought like the
very Devil. Three in the bag and it was only 10
a.m. I backtracked upstream in order to cover the
rest of the wash. About halfway down into it this
time there was a big swirl but no weight; I let the
fly continue to swing, slowly stripping in line. When
it was almost directly downstream from me, there
was a bow wave from the direction of the wash
and then an almighty slash at my fly, and line
whizzed out under considerable strain. Backing up
to the pebbles I settled down to slug it out; I was
quite obviously connected to a good fish. Although
he broke the surface with a lot of spray a couple
of times I did not see him fully during the first
ten minutes. But when, with him complaining
physically, I brought my charge to within 15 paces
of the bank, I suddenly saw that the fish (about
an eight-pounder) had a mate keeping close station—
a phenomenon I had witnessed previously with
trout. Together they put on a battle in the shallow
water that had me thinking for a while that the
leader had caught around the second fish and I was
trying to land a double-header! But it was not to
be; suddenly the mate broke formation and headed
for the deep water. My hooked friend followed with
such suddenness and ferocity that there was a quick
PING . . . as the hook pulled out and I was left
wondering if this was a well-rehearsed battle tactic.

As we returned for lunch, Ingo inquired whether
my first fish that morning was, indeed, my first
landed, live Atlantic salmon? After considering the
landlocked fish I had caught in Australia and New
Zealand, the wild Pacific salmon from New
Zealand's South Island, and remembering I had not
actually *caught* a salmon in Scotland in the 1950s,
nor in Norway some weeks before my visit to
Iceland, I had to admit it was. Doubling up with
mirth, Ingo announced that there was an ancient
ritual in Iceland that had to be performed by the
angler on landing his first Atlantic salmon. Thinking
dark thoughts about pagan Viking rituals (did I have
to chew out its liver while it was still kicking?),
I hesitatingly asked what this ritual required of me.
Between shrieks of laughter Ingo indicated that,
back at the lodge, in front of my fishing companions,
I had to grasp the fish and ceremoniously bite off
its adipose fin.

YUK! My black thoughts weren't that far from
the truth!

Some will recall just how firmly an adipose fin
is attached to the upper backbone structure of a
salmonid, particularly if they have had to strip a
fish after smoking it. I certainly wasn't looking
forward to it all when they placed me with my fish

Fishing Laxfoss, the Nordurá River in Iceland. Some
of the best fishing in the world.

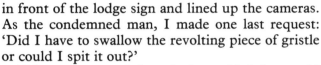

Success! The author returns with three good *lax* . . .   . . . and bites the adipose fin from his first!

in front of the lodge sign and lined up the cameras. As the condemned man, I made one last request: 'Did I have to swallow the revolting piece of gristle or could I spit it out?'

'Of course you spit it out', they said, 'who would be so stupid as to eat it?'

Mumbling something about 'anyone stupid enough to bite it off', I grasped the fish in both hands like a piece of watermelon and sunk my teeth into the fin just above the line of the back. Thirty seconds later the revolting morsel was lying at my feet, congratulations and laughter enveloped me, and the bubbly flowed like the water in the river!

Strangely enough I *did* eat lunch—the morning had been so invigorating—and was eagerly back in the river, this time in the home beat in front of the lodge, at 4.10 p.m. I fished a flat, quickly gliding rocky pool, close in by the bank and not far from the lodge. For the first hour and a half, although salmon were jumping all around me, I couldn't seem to hook one. Then I remembered to 'think trout' again, switched to a seven-pound tippet and a size-14 fly, and promptly landed a five-pounder. Ingo was asleep on the bank in the sun but joined me after I had landed the fish and we walked up to Laxfoss to fish the white water for the remainder of the session. When we arrived I noticed the Frenchmen on the other bank (chosen by them) giving the water a fair pounding but apparently with little to show for it. Ingo lead me to a good white-water run almost under the falls and changed my tippet to ten-pound Maxima keeping the small Blue Charm in place. On the third cast I was well connected to a five-pounder and understood, by the time I landed him, the need for a stronger tippet in that particularly strong run. Before Ingo had reached the bank to bag that salmon I was hooked to a second one of much the same size. I only wished

at the time that I'd had my camera with me to record the Gallic expressions on the other bank (although we became good friends later).

A short while later, and a little further downstream, I hooked another fish and, despite the hook pulling out, I knew I could do little wrong and was in the very grip of one of those truly red-letter days the like of which even regular fishermen experience only once in every two or three years. As we walked back to the falls to fish the white water again, I indicated to Ingo that, as I now had six salmon in the coolroom (potentially 20 pounds of Graflax for Gini to take back to London for our friends), it would be greedy to take any more and that, unless I took a particularly evil looking jack fish or a trophy-sized monster, we should practise catch-and-release for the final hour. Fifteen minutes later a good henfish took my fly and gave me an excellent ten-minute fight before we gently beached her. If the expressions on the fishless Gallic faces on the other bank had been worth photographing earlier that evening, then the looks of total disbelief as the crazy Australian actually put his fish back in the water could have written a million words. Then, through the mosquito netting, polaroids and hats, I actually saw a couple of faces go chalk white when I made it obvious to Ingo, with 15 (expensive) minutes of the session still remaining, that I'd had enough for one day and started to head back to the lodge.

I was acclaimed 'top rod' that day, a matter of little importance in true fishing terms to me, it was all wonderfully enjoyable and I had to admit to the highs and lows we fishermen endure as I compared Iceland and Norway, happy in the thought that I could change nothing anyway. Red-letter days must be accepted happily for what they are, as must the many blank days because of the expectations which

Celebrating at midnight dinner.

always follow. Fly-fishing needs both—roughly in the proportions that they naturally occur—if it is to maintain its incurable mystique.

For once I could say: 'You should have been there on Monday . . . *and I was there!*'

The next morning I arose out of the mushy trance of insufficient sleep, too much celebration, aching muscles, and with a horribly sore throat, to greet a cold and bleak morning. I had graduated from my three sessions covering each of the beats with Ingo and was on my own for the next three. Ingo had returned to Reykjavik, where he also worked as a flying instructor, and was arranging an evening flight for Gini and me to look over Gullfoss and other famous wonders when we returned to Reykjavik three days later. Meanwhile he had loosely teamed me up with the two Germans and their guide, Kristián, in case I needed further advice or help. It was a kind gesture and I thoroughly enjoyed their company. The older German, Bernhard, had fished the Nordurá for 16 years; indeed, he had also fished Norway and a great deal of Europe, Alaska, Canada and South America ('Argentine and Chile were best in the 1970s'), and he had personally fished with Charles Ritz and other famous fishing identities. Yet he was an unassuming and quietly spoken man; he said he had a philosophy about the three stages in a fly-fisherman's life. 'The most, the biggest and the most difficult'? I proffered. 'No', he said, 'catch fish, help others to catch fish, watch others catching fish'. I silently bowed to a superior, wise and humane philosophy.

His companion was a first-timer to the Nordurá who spoke little English (he had an equal right to say that I spoke little German), but who had a wicked and engaging sense of humour. Their guide, Kristián, was a multi-lingual Icelander, an excellent fisherman of long standing, a member of the SVFR

and a great help to me with his knowledge of the area.

That morning we returned to the downstream beat to fish the horseshoe bend. After a fruitless hour together fishing two rods on one bank, Kristián suggested that I cross to the other side, saying that the Germans were keen to stay put and that he would help me to cross the river. I thus found out how sensible the Germans were. With arms locked together and Kristián sporting a staff, somehow we crossed that maelstrom and, what's more, Kristián returned on his own—finding a somewhat less perilous track than our outward route, which we used together for my eventual return.

I climbed the hill, around which the river curved in its horseshoe formation, to fish the distant side while Kristián, who had returned to the opposite bank by then, directed me into my starting point with whistles and pointed arms. It was so cold that I was wearing long thermal underwear, my normal fishing attire with a thick jumper, my black oiled fishing coat and silk balaclava and gloves. My throat hurt like hell and I couldn't seem to find my deadly Blue Charm tube from the day before. How the mighty had fallen.

At least my position was sheltered compared with the Germans fishing on the other bank around the corner. So I sat on a rock and 'manufactured' a small Blue Charm by cutting off the first half-inch of a huge Norwegian tube fly of similar colouring, and giving it a substantial haircut. My spirits rose with the results and I started casting from the sloped rocky shore into the tight, fast white water in the first running pool. Below it was a short waterfall after which the fast water broadened into a very long, deep pool surrounded by cliffs on the far side but with a good rocky beach on mine.

Cast, swing, step . . . cast, swing, step . . . It looked to be good fishy water and, even through the cold, I began to re-kindle sparks from yesterday. Some 50 paces downstream from my starting point, and a similar distance to the waterfall, my fly swung over a submerged boulder into the deep green water beyond, to become snagged on the bottom. At least I thought it was snagged on the bottom until the 'bottom' began to shake its head!

But let us return for a moment to the evening before; around midnight, flush with success (and red wine) at dinner, a Norwegian chum and I were agreeing that we ought to 'go smaller' in this river. We reckoned we should 'raise the tone of the place' by fishing with trout rods, seven-pound tippets, and very small flies.

So there I was, at 8.25 a.m., eight hours and 25

Fishing the Nordurá upstream from the Horseshoe.

The midnight sun through the scratched Piper perspex.

minutes later, connected via a Fenwick eight and a half foot trout rod, seven-weight line, seven-pound tippet, and a size-14 bastardised Norwegian tube fly, to the 'bottom' of Iceland which, at the time, happened to be shaking its head violently!

How do I get myself into these predicaments? I had plenty of time to think of the answers because the 'bottom' held position behind the boulder, totally in control, effortlessly shaking his head and sometimes moving a foot or so in any direction. He just wanted to let me know he was a fish, and a fish in total command of the situation.

At eight forty-five he slowly left his rocky home and moved out midstream for his morning exercise. I could do nothing. I've never felt quite so helpless. Then he allowed the water to ease him slowly back towards the waterfall, shaking his head more aggressively, and stopping just short of the brink, to demonstrate his strength. After a further ten minutes he allowed himself to drop over the falls then, with a rocket-propelled burst, shot down the long pool as I stumbled over the rocks trying to catch up while dacron backing came howling out from the little trout reel.

With nearly 70 of my 120 metres of backing beyond the tip of the rod, the fish turned and finned

the current. I kept the pressure up, regained most of the backing and started to move downstream to get below him. It was just after 9 a.m., 40 minutes from hookup, when the fish thought I should see what I was up against and leapt. Fifteen? Eighteen? Twenty pounds? Who knows? Who cares, because in crashing back into the water he broke my silly little seven-pound tippet and I immediately upped him to an estimated 22—he deserved every bit of it.

Kristián helped me to recross the river as I mumbled incoherently about 25-pound monsters; I think he had probably heard it all before. Anyway I stopped fishing then, gave Kristián my final two rod hours of that session and returned to the lodge to lick my wounds. As ever, I shall later recall all the details of that fish in Iceland; at the time, I couldn't remember even the number of fish I had caught the day before. This fish had undoubtedly joined my private Hall of Fame; along with the Rakaia Monster, the double-figure brownie near Adaminaby in the Murrumbidgee, and the 'Fossen Monster' from the falls on the Forra in Norway . . . he had joined those who had beaten me resoundingly. Victory and size were their only common facets, in all other characteristics they were truly mighty individuals.

The 4 to 10 p.m. session was a cold zero for me, bringing home once again the extraordinary ups and downs that make fly-fishing so alluring. But I did manage one success that that day; the lodge chef, who fed us magnificently, agreed to Graflax my salmon so that Gini could, indeed, take them back to London. I think his recipe is the best I've tasted and he agreed to part with it for publication:

"Jeannie"

My final fishing session lasted from 6 a.m. to 1 p.m. on Wednesday, 15 July, using the home beat on the bank opposite the lodge. I started at the Laxfoss end, with the Frenchmen across the river from me, trying unsuccessfully to find the secret spots that I had fished two days before. I fished without success until I was below the lodge. Kristián and my German mates had worked from the bottom towards me, also without result. Around 11 a.m. I moved to the very bottom of the beat where the water runs fast through a rapid and into a long, deep pool before entering the canyon. One of my French friends was on the other bank fishing the

Gudmundur Vidarsson's Graflax

3 cups salt	1 cup dried brown dill
3 cups sugar	½ cup pepper
2 cups dried dill	½ cup fennel

Mix together and sprinkle on an oven tray. Place the salmon fillets (skin-side down) in the tray, laying one on top of the other with a good sprinkling of the mixture between the layers.

Leave standing in the kitchen for 24 hours (assuming a temperature of about 20°C). Then place in the fridge for *at least* 24 hours.

Serve with the following sauce:

1 cup sweet mustard	1 cup vegetable oil
1 cup hot mustard	½ cup honey
1 cup brown sugar	¼ cup cognac
1 cup dried dill	

Mix together all except the oil and cognac and allow to settle. Then stir in the oil and the cognac and allow one hour to settle before serving.

"The Jock Scott"

lower part of the rapid, so I climbed into waist-deep water among the boulders at the head of the white water to thrash it with another homemade Blue Charm, this time using a 12-pound tippet. I maintained a set position because movement was extremely difficult and, anyway, the salmon *had* to pass within eight metres of me if they were to continue up the river. After a number of casts, I was firmly connected to a good fish and faced the problem of getting both of us clear of the rocks and white water into a position where I could play and land him. But it was wonderful weather again, I was back on top, and ten minutes later I beached the five-pounder without difficulty.

As I was redressing my tackle, my French friend hooked up opposite me; it looked like a good spot. Unfortunately, however, his hook pulled out moments later and I had to sympathise with him; every time we fished near each other, he seemed to bring me good luck while I brought him bad. And this theory took on an absurd reality when, having returned to my rocky rapid, a few moments later I hooked another five-pounder on the second cast. So, as I landed it, remembering Bernhard's philosophy, I suggested to my friend that he take over the top part of the white water which had been so good to me, an offer which he readily accepted, unfortunately without success.

Thus, I concluded a fabulous fishing period with two more fish which I gave to Kristián. And I was very pleased to add that, on the next day when I was no longer fishing, my French friend landed a 12-pounder.

After celebratory champagne and lunch, and in the knowledge that I had fished hard for three days in one of the world's best fisheries, I fell onto my bed and slept until dinnertime. Meanwhile, Gini had covered some interesting territory in the car and had probably seen a lot more of Iceland and, indeed, read more about its fascinating history, than I had. But my business was to fish and to describe it and, in that, I was well content.

I worked throughout my final day at the lodge; a necessary song for my fishing supper, but it was by no means an easy song to sing. As I worked, my eyes kept drifting to the window, to the lava cliffs, and down to the river where other lucky fishermen were chasing the elusive *lax*.

We left the lodge rather sadly on the morning of Friday 17 July and returned to Reykjavik in time for lunch. Ingo dropped in at lunchtime to give us flight details for the evening and, in the afternoon, Gini took in more local culture while I had to stay at the hotel catching up. One day I'll get it all together but, in order to do so, I'll never try to combine fishing with anything else again; certainly not sight-seeing and touring with writing about fishing!

We took off in the little Piper Cherokee at ten that evening; a beautiful Arctic evening with multicoloured clouds occasionally hiding a blood red sun as it dodged between the mountain peaks. I wound the Nikon into manual and played with the scenery as best I could through the distortions of the scratched perspex canopy. Ingo chatted on about the scene below, his knowledge increasing as we crossed rivers and diminishing when we flew over country not immediately related to the *lax*. The highpoint was ten minutes, almost at ground level, tightly circling Gullfoss—the most famous waterfall in Iceland. The sheer power of that milky, glacial water, as it thundered over the abyss into an incredibly narrow canyon which it had carved over the centuries, was simply breathtaking. To see it from 200 feet up, and from every angle, was something even I hadn't planned for in my two years of safari research; it was a view which will live with me for a very long time.

Ingo invited me to fly the Piper back to Reykjavik circuit, a thrill at the end of a week of thrills for me, although it must have been pretty obvious to him that I hadn't flown for some 30 years. Thoughts of Lossiemouth and Tiger Moths went through my mind, invoking a sense of both history and peace; a great deal of fly water had passed under the bridge joining Scotland in the 1950s to Iceland in the 1990s.

It was the perfect finale in another country of my travels which I personally rated as Heaven on a stick, and a fitting point from which to go on, through Greenland, to Baffin Island for the next Arctic adventure. Sadly, Gini had to return to London (with the Graflax), and to Europe where she would meet our daughter, Katharine, for more eastabout travels before returning to Australia at roughly the same time as I would, travelling westabout.

19
Greenland's Icy Mountains and Arctic Char in Baffin Island

It was Graham Lochhead, of the Canadian High Commission in Canberra, who in 1990 persuaded me to go to Baffin Island and Pangnirtung—'Pang', he called it.

'The water boils with fish at midnight,' he told me one quiet evening in Canberra. 'You go out on ice-floes and cast among them, but you should wear spikes on your boots; if you connect up, they pull so hard they'll skid you right off the ice! Ross Peyton, up at Peyton Lodge, is the man to fix it for you. I'll give you some details . . .'

Fishermen's stories are elastic. Spiked shoes? . . . fish powerful enough to pull a man off an ice-floe? But the bait was awfully tempting; tempting enough anyway to go through the full research program, resulting in my flights through Greenland to Iqaluit (the old Frobisher Bay), and from Iqaluit to Pangnirtung and Peyton Lodge (which had changed hands by then to become Auyuittuq Lodge). Ross Peyton was still on the scene, however, to provide the final leg by Inuit (Eskimo) canoe to Clearwater Fjord to fish for Arctic char, inside the Arctic Circle. By telephone and fax, Ross had tried to persuade me, in my planning, to allow for the use of spinning tackle. 'Can't catch char on the fly,' he had said. My research indicated, quite clearly, that fly-fishing for Arctic char had been successfully undertaken for decades and I told him so. He was still unconvinced, and we let the matter rest in the knowledge that I would bring only fly tackle, he would bring spinning gear, and there was a wager resting on my taking a char on the fly.

I left Keflavik at 5 p.m. on Sunday 19 July, and flew to Nuuk (the old Godthaab), the capital of Greenland, where I stayed for two nights waiting for my flight out to Canada's Northwest Territories. I thought I had used up my quota of scenery superlatives when the little DASH-8 left Keflavik airstrip. Indeed, as I settled back in the front window seat but one (in fact five aisles back because the front section of the cabin was devoted to freight), I was content to read a magazine for an hour or so and catch up with world events. Then, about one and a half hours out from Iceland, I took off my glasses to rub my eyes and happened to glance out the window (sorry, Theroux, but this is necessary). I have never seen such a sight. At 25,000 feet we had just crossed into the icefield, flying a great circle route into the Arctic, west into the sun on an immaculately clear evening. It was as though someone in the midst of a sunlit mist had just painted the floor with deep ultramarine turquoise, then sprinkled the wet paint with the purest rock-salt! It was unbelievably beautiful and even the diehard locals on board happily jostled with me to put Nikon and Canon lenses against the perspex. It was the most superb shading of blue monotint imaginable, enhanced by the appearance, a few minutes later, of the ice rock, towering skyline of Greenland's east coast as it emerged in the same colours out of the mist. I won't forget that sight; the exaltation stayed with me as we crossed the coast, when the rock-salt became one continuous carpet of pure white. The scene was similar, but reversed, when we descended into Nuuk, passing through the towering peaks guarding the fjords.

Only four people were on duty at Nuuk airport; a parking marshal, two baggage carriers and a girl at the flight booking desk. No immigration, no

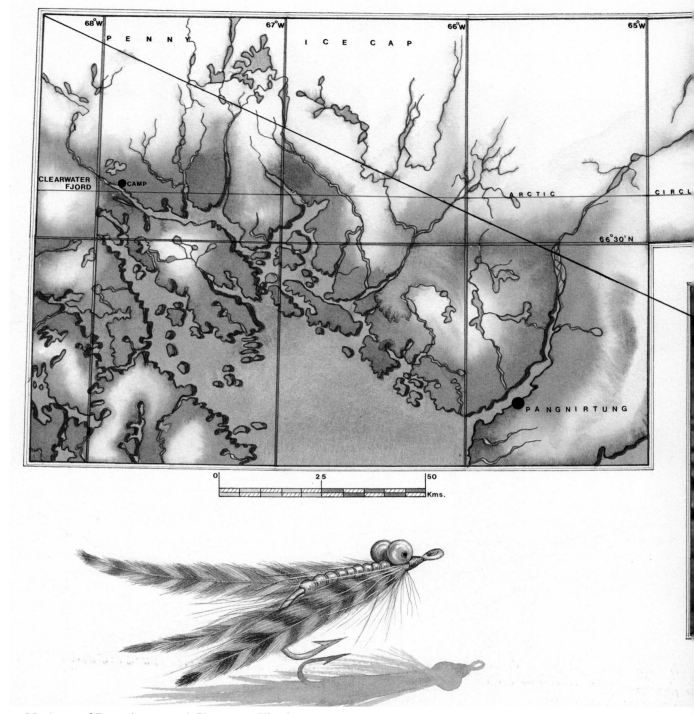

Mudmap of Pangnirtung and Clearwater Fjord.

customs, no hassles, no nothing. Nuuk immediately became my most favourite international airport in the world. But there were also no porters at the hotel and I had to lug my 60 kilos up to my room unaided. I hadn't even caught a fish but it had been a wonderful day, and a dinner of smoked puffin followed by curried reindeer and a bottle of German hock sent me to bed thoroughly contented.

Unfortunately I had only one full day in Greenland (Monday 20 July) and that was fogbound so, apart from exploring Nuuk, I worked away in my room for most of the day. I made a mental note to explore more of the country if ever I returned to the Northern Hemisphere; I felt I was short-

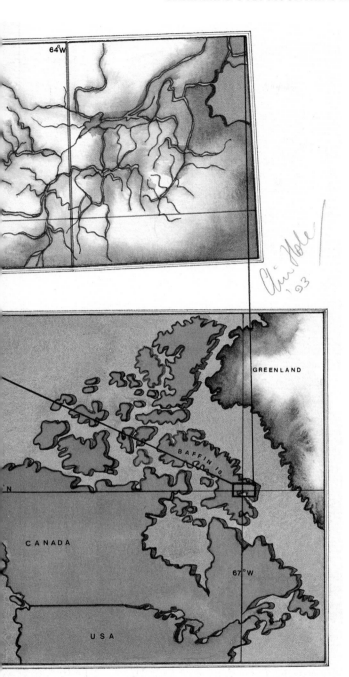

'Porthole gazing' . . . the east coast of Greenland

. . . and Greenland's icy mountains.

The coloured buildings of Nuuk.

changing myself and, at that point, very nearly abandoned the idea of a book completely so I could properly enjoy the rest of the world. I did have time to notice, however, that in direct contrast with Iceland, where the buildings are white and the roofs brightly coloured, in Greenland the houses had uniformly dark grey roofs but the walls were the brightest of colours. In those bleak Arctic countries, bright colour must mean a great deal to the inhabitants, especially in winter.

My flight through Iqaluit to Pangnirtung was meant to leave Greenland at 8 a.m. on Tuesday 21 July. Having set the alarm for six, and on checking in at Nuuk airport an hour later, however, I was given my first taste of the overpowering control of Arctic weather. Dense fog rolled in from the Atlantic, totally blanketing the airport and delaying our departure until midday. I shared the wait with a French botanist whose onward connection to Resolute started to look very shaky. He was worried because there was only one flight each week from Iqaluit to Resolute, where he was due to join a sponsored international team to camp on the ice cap in the vicinity of 80 degrees North latitude, where he would identify Arctic flora. In the end, he made his destination while I found myself stranded in Iqaluit as movement in and out of Pang had been stopped three days earlier by gale-force winds and poor visibility in scudding, ground-level cloud.

I booked at a local hotel and telephoned Pang to let Ross and the lodge know of my delay. They had heard it all hundreds of times before and frankly wondered why I had bothered to call. I must admit I found it fairly easy to accept the inevitable myself. I realised that the Arctic was in total command of my movements and that there was absolutely nothing I could do about it.

I walked downtown through the wind, cold and mist. It was around minus 5 degrees Centigrade, heaven knows what the wind-chill factor was, and I noticed that the immediate shoreline was packed with wind-blown rim ice from the 'beach' out for some 200 metres to seaward. Because of the relatively dry air, it didn't feel that cold, or so I thought until I had walked for 15 or 20 minutes and realised my thinking had slowed and I really needed to get indoors and warm up fast! I sent postcards to my family and to Graham Lochhead back in the Canadian High Commission in Canberra and, after dinner, went to bed hoping that the morning would bring weather that would allow me to reach Pang.

It didn't look too promising at first; cold, grey, overcast and drizzle, but at least the wind had dropped. I rang the airline, they told me it was all clear in Pang, and so I hurriedly put my overnight belongings together and returned to the airport. My luggage had already been booked but I rechecked it with the ground staff, noticing that my rods and folio case were separated from the remainder. 'Odd shape,' I was told. 'It will go with you.'

We took off at ten that morning and arrived 50 minutes later among the snowclad peaks of Pangnirtung Fjord in brilliant, clear sunshine. When we landed, three shocks were in store: my rods and folio case were missing; Pangnirtung is an alcohol-free zone—genuine Prohibition—and lasagna was on the menu for lunch! I can't stand lasagna; I ascertained that the missing luggage would arrive on the afternoon shuttle (which it did); then, on arrival at Auyuittuq Lodge, I locked myself in my room and had three quick scotches while I read the notice on the inside of the bedroom door, which said:

ALCOHOL IS NOT PERMITTED IN PANGNIRTUNG. THIS INCLUDES THE LODGE. ANYONE VIOLATING THIS WILL BE REPORTED TO THE R.C.M.P.

I sorted out my gear, leaving much to be stored at the lodge, then went in search of Ross Peyton to determine the plan of action. Ross told me that there was still some ice around Clearwater Fjord; indeed, there were weekend fishermen caught out in it unable to return to Pang. He was in radio contact with them, keeping up to date with the weather and ice forecasts, and considered we would have a reasonable chance if we left at about nine the next morning, two hours before high-tide. He added that, if we couldn't get in, we would fish elsewhere anyway.

It sounded a fine plan to me and I spent the evening walking around Pang. It struck me very much as a frontier town, desolate in its remoteness despite the summer fjord scenery, yet with a strong spirit, born no doubt of that remoteness and the need for survival. Shanties lined the sand and gravel roads, the sequence being broken occasionally by one or two more modern buildings—the visitors' centre, the weaving and art shop, and the lodge. There was a feeling of relief and enjoyment of the short summer's respite from the dark cold of winter, evidence of the Inuit hunter was frequent and there was still a Hudson's Bay Company store on the main street—one of three stores to serve the town's 1,400 inhabitants.

Pang is situated on the east shore of Pangnirtung Fjord which flows into Cumberland Sound where regional history can be traced back 3,500 years to Siberian migration. More recently, in the tenth century, Thule culture, from which the present Inuits descended, invaded the area. It is also possible that Vikings explored the area before 1585, the date of the first recorded European visit by the explorer John Davis, who named the sound after the Earl of Cumberland. During the nineteenth and early twentieth centuries the area became better known as a trading post for trappers under the control of the Hudson's Bay Company.

As ever, my wanderings led me to the water where, at high-tide, the locals were standing shoulder to shoulder on the rocky edge (like the 'picket fence' in New Zealand), thrashing the water with spinners, trying to jag Arctic char. Apparently the fish were not feeding close in by the town, and they had to be foulhooked with massive agricultural trebles— a method legalised only for the locals. I watched as one mother in waders with her baby in a papoose on her back, up to her knees in icy water, foulhooked and dragged in a five-pounder! Then another local gutted his fish, revealing a stomach bulging with very small smelt; to this vital piece of information, Ross added that the char fed off sea-lice and small shrimp further out. I figured that a sink-tip line, small White Smelt flies, and size-12 Swanundaze Nymphs might be a good starting point.

The next morning I packed up and moved my gear down to the water's edge at eight-thirty and the five of us left an hour later: Ross Peyton and I, an American, David Parker, who happened to tag along, the boat skipper Jaco, a solidly built, shortish Inuit, and his son, Garry.

The boat was a 23-foot, canvas-covered wood half-cabin Inuit canoe, with a 70-horsepower Johnson outboard on the back. Our gear, provisions and fuel filled the half-cabin and some of the open cockpit, leaving just enough room for the five of us to settle uncovered but comfortably. It was a clear morning, but cold, with a stiff breeze blowing into the fjord. I was dressed in long thermal underwear, two pairs of socks, rough shirt and trousers, two jumpers, silk balaclava and gloves, and a black oilskin fishing jacket. Even so, I learnt the very meaning of the word *cold* and was further subjected to a personal explanation of the term *wind-chill factor*: once we cleared the fjord, the wind dropped and the only air movement was caused by our passage through the water at about 15 knots; that was very cold indeed, but when we stopped, and the relative wind disappeared, things were quite comfortable. It was a salutary lesson.

The trip that morning was meant to take about four or five hours. But two hours out we met the pack ice, and then spent another nine in that open boat, searching for leads, pushing the ice aside, making very slow progress and sometimes going backwards. There was often ice all around us, then clear water; towering snow-capped cliffs above us, then more ice; out of the ice again, and the Inuits shot a seal—their right (and a necessity if the fishing

industry is to survive); then icy cold breezes, followed by clear still periods. We caught a good Arctic char on the way and Garry made a wonderfully sustaining fish stew/soup. Going north we crossed the Arctic Circle and celebrated with hot tea and Inuit bread. A whole book could have been written about that 12-hour day—it was totally fascinating.

Eventually the ice cleared and we spent the final two hours moving up the fjord to its beginnings in the mouth of a river, and there was the camp. Seven accommodation huts faced seawards on the sloping rocky and icy beach, and various cooking, eating, radio, maintenance and bathroom huts stood nearby. We were the first to pass through the ice by sea that year, although hunters had obviously been through by *skidoo* before us and had made a mess of the place. It was primitive, but in the days that followed, particularly in the warm summer sunshine and clear skies when we caught fish, it became a veritable haven for our little group.

I think we all sank into dreamless sleep that night; I know I did. But Ross was already up and working on the plumbing, generators and other things when I left to start fishing at six the next morning. The weather was absolutely perfect. Clear blue sky, snow-clad mountains, glassy clear water, no wind, and a low-tide exposing the rocks beyond which I could wade in waist-deep water (in two layers of thermal underwear under my neoprene waders), polaroiding for miles. I spotted my first Arctic char—in fact four together—before I had taken more than two steps. But I went through a selection of Bonefish Specials, Horrors and White Smelt flies, all of which the fish followed but would not take, until I tied on a Gold and Brown Shrimp. It was really top quality stalking and polaroid fishing at its very best; *and* above the Arctic Circle, *and* in perfect weather!

The Shrimp did the trick and, at seven that morning I was connected to my first-ever Arctic char. They said they wouldn't take flies, they said they wouldn't jump, they said they don't take off the top . . . they even once said the world was flat. Utter piffle!

My fish, although only a three-pounder, did all that a top rainbow or brown would do, and with twice the vigour. A wager was never more easily won.

Before stopping for breakfast I took two more fish (one a seven-pounder) and released them both. I also lost two fish when the hook pulled out, the second as David joined me to take several fish on his hardware. I rigged his fly rod for him later that

The trip to Clearwater Fjord in Jaco's canoe (above), through the ice (below),

Clearwater Fjord Fishing Camp.

. . . and more ice.

morning, only to find later, when I was up in my 'cabin-studio' looking out over the million-dollar view and working, that he was hauling in more fish using his lightweight spinning gear. Shame, Dave! Shame!

After lunch we cleaned the fish and packed them in ice, then I worked until half low-tide, around four, and went back to the char.

It has always been a secret fear of mine that, one day, I would catch so many fish that, for a fleeting moment, fly-fishing would become boring. This awful nightmare also had me handling backing more frequently than fly line; and, in my worst

Out of the ice and into Clearwater Fjord, Thursday 23 July 1992 at 8 p.m.

dreams, my quarry were all close to double figures. Surely the dream would never to come true; it could never be a perpetual red-letter day; I would awake and find that I had returned to the frustrations and joys of real fly-fishing eventually. However, that late afternoon, between six and eight, the dream became horrifying real. I spotted, cast to and hooked monster after monster; I certainly handled more backing than I do when rigging up in spring or unrigging at the end of the season. Perhaps I lost a few when I was broken or when the hook pulled out; a greater loss was the count and weight of the number I took (and released), and the greatest loss was that, for a nightmarish lost epoch in time, I actually became bored with fly-fishing.

Naturally I suppressed my reeling senses by stopping for dinner, and by telling myself that it was all some wonderful Arctic hallucination, brought on by the northern lights and Prohibition, and in three days I would probably never see it all again anyway. I therefore went to bed in bright twilight around eleven in the very satisfying knowledge that, at worst, I would have to put up with only three more such fishing days in Paradise before I was due to leave for Pangnirtung, and then imminent boredom would be replaced by the normal, frustrating, exciting uncertainties, failures and rare successes of true fly-fishing.

Saturday started a little more slowly. Ross persuaded me to have coffee and breakfast with him before fishing the low-water on the incoming tide from half past seven. Ross comes from a family of six other brothers and seven sisters, and has lived all his life in the north based on Newfoundland and Baffin Island, so his information-packed banter over bacon and eggs was fascinating. He had worked with the Inuits most of his life; from his early days in Pang with the Hudson's Bay Company, through his lodge days and fishing camp management days, to his looming retirement when he plans to sell the camp to his son, Jeff, who has plans to upgrade it to a year-round facility catering for both hunters and fishermen. I could not have been put in better hands for my Arctic sojourn.

Again the day was a heavenly mixture of washed blues, bright sunlight, crystal clarity, and water that looked like a polished mirror; more difficult conditions than the previous evening and I'm sure the fish also were beginning to learn a thing or two. It took me 15 minutes to hook the first one (which I released as I did all my fish that day), and 15 minutes later I was broken by a monster, an event which emptied my flybox of Gold and Brown Shrimps. I thought a Gold Crazy Charlie looked

The author and Ross Peyton outside the radio shack.

similar, although it is an Equatorial bonefish fly, so I tied it on and promptly hooked another fish, only to have the hook pull out. I landed (and released) one more good fish on that fly before I thought: Some of those fish are taking off the top, let's try a dry. Remembering that my dry-fly box was back in the cabin, I borrowed a Mayfly from Dave, changed to a fully floating line and cast out among the fishes. They approached, inspected, but wouldn't take. It was fascinating watching them through that gin clear water, and I thought that, later, I might try a small Black Gnat or something that resembled the mosquitoes which were huge, always around in droves and probably the only flying insects in the area. I had certainly seen snouts come out of the water to take; it was just a matter of finding out what they were taking.

In the meantime, I reverted to the Crazy Charlie and took (and released) a seven-pounder to complete the morning.

More work, followed by caribou steaks for lunch, then David and I took off in the boat with Garry and his father to look at an old whale-breeding ground. Decades earlier, when the water table at the head of the fjord was apparently much higher, white beluga whales used to move up there in spring to breed. Of course the hunters of the time realised the whales had only one way out, and they would trap them inside and slaughter them for meat and oil. Sunbleached white bones above the high-tide mark were the only sad reminder of those days.

Garry shot a young buck caribou while we were there. He skinned, gutted and divided it in less than 15 minutes and put it in a tub in the boat to take back to his family for food. I though no more about it until we approached the camp landing, where I was to be offloaded so I could continue writing while the others went out to fish again. As I climbed out of the boat, my back foot became caught in the caribou antlers and I went backside-first over the side, fully clothed clutching camera bag and fishing rod, *splash* into the icy waters of the Arctic.

It was breathstoppingly cold!

I stumbled ashore apparently undamaged, apart from hurt pride, and luckily my camera case was secure enough to prevent any ingress of water during the brief time it was submerged. Dry clothes, a clean-up and a glass of malt whisky had me back at the desk 15 minutes later. I noticed, however, that there were only four snorts left in the bottle, then total prohibition until Ottawa in five day's time. So I joined Ross, and we—a Newfoundlander and an Australian in remote country above the Arctic Circle—demolished the last few ounces of Laphroaig from the Isle of Islay. Somehow it all seemed very appropriate.

Low-tide was later that evening, so I didn't start fishing until after seven. At lunchtime the wind had sprung up from a new direction, from the west down the fjord, and there was absolutely no movement and no fish. I returned to the camp to join the others for something to eat, then resumed fishing half an hour later. The wind was still in the west, veering to the north; and still there was nothing, absolutely nothing. Until then, fish had always been visible, both by polaroiding the water and by watching them break the surface to feed and move. That night, other than a gentle wind ripple, there was nothing to be seen on or in the water. Apparently the bay was totally empty, the only new factor being a 180-degree swing in the prevailing light breeze which could possibly have been accompanied by a change in pressure; I'll never know because we didn't have a barometer.

It was all fascinating stuff for the scientific salmonid observer. To me it simply meant that the red-letter day was over and that I had returned to reality.

So I took a cupful of banded miniature shrimps to study and photograph in the morning, because the striping on their backs was very similar to the teal-like striping on the wings of both the Brown and Gold Shrimp fly and the Crazy Charlie. I'd had a heap of very valuable lessons put before my eyes in 48 magical hours, more than I had sometimes experienced in a full season's fishing.

Next morning the weather conditions were similar. As Dave and I approached our favourite bay, however, the wind died right on low-water, giving us an hour or so to polaroid and spot before the water became too deep. I spotted only one lone cruiser and two surface splashes. Although I

managed to take one of the fish that broke the surface (a little two-pounder, which I released), it was evident that the big shoals of fish that had given us a 36-hour bonanza had departed elsewhere. By then the wind had swung to the east and increased to about 15 knots. The problem was: where to find the fish.

Local advice seemed necessary. Garry recommended that, once the tide lifted the boat off the rocks, we should go down the fjord and fish a favourite river mouth of his until high-water. As we had already discovered, if the char are there they only seem to feed on the rising tide and that gave me three hours in the 'studio' before we left in the boat after an early lunch.

But, once again, the salmonid family fooled us; we caught no fish and sighted only five all afternoon. I wasn't surprised because the others, using hardware, wanted to anchor and fish deep. When we returned to the camp and the shallows, even though it was a falling-tide, I managed a three-pounder on the Crazy Charlie, third cast.

That evening, the team decided to return to Pang the next day. Who was I to argue? Jaco and Garry had the only boat, they wanted to go home, and I would have looked pretty silly sitting in Clearwater Fjord all by myself with no means of getting out had I wanted to stay. I'd had three simply perfect days and there were still two more low-water, rising-tide fishing sessions to go.

After dinner we had our penultimate fishing session and the 'awful fantasy' returned to haunt me. It was a much colder night and I put on an extra jumper and my silk balaclava. The southeast breeze dropped around the time of low-water and conditions were perfect. But nothing much happened until the tide started to come in when I took and released a five-pounder and was broken by something much bigger. Tying on my last but one Gold Crazy Charlie , I worked into a pool at the mouth of a river as the tide began to fill the pool. As I strip-retrieved in short strokes I had a light take; then heavy weight; then totally uncontrollable and untamed fury! The fish took the fly and headed down the fjord at right angles to the direction of my cast and rod tip at unbelievable speed. In a matter of seconds, with me still facing the spot where I had hooked him, he was disappearing into the distance to my immediate left, with backing stripping off the Sunbeam as I have never seen it strip before. He jumped and cartwheeled like some prehistoric monster and powered down the fjord with such acceleration that the Sunbeam flyreel, set to absorb a fight using

The tourist viewing-platform at Pangnirtung, NWT.

The 'studio' at Clearwater Fjord.

Arctic 'fishing costume' . . .   . . . and the result 20 minutes later!

a ten-pound tippet, simply over-ran like a badly handled bait caster. The outcome was inevitable: a jammed reel, a stretch to breaking point, and PING! That was that! Never in my fishing life had I experienced such sudden power, and never before had I experienced an over-run flyreel.

I knew there were still fish in that pool which was filling with the tide; I cleaned up my tackle, tied on my last Crazy Charlie using a 12-pound tippet, and adjusted my drag to to try to meet the requirements of over-run prevention within the limits of the tippet breaking strain.

Next cast: WHAM!

It was almost history repeating itself, but this time it was a smaller fish and I had my tippet and strain solution under control. A 15-minute fight and I landed a superbly conditioned, beautifully coloured nine-pounder (which I kept). A few moments later I caught and released a five-pounder then, as a fitting finále around sunset at 10.30 p.m., I hooked another Arctic express. This one fought for half an hour—he just wouldn't accept the pebbly shore and made at least six dashes for freedom. I finally beached him, a 14-pounder, and called it a night in order to get some photographs and clean the fish before it became too dark.

There were no dreams that night, it was the deepest sleep I'd had for a long time. I'd been thinking, as I had played those big fish: You are actually inside the Arctic Circle. You are fishing in conditions and under circumstances that one only dreams about, and you are connected to a monster with the promise of an unending supply to come. To use a highly abused and misused teenage description—literally this time—Man, it was *unreal!*

On the final morning, Monday 27 July, the camp became domestic after breakfast: cleaning up, packing gear, bagging rubbish and burying degradable garbage. It left one final fishing session from ten-thirty, before lunch and departure, and that session maintained the pace. I caught and released six more fish (but only around the three-pound mark) before saying goodbye to that little piece of Paradise. I'd caught (and mainly released) 140 pounds of Arctic char in three and a half days' fishing; an average of eight, five-pound fish each day, with the biggest topping 14.

If Patagonia was Valhalla on a 40-foot pole, then Clearwater Fjord was Eldorado on the roof of this planet Earth.

We loaded the canoe and set out down Clearwater Fjord, bound for Pangnirtung at 3 o'clock that afternoon. And what a contrast to the outward passage was the return. In sullen steel-grey overcast, we sliced through the ice-free, gunmetal-coloured flat calm water in a direct line at over 20 knots, completing the trip in just over four hours. Without direct sunshine, the weather conditions were colder on the inbound voyage and it was a relief to return to the warmth of the lodge that evening.

A picture was beginning to emerge.

The best fishing, the most imposing scenery and the cleanest areas, my favourite places, always seemed to be the most remote. And more often than not they were also the best managed or if management appeared slight and the area was still attractive, it was simply because man had not yet made a mess of it. New Zealand, Patagonia, Iceland, perhaps Norway, and certainly Baffin Island stood head and shoulders above those other countries (including my own) which, although all delightful in their own way, suffer from what might be termed the pollution of population. Moreover, where this pollution exists, sport fishery management often makes it worse by going to one extreme or the other: either to abandon proper management in the face of populous pressure and allow almost open slather, or to over-manage and to create artificial fisheries of little sporting attraction but at very high cost.

As I left Baffin Island I still had some contrasts ahead of me: Labrador where conditions might still be remote but where there was an established sport fishery; Idaho and Montana where, if one believed the written word, a magnificent but now highly pressured fishery was striving to retain its wonder through very exacting management plans; British Columbia, of which much the same could be said as of Labrador; and Kiribati, whose advertised remoteness could belie its juxtaposition with Honolulu, and whose salt-water fly-fishing could deteriorate if not properly managed.

I had already travelled 120,000 kilometres but there was still much of interest to come.

20
Michael's River, Labrador

Change is inevitable. Sometimes it is welcome and at others it can be frustrating and aggravating. Nonetheless, it is very often beneficial.

My flight plan from Pangnirtung to Goose Bay—even without a change, a mysterious adventure involving an extra 3,000 kilometres via Ottawa and Halifax simply because there were no direct connections—had to be changed because I had been booked on flights that simply didn't exist. In this case, however, the change was both beneficial and pleasant. Although I had to leave Pang 24 hours early (a distinct sorrow), it gave me a night in Ottawa at airline expense because they admitted the initial booking mistake, and arrival—albeit via Halifax—in Goose Bay on my planned date, but much earlier in the day, allowing a buffer zone for bad weather.

The change also gave me access to modern hotel facilities in Ottawa where I could contact my family with the latest news (exaggerating the size and number of Arctic char in the ice, and highlighting life north of the Circle—which they all picked immediately) and could top up a completely exhausted supply of 35mm slide film.

Lasagna again (but there was an alternative on the flight to Ottawa) was the only aggravation. My nose tweaked to the sickly aroma of sour-milk-cheese even before the seatbelt sign lit up for take-off. I'm not normally fussy about food, indeed my dislikes can be counted on the fingers of one hand after a wood chopping accident. I thoroughly enjoy good eating and even dishes such as kangaroo, caribou, water buffalo, seal and other necessities in the wild don't worry me at all; in the main I enjoy them. But the layered slop of lasagna, like tripe, wire coathangers and dead toenails, is something I never want to see again.

On Thursday 30 July, 70 days since I left Australia, I was once more on my way.

Had I been approaching Labrador direct from the south (other than the diversion to Ottawa, I considered myself to be approaching from Baffin Island in the north), I would no doubt have been feeling very excited about fishing so far north, and in such famous fishing territory. As it was, I felt somewhat an old hand at the northern game by then. I was, however, not foolish enough to let this feeling take control. Even a modicum of fly-fishing experience, I have learnt, must be divided subsequently into a small degree of confidence based on the level of knowledge and success gained through that experience, balanced by the need to examine very carefully the next new environment. Other than lasagna, to me there is nothing more sickening than the I've-been-everywhere-I-know-all-the-answers angler, and nothing so demoralising as the 'success story' who hits rock bottom on the very next river due to over-confidence. Every situation must be studied using past experience, then played for what it is worth. Confidence and success should be treated as elusive and always respected qualities, lest over-confidence takes control to the detriment of success.

Thus it was that I approached Michael's River in Labrador, on the flights from Ottawa, via Halifax and Deer Lake to Goose Bay. I shared the final leg in the pleasant company of a group of old-hand Labrador anglers who told me that 1991 had been a disastrous year. Apparently both Atlantic and Arctic ice had remained onshore well into the season, driven by easterlies created by the ice's very existence. Thus the salmon could not reach their rivers to spawn, there was no significant fishing, and countless thousands of fish dumped their roe and returned to the ocean. However, 1992 was expected to be a good year because those older, fitter and bigger fish were expected to come back to their rivers, which were now clear of ice. Maybe I was in luck again, but one can never tell when a salmon cycle is disturbed.

I landed at Goose Bay at two that afternoon and transferred to the Labrador Inn, expecting that I would have the next day free to work and explore before flying into Michael's River on the Saturday. Bill Bennett met me at the hotel and I decided that, if Ross Peyton was the wildman of the north—the 'mayor' of Pangnirtung—then Irish-Canadian Bill Bennett was his equivalent in Newfoundland. Bill owns Gander Aviation in Newfoundland, and fishing lodges at Michael's River, Sand Hill River, and Wulff Lake (named after the late Lee Wulff) in Labrador. In passing on a great deal of information, stories and local fishing lore that afternoon, Bill managed to suggest that, if I wished, I could travel with him to Michael's the next day—a day early—because he had to fly in some freight and return with a fishing party at the end of their visit.

'Yes please', I said.

The weather had been pretty miserable since my arrival in Goose Bay: cold, with rain and low cloud. Although it was forecast to improve, when we took off in the Twin Otter the next morning for the hour's flight to Michael's, the cloud base was still down below 400 feet, and we flew at treetop level most of the way. To add to the excitement we landed on the sandy peninsula at Michael's with the storm-tossed Atlantic on one side and the lodge and the mouth of the river on the other. I exchanged fishermen's discussion with the outgoing party, to find that one of them was the internationally known artist, Shirley Deterding, who had just published *Rivers of Joy*, an *exposé* of fly fishing scenes similar to my own undertaking, incorporating, in a coffee table edition (of less detail and geographic scope), her artwork together with writing by John Bailey and a foreword by Hugh Falkus. We quickly swapped addresses and notes but, all too soon, the Otter had to leave. I would have liked to have spent longer talking with her. Maybe some other time in some other place?

The lodge, built by Bill in 1968/'69, was well up to the standards I had seen around the world. It had five double-bedrooms (I had one to myself and moved the desk under the window to get the best light), two suites, two bathrooms, a big living and dining area with open fireplace, a basement for rods and waders; kitchen, staff quarters, and adjacent huts for the guides. It faced toward the Atlantic Ocean, looking east and south, while over one's shoulder Michael's River emptied into the Atlantic, looking a perfect haven for incoming Atlantic salmon, Arctic char and searun trout. It struck me immediately as well thought-out retreat.

A de Havilland Beaver and Cessna 185 floatplane were moored in the river, and outboard-powered canoes were drawn up on the bank not far from the front door: transport to any local fishing area was thus immediately at hand.

When I first stepped inside the lodge I got quite a shock. It looked like the aftermath of a bombing raid. Wall panels were smashed in, windows broken and temporarily covered with plastic sheet; huge scratches were evident on most of the woodwork, and the staff were busily carrying out running repairs. Apparently a Polar bear had broken in during winter and had had a field day searching for food . . . he even tried to eat the microwave oven! Didn't I say that fly-fishing was a lot more than . . .?

After unpacking I worked in my room for the rest of the afternoon as the rain and wind continued outside. Then, in the late afternoon, the cloud started to lift and the overall picture improved quickly. In our discussions, Bill had already told me something of Newfoundland sport fishing. He told me that netting had been stopped around the island of Newfoundland for five years at buy-out expense to the government, and that similar measures were being introduced, initially in an option program, for the coast of Labrador. Sport fishing, apart from the ice-caused disaster of 1991, was consequently said to be improving (a commensurate increase in poaching notwithstanding). Also, I found that I had apparently arrived in Michael's at the calculated right time for the salmon and grilse runs; earlier they had run in rivers to the south, and in two weeks they were due to start running in rivers further north. That was, of course, all things being normal, but are they ever? Bill was a fount of knowledge in these matters. So, with the lodge to myself apart from the staff, after an early dinner, I decided to try my luck. The signs were good but, as I've so often indicated, I no longer expect things to be exactly as anticipated.

I met Reg Vivian, my very pleasant and able guide, down on the banks of the river where the canoes were drawn up, only two minutes' walk from the lodge. Although we subsequently had a great time together, I think I seldom understood him ('gonna gitchee bigsammun, Bayhee, biddabilivid!'); and he probably didn't understand me too well either. We pushed off up into the fast current, with me sitting in the bow and Reg standing in the stern working a punter's pole and the little 6.5-horsepower outboard, dodging the rocks and shallows. As with Santi in Patagonia, it was a case of pulling up at the top of a good run, jumping out and fishing the

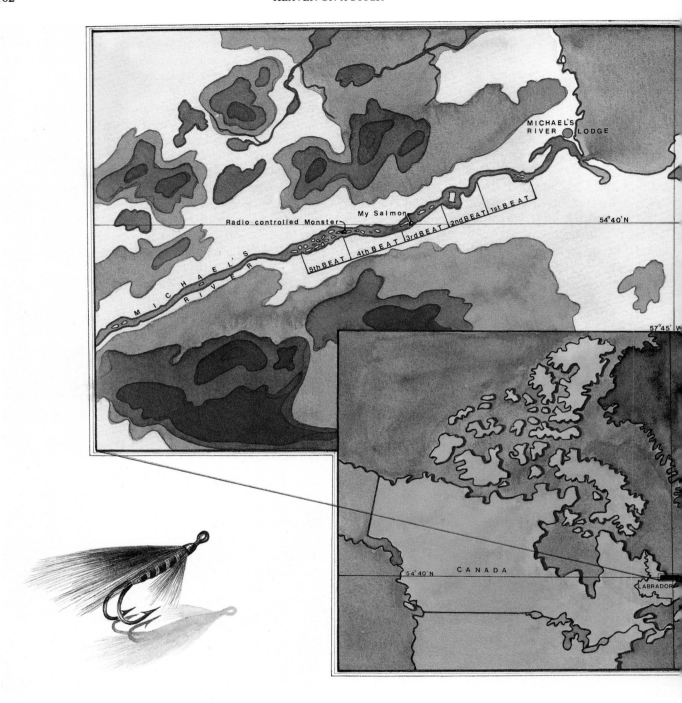

Mudmap of Michael's River in Labrador.

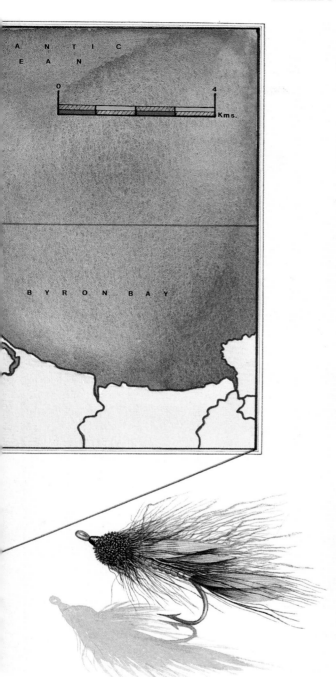

Michael's River Lodge.

Reg with one of his two salmon.

Bill Bennett and Shirley Deterding on the Lodge verandah.

run from top to bottom. We had only two or three hours that evening and the river was up after the heavy rain so the salmon were unsettled, but in the third pool on the way home I hooked my first Labrador salmon, or grilse to be precise. I was using the old reliable 'big' Hardy again, a WF8F line, and a size-12 Hairy Mary. It was only a four-pounder, but it fought hard taking me out once to that now familiar backing, and hopefully (I thought at the time) it was indicative of the start of the grilse run to come. Anyway, it seemed a good omen and the weather was improving rapidly.

As I went to bed that evening I took time to study the Canadian 1992 *Anglers' Guide* with respect to Newfoundland. I found it to be a comprehensive précis of effective management and control over a valuable sport fishery. For example, salmon bag limits were restricted to two fish daily and four others caught and released; season limits were set at eight; licences were mandatory and had to be carried; fishing was with fly only and limited to one rod and one fly; treble hooks were prohibited; size limits were placed on retained fish; fishing was only permitted between one hour before sunrise until one hour after sunset in the season; barbless hooks were encouraged and the season restricted and allocated into zones. It appeared to be a very

workable, very efficient and well-supported system of which locals and visitors alike were proud to the extent that such programs as Report a Poacher and River Watch (community law enforcement programmes similar to Neighbourhood Watch) were actively supported. I went to sleep that night in the hope that, some day, we would be sensible enough to embark on similar programs in my own country.

Next morning, 1 August, the day dawned clear, calm and perfect. Sitting at the breakfast table, I couldn't get over being able to look out over the beach and the ocean knowing that, on the other side of the house, one of Labrador's best salmon rivers ran fast and deep.

With a packed picnic, Reg and I motored up the river for a full day's fishing in that remote paradise set about with black spruce and bright green alder trees. I made the point, early with Reg, that I didn't want to be fussed over too much. I was quite capable of tying on my own flies and retrieving them from bushes when I had to, and I didn't necessarily expect anyone to net for me. On the other hand I said that I would appreciate all the local advice available and, equally importantly, I reckoned that my guide should fish with me. Such an attitude may cause the odd Scots laird to shift in his grave, but I like to operate on a personal and friendly basis with those good enough to guide me and acknowledge that, on most occasions in their home territory, guides can be more successful fishermen than I am.

So it was that Reg followed me down each pool that day; we fished as a pair in heavenly scenery, in warm sunshine and under a faded blue sky. The river was superbly clear with that peat (or tea) coloured tinge which reminded me of the Taieri in New Zealand. As Reg was following me it was nothing but my own fault. I'd covered the water ahead of him, but he took the two salmon that day, a ten-pounder and a 12-pounder, while I had an empty creel. It didn't upset me, although the tartan lairds may have been chuckling in their ashes. As it was, when Reg hooked his first fish he gave me his wildly gyrating rod while he ran back to the canoe to collect the net and my Nikon . . . that's what I call guiding! When he returned I gave him back his rod—luckily with the fish still attached—and used up nearly a whole roll of film photographing the playing and the landing of his fish.

Later in the afternoon we moved up the river to the top beat to cover a number of pools but without success. As we packed up and pushed the canoe into deep water to return to the lodge, Reg called out: 'Christ, look at that!' Close beside us, in a relatively shallow but fast run past rocks, was a colossal shadow. At first I thought it was also a rock, then it moved and changed to a light green colour. It was an extremely big salmon indeed!

We beached the canoe and stood knee deep in water only five paces from this 'Michael's Monster'. At that range I couldn't cast very well so I simply let six inches of fly line out beyond my rod tip and allowed the leader and fly to dance in front of the fish's nose. It was, somehow, like standing behind a one-way mirror, protected by a cloak of invisibility, watching a bizarre performance . . . or maybe the fish was behind the mirror and the two human beings were playing out the drama?

I tried most of the flies I had with me. From respectable salmon flies I switched to unrespectable ones; I discarded Crazy Charlies and tied on the massive Saltwater Smelt that had worked in Norway; I tried pink flies, orange flies, blue flies and red flies, I tried nymphs and shrimps . . . I tried everything, but nothing moved him. The closest I got, I guess, was with a small, sparsely tied white fly. The Michael's Monster rolled, partly rose to the fly, rolled again and returned to his lie. Then, 15 seconds later, like that awful scene in the movie *Jaws*, when the great white shark is seen for the first time from the stern of the fishing boat and our hero says: 'I think we need a bigger boat!' the monster unexpectedly leapt. He was so big and so close he nearly knocked Reg and me over. I thought he was going to eat us. He was huge! Twenty pounds? I don't know but, like Doug Stewart, let's leave him at a conservative 25.

We kept at him for another hour, but he had seen us when he jumped (if not before) and was in total control. He was just playing with us. So we stood tall, saluted him, jumped into the canoe and returned to the lodge. When you miss them, they are always memorable but this one, like the Rakaia Monster and one or two others, was especially memorable. I wondered that night whether he too was radio-controlled.

Back at the lodge the next fishing party had arrived, some of the anglers guided in by Tarquin Millington-Drake whom I had previously met at Nordurá in Iceland. My fellow fishermen were mainly from England but included one American and two Canadians, and we were joined the following day by Harry Birks, an expatriate Englishman from Spain. Most fished the river mouth for Arctic char that evening and were greeted by mosquitoes and a mass of very small searun speckled-trout. One or two Arctic char were taken during my visit and

The author and his eight-pounder caught on the dry.

one or two larger trout, but the best was less than four pounds (a returnable minnow at Clearwater), and the char were taken on spinning tackle which strangely was permitted in the estuary.

The next morning, while I worked, one party flew to the head of the river at Michael's Lake for the day while the others took up the five beats on the lower river. Those fishing the upstream beats seemed to do best, taking two grilse and one salmon, while the lake produced practically nothing. In the afternoon, Reg and I fished the lower beats, sighting five jumping fish moving upstream, but we didn't take a single one. The evening pilgrimage to the river mouth, while cold and free of mosquitoes, produced the usual run of small trout and I had a lot of fun taking and releasing 20 or more of these fish using a small Royal Wulff.

When Harry joined Reg and me for another full day on the river on Monday, 3 August, the weather was still fine and clear. Fishing the middle beats this time, it was Harry's start that morning. Having fished together unproductively for two hours, we moved downstream to the area where I had seen fish jumping the day before. Harry soon hooked a good one using a beautifully restored, 50-year-old ten-foot Hardy Palakona split-cane rod. After a 35-minute fight, Reg was about to net the fish

and raised the rod tip. I was connected.

It was a satisfying 15-minute fight. He jumped twice, throwing a lot of water, and I sighted white dacron once before he was subdued enough for Reg to net him. He was a well-conditioned, fresh-run fish of just on eight pounds, but he carried the scars of a seal attack and an escape from the nets. The seal had bitten off a large part of his tail fin and it amazed me that he could fight and jump so well. What extraordinarily strong fish they are.

After dinner I went upstream again with Reg, but we took nothing.

The following day found us putting in another ten hours on the river in the middle beat which included the pool where I had caught my fish. We must have sighted at least a dozen salmon that day and fished to more than half of them but, no matter what flies were presented—including the Muddler—there were no takes. Except for two anglers on the very top beat who managed one grilse and two lost salmon (one of which may have been the radio-controlled monster), all the others experienced the same frustrating day. As the afternoon wore on an extremely cold Arctic sea smog came rolling in from the coast. We theorised whether the concomitant very low surface air temperatures were responsible for the fish not taking. It was

when it took one final run around his legs and broke off.

Later in the afternoon we returned to the pool where I had caught the grilse on the first evening. Reg, whose polaroiding ability I have only seen matched by Phil Waldron in New Zealand, spotted a good salmon at the top of the run, quite close to the near bank and clear of the main current. He called me over, and I too could see the fish clearly through my polaroids. The wind was blowing upstream and it was difficult to get a very short cast out into position, but I managed in the end by flicking the fly upstream with the wind and letting the current swing it over the fish. I put two recommended salmon flies right over his nose with barely a twitch in response; something more dramatic was called for. So I hunted through my boxes and came up with a large, hairy, scruffy Muddler Minnow which I tied on and greased liberally.

First cast and the fish slashed at the fly with totally unexpected ferocity.

Next cast and he came again to take but, although I waited for the visible downturn, I only pricked him. This was dry-fly fishing at its best.

Third cast and he took heavily. I waited until he had turned away dragging the leader with him

possible; on the other hand they were also ignoring sunken flies in constantly cold temperatures in the depths. Only one angler ventured out to the river mouth that evening; it was bitterly cold and damp in the fog and he soon returned. Most of us stayed up, talking around the fire until eleven or so; topics strayed from fishing to travel, then to politics and back to fishing. There is a wonderfully relaxed common bond among fly-fishermen; sure, they bore others at times, just as they become bored with meaningless social chitchat; but when their numbers include members of many nations with a lot of international experience, I find the discussion— which often has little to do with split-cane· and windknots—very enlightening.

On Wednesday 5 August I called a temporary halt to my fishing and left the second top beat to Harry and Reg while I worked at the lodge. I badly needed to catch up; moreover I found that, as was the case in both Norway and Iceland, the effects of continuous fast water fishing 12 hours a day can be cumulatively exhausting, and one needs a break. I was also beginning to experience a growing fatigue similar to the latter stages of the Southern Hemispherian trip. While the will to fish had if anything increased, the body was beginning to tire and, in my case, the backlog of writing and artwork, which was also growing, was beginning to impose an uninvited need to stop fishing for a while. I had two weeks ahead of me with Don Haines in Idaho and Montana, and I knew Don's great program would allow little chance to record and paint until I reached Vancouver at the end of it. Then I had Bella Coola and Kiribati to come, with only one or two days' respite in between. Of course there would be ample time to put it all together once I returned home, but that didn't remove the need to record feelings, colours, shades, people, places, events (and fish!) while they were still fresh, otherwise the subsequent homework would produce a flat and lifeless picture. So I beavered away until the others returned at six that evening.

It was an ironic return. Between the eight experienced fly-fishermen, only one salmon was returned to the lodge, while the chef, busy at his allotted task and inexperienced as a fisherman, had wandered down to the estuary for an hour after lunch to take a salmon, a grilse and a sea-trout on his spinning gear. In a way it highlighted my growing beliefs about blind, across-and-down salmon fishing. It *must* be largely luck.

Later in the evening, Bill Bennett arrived, flying the Cessna floatplane because he wanted to get in before the weather turned bad. It was already beginning to rain and the cloud level was falling. The next day brought cooler weather and showers when Harry, Reg and I departed for my final full day's fishing.

I don't think I've ever worked harder for fish without a result. Harry took two small grilse representing two-thirds of the day's take, otherwise most of us went fishless. I'm sure that conditions and luck play a large part in salmon fishing; Iceland was certainly magnificent, and Labrador, like Norway, demonstrated great potential for excitement. But I remain unable to comprehend why so many people go to such vast expense and trouble to stand in beautiful but very cold rivers, blindly casting away for something that, more often than not, does not appear; in direct contrast with my other experiences of salmonid fishing, when the fish is spotted, stalked and, if hooked by the angler, done so by him demonstrating considerable skill. Yet,

Michael's River transport.

strangely, after my experiences, I am still drawn inexplicably to the lure of Atlantic salmon.

In such a frame of mind I worked until lunchtime on my last full day and fished the afternoon without adding to the four salmon fillets I already had in the deep freeze. Let not my own views of the skill, chance and cost factors of salmon fishing, however, detract from Bill Bennett's lodge organisation in Labrador. Michael's was very comfortable, well-run, filled with interesting people and situated among some of the best remote scenery in the world. Guests who had also visited Sand Hill and Wulff confirmed this opinion, although many were disappointed in our particular fishing results at the time, theorising that things probably hadn't settled since the ice disruption of 1991. It is also of considerable interest that Bill is a director of the Labrador Outfitters' Association and a member of the Sports Fishing Advisory Committee to the

Federal Department of Fisheries and Oceans, the very department responsible for the creation of the sensible rules and guidelines I have already mentioned. Moreover, this committee was due to meet at Michael's Lodge as Bill's guests the week following our departure. And it is even more noteworthy that the power which created the Committee was the power which, after many years of effort, managed to convince the federal government of the need to support and preserve sport fishing, commensurate with the money spent on the sport and the need to ensure its continuity.

Although we hadn't hooked huge quantities of salmon, dinner on our final evening, Friday 7 August, was a very happy and relaxed affair. The last of the wine was drunk, addresses exchanged, borrowed flies returned, and promises of future meetings made in the knowledge that they would probably be broken. Our chef, Leslie Normore, excelled himself, presenting us with a magnificent baked, stuffed salmon. It was one of the many recipes that I enjoyed in my travels, but on this occasion Leslie gave me his permission to quote it, and I do so as follows:

Leslie Normore's Baked Stuffed Salmon

2 cups savoury dressing (see recipe)
3 teaspoons salt
2 teaspoons pepper
3 tablespoons lemon juice
1 cup barbeque sauce (Canadian style; European may be more spicy)
Split one salmon (of five to six pounds) down the centre and debone. Place the fish skin side down and sprinkle with the salt and pepper, then rub the lemon juice over the flesh. Spread the barbeque sauce over the flesh and place the savoury dressing in the centre join. Fold the salmon back together, sprinkle with the remaining salt, pepper, lemon juice and barbeque sauce. Wrap in foil and bake at 350°F for 25 minutes.

Savoury Dressing

2 cups breadcrumbs
¼ cup butter
1 medium onion (diced)
¼ cup mixed dried herbs
Melt the butter in a saucepan and add the onion and herbs. Simmer for five minutes then stir in the breadcrumbs.

The next day it took two Beaver trips and one in the Cessna to return all of us with our luggage to Goose Bay. I stayed at the lodge until nearly lunchtime as the others had close flight connections to make, I had no need to leave Goose Bay for a further 24 hours and it gave me another half-day at the desk. The trip went smoothly and I again spent the night at the Labrador Inn, rearranging my luggage, completing last-minute tasks with Bill and bringing some of my notes up to date.

Labrador had been an extremely worthwhile experience; the comfort of that lodge and the efficiency of the organisation were praiseworthy, and the scenery outstanding. Fishing successes come and go and, over the years, Labrador has been a great salmon fishery and is likely to resume that status very soon. The provisions of Bill's lodges do not fluctuate, indeed they progress and, given the chance, sure, I would go back again . . . and probably again and again. The spruce trees and alders, the loamy cliffs, the powerfully deep, tea-coloured water, the bear tracks on the sand and the birdlife; the Newfoundland people and their guests, that wonderfully remote lodge, and the almost unbelievable juxtaposition of the Atlantic Ocean's sandy shore with the freshwater clarity of a mightily salmon river, all under a canopy of cobalt tinged with white, grey and rustic tints, was very hard to leave. But I didn't really leave it all behind . . . it became one of the vivid and living memories of my trip, and I would suggest one of the best Atlantic salmon fisheries in the world.

21
Fly-fishing in the Rocky Mountains, Idaho, Yellowstone and Montana

She was probably in her mid-twenties; tall and shapely in a very positive way, with an organised tangle of blonde hair tumbling towards floor level where her legs started and seemed to flow upwards forever, barely concealed by the tight, black hairdresser's smock. And she called everyone Honey.

After my sad experiences in barber shops in Auckland and Devon, I had at last struck gold in the ground-floor beauty parlour (where they also cut men's hair) of the hotel in Montreal where I stayed for two days on my way to Sun Valley in Idaho. She cut hair beautifully too, and I left that salon, walking some distance above the floor, imagining myself to be a sort of sunburnt Tom Cruise—how we deceive ourselves in our second half century! Anyway, it was an enjoyable interlude and I suddenly started to believe in Robert Traver's mermaid.

Don Haines was a very successful American architect whom I had met regularly in New Zealand, where he liked to fish in his retirement. He and his wife, Gayle, a one-time scratch golfer and women's amateur champion of Texas, persuaded me to join them on a visit to Sun Valley, where they had lived before moving to Washington state. Don, an excellent fly-fisherman of long experience, had told me much about fishing those famous rivers in Idaho and Montana: Silver Creek, the Snake, the Madison, Yellowstone, the Gallatin, the Big Hole, Firehole and the Big Horn. He brought Norman Maclean and other great American writers to my

mind, and was instrumental in persuading me to make two circumnavigations of the world in order to experience the best fishing periods in both hemispheres. So it was that I flew from Goose Bay to Montreal, where I stopped for three nights, onwards through Chicago to Boise, and finally to Sun Valley in Idaho where Don met me in the early afternoon of Wednesday 12 August.

Don had been very thorough in his planning, sending me maps, photographs, descriptions and magazine articles covering all the areas we were to fish; he had also mapped out a program for my visit with military precision. Indeed, he even warned me earlier, by fax to London, that his area had been experiencing a bad drought, and perhaps I should delay my visit for 12 months. But by then we both knew I was committed. It was indicative, however, of Don's thoughtfulness and thoroughness, facets that I much appreciated. It was a delight to meet him again when I stepped off the plane in Sun Valley, where the temperature was in the high thirties, a dramatic change after Baffin Island.

Although Don had moved his home to Washington state, he still had many friends in the Sun Valley area, including Bud and Ruth Purdy of the Double-R Ranch at Picabo, about 25 minutes' drive southeast of the airport. We were kindly invited to stay in their guest cottage (the original homestead), right on the banks of Silver Creek.

This area will be familiar to both Ernest Hemingway followers and international fishermen. Hemingway spent some time in Sun Valley, fishing

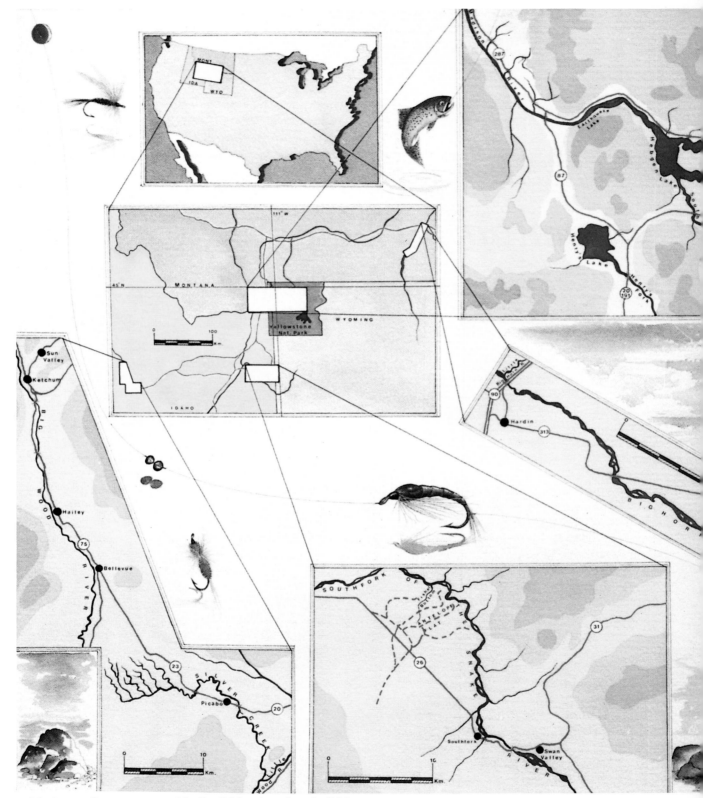

Mudmap of some memorable fly-fishing locations in Idaho.
Yellowstone and Montana.

Don Haines 'tubing' Silver Creek.

The author 'tubing' Silver Creek in the evening. (*Don Haines*).

Silver Creek and other rivers and hunting in the surrounding mountains. And Silver Creek is certainly one of the most written about trout streams in the world, up there with rivers like the Snake, Beaverkill, Itchen, Test, Letort, Madison, Big Horn and Mataura. The countryside reminded me very much at first of parts of Australia, even though the mountains were higher and the entire area began some 5,000 feet above sea level. The heat and the summer colours were very familiar: faded blue mountains with an underlying ochre colour, colours which deepened to dark blues in the evening; with dry, dusty, harvested flats broken by a patchwork of irrigated fields. As twilight descended that first evening the colours became more intense, not softer as they do at home. And the river was very clear, abundant in straggly green weed, with trout visibly rising in large numbers.

I managed an hour or so on the river that evening before sharing a late dinner with Don. I was tired after 12 hours' travelling, two time zones and arrival in baking heat at relatively high altitude. The river was blissfully cool and totally relaxing; moreover, Don talked me into using a fishing tube to float downstream with the current, casting very small dry flies to rising fish, mending the line as I went. It was a new style of fishing for me which I found both enjoyable and very comfortable; indeed, Dave, who owns the 'Best Goddam Sandwich Shop' and angling store in Adaminaby had been extolling the virtues of tubes for sometime before I left Australia, and now I had to agree with him—at least for use at home in places like Lake Eucumbene.

Two trout immediately attacked my size-18 Adams but I missed them both. At dinner, Don warned me that good presentation, small flies, very fine leaders and low-profile movement were all essential for success in those Rocky Mountain rivers. As they are on the basalt plain of the Monaro, I thought to myself. Additionally, it was a strange experience for me to fish a dry fly downstream, and I found it difficult, initially, to persuade myself to throw enough slack on the water to prevent drag. What's more, I'd just completed a month of casting eight- and nine-weight outfits in fast water and, no matter how much fishing practice one has had, there is always a need for minor adjustment. Next morning, concentrating hard, I took two rainbows of about a pound and a half each and lost two others, one of which may have been more than two pounds. They all fought like the very Devil.

We were observing a mandatory catch-and-release policy with barbless hooks on Silver Creek. Moreover, with riparian rights, access to the river

in that area was determined by the Purdys. They had formed a club to control access, which now has 300 members, and every effort was made to preserve the water and the fishery. While similar controls are evident in many other privately controlled areas throughout America, conservation and preservation are also the over-riding requirements on the more extensive public waters and fisheries. The angling population has been educated that, without such measures, their important and valuable resource will deteriorate rapidly and, in some cases, eventually even disappear.

That evening we had dinner at a nearby ranch with several of Don's old fishing and business friends, people who had hunted with Hemingway, fought with MacArthur and fished with Ritz and Schwiebert. It was fascinating talk as we ate a barbecued boneless leg of lamb, before meeting again the next morning to fish Silver Creek together.

The river beat me totally that morning. Fish up to three pounds were rising all around me, but I couldn't get one to take in three hours in spite of 30 or 40 changes of fly. My companions rose six and caught and released one before we returned to the cottage for bloody Marys and sandwiches. The talk was about another angler, fishing nearby that morning, who burst into a victory yell every time he hooked a fish. I said that at first I thought he was drowning and needed help, only to see I wasn't needed. One or two of the others admitted to similar expressions on hookup, and I concluded that, if one chose the right fly under such conditions, why not announce success? But admitted that it was frustrating to listen to these cries when one could not entice a fish to rise oneself.

I worked for a while after lunch, but it was another very hot Idaho day and I was glad when the sun started to dip and Don took me (and the tubes) to another part of the river. We fished for three hours in warm, still conditions. The trout were very spooky and only a few were rising. Don hooked and released three or four fish that evening, and I hooked and lost four. The colour changes on the mountains in the setting sun were so eye-catching that, for once, fish didn't really seem to matter to me. The scene was almost surrealistic in its clarity; stripes of colour—cobalts, purples, greys and tans in the mountains; tawny-coloured dried corn in the fields, dramatically changing to the deep green of rushes at the river's edge, then deep, repeated reflections in the water—all starkly enhanced in the dry air of the dying day.

The next morning we were up at six, packing

our gear and cleaning the cottage. We signed the visitors' book and I left a small watercolour fly painting for the Purdys before we drove away, eastwards on Highway 93/33. Skirting the southern extremities of the Rockies, we headed for Rexburg near the border with Wyoming. It was a morning of contrasts. We left the mountains and crossed a dead lava plain before emerging on flat sagebush desert which shimmered in the midday heat, only to be relieved by reaching the famed Henry's Fork of the Snake River just short of Rexburg. Following the river north, I persuaded Don to stop near Last Chance so that I could photograph this famous trout water as it passed through the ranch of Averill Harriman, the former American statesman who had donated it to the American nation.

After lunch, we climbed into the Rockies again, crossing into Montana with the Centennial Mountains on our left and Yellowstone Park in the distance on our right. The road was lined with spruce, Douglas fir and lodgepole pines often denuded by beetle attack, and these species continued to our destination, West Yellowstone, a major tourist stop near one of the five entrances to Yellowstone National Park.

Don suggested a little shopping in town, and what an experience it was.

Processing millions of tourists each season, West Yellowstone is, of course, a major centre: motels, souvenir shops, pancake parlours, restaurants, takeaways, laundromats, saloons and museums abound. All are immaculately presented, attractively packaged and squeaky clean—real drawcards for the free spending tourist. On the top of my list, obviously, were four magnificent fly-fishing shops—outfitters they call them. Every possible item of the most dreamed of equipment was there on the shelves for sale. Not only that, but it was attractively packaged, well marketed, and priced to attract even those who had spent the last eight months travelling the entire world, fishing. They even had shelves of brooches, silver and glassware to console the most despondent of fishing widows.

But, apart from buying essentials such as licences, flies and maps, Don made me promise to keep my hands out of my pockets and confiscated my plastic money each time we crossed the threshold of any of these wonderlands—an act I silently thanked him for on return to Australia, when I accounted for my travels.

Finally we left these Aladdin's caves and drove a short distance south, back down the highway to a settlement set back from the road among the firs near the South Fork of the Madison. Here we planned to stay for three days in the guest cabin of Bob and Betty Klemann, more old friends of Don's. A retired Florida businessman, Bob was a naval aviator in the Pacific during the Second World War, a subsequent adviser on naval operations and, with Betty, a lover of the outdoors and particularly of hunting and fishing. They were both excellent fly-fishermen: there were trophies on the walls, Bob's fly production (from a little table on the verandah) never seemed to stop, and Betty had won some excellent graphite rods in competition. Bob had had the occasional scrape with bears and seemed to have an endless fund of experiences which he was happy to share, but only if asked. I learnt some of this at dinner that evening and more as we fished together and travelled some of the Montana and Yellowstone countryside in the days which followed.

We rose early the next day and drove to Lake Hebgen where the Madison River is dammed soon after it leaves Yellowstone on its long journey to join the Missouri at Three Forks. Bob and I fished from Bob's aluminium dinghy while Don took his co-in-law, Walt Monter, in his rubber Avon. When Walt later left the relative comfort of the Avon to fish the lake that morning from a tube, he was the first to take a fish.

Tricorythodes, a miniature mayfly dun, hatched spasmodically early in the morning, followed by *calabaetus* (a larger—size-18—dun) some time later. But that morning the sun shone on the water, the hatch was reduced, the rise faltered and the fish became pretty spooky. Tippet ends that curled up and became obvious above the water—even 7X—were enough to cause problems. So the morning gulping session (as it is known) was not quite up to expectations, although fish rose spasmodically. Around midday, I managed to hook a two-pound rainbow using the earlier and smaller dun; it was a fish that fought hard, throwing the hook only to have it snag in a pectoral fin which added to the battle before release.

The scenery surrounding Hebgen that morning was more of the contrasts evident near Silver Creek in Idaho. As if to add to the kaleidoscope, cumulus clouds stacked on top of each other above the mountains, providing a canopy in blues, whites, greys, blacks and pinks. Below this painted ceiling, on the glassy surface of the lake, pelicans worked with merganzers to round up fish for a common buffet; wildlife in harmony and extreme.

Bob and I finally returned to his house for sandwiches and I worked through the afternoon until time for drinks and a delicious lamb barbecue cooked by Walt. Again I knew I was being spoilt

The author beside Henry's Fork of the Snake River. (*Don Haines*).

Lake Hebgen—and Walt hooked up!

Fishing Lake Hebgen from the dinghy, Bob Klemann (below, left) and the author (below).

but, once again, I was loving every minute of it; relaxing with fly-fishermen of many, varied and fascinating backgrounds. Next morning, with a well-meant show of independence aimed at relieving Betty in the kitchen, Don and I breakfasted at Momma Bear's Pancake Parlour before floating a full day on the Madison River. With a full stack of pancakes, bacon, orange juice and coffee in front of us, we made a pact (that we knew we would not keep) that lunch would be an apple, and dinner a lettuce leaf.

We joined Bob Jacklin, of 'Jacklin's Outfitters for the World of Fly-fishing', at 8 a.m. and set out in Bob's car, towing a Madison River float boat. Bob, a thoroughly dedicated fly-fisherman, had spent 20 years running his business; he proved to be totally dedicated to the preservation of American wild trout, and he is an active member of Trout Unlimited and the Federation of Fly-Fishers. I was told that he lectures regularly to sporting organisations and demonstrates fly-casting at many international sports shows. In any event, he was an ideal and humorous guide with numerous friends and associates including the list of authors responsible for the fishing books on the shelves in his shop.

We drove to the Madison on the meadows well below Hebgen Lake, launched the boat and began another wonderful day of fly-fishing, floating eight miles down the river through the meadows, with those colour coordinated mountains as a backdrop. Don was seated in the stern, I was forward, and

Lake Hebgen—'As if to add to the kaleidoscope . . .!'

The author releasing a Madison River brownie. (*Bob Jacklin*).

Bob manoeuvred the boat from amidships, using oars and a quick-release stern anchor. We cast, and dead-drifted as we went and, as in Argentina, pulled up every now and then when there was a good run worthy of detailed examination, to fish from the shore or by wading. Again it was this unusual (for me) downstream dry-fly fishing and, again, I initially found it awkward to throw enough slack to allow the fly to dead-drift. Once I became used to it, however, I had to admit it was quite a good way to fish. Firstly, one was moving downstream which, with the strong flow, was much easier than working up; and, secondly, it meant the fish saw the fly before the possibility of sighting the leader. On the other hand, it meant that a strike caused the hook to be pulled away from the fish whereas, with upstream fishing, the cast can be made to obscure the leader and, more importantly, the strike causes the hook to be pulled into the fish's mouth. Probably, each situation should be examined to see which method is best suited. Certainly I found that, in most places on this visit, except when dead-drifting from a boat, the nymph was fished predominantly upstream but, as is the case worldwide, it is allowed to move downstream from the angler before retrieval (at which point it is often taken).

We rose only two fish before lunchtime, when Bob found a puncture in his waders and completed the day in sky blue long johns. Although it was another hot day and I was sweating inside neoprene waders, the water was very cold and Bob had turned positively blue by dusk.

After lunch (delicious sandwiches which made Don and me forget our pancakes), the action picked up. We started fishing one particular run in rotation; me first to rise a brown under a tree by the far bank and miss him. Don followed but the fish remained sullen and wouldn't rise again, so we

invited Bob to have a go. He rose and hooked the so-and-so in the exact spot where I had moved him but, seconds later, the hook pulled out.

We floated further downstream and stopped at an island where Don fished the immediate run with success, and from where Bob and I walked to the next run for me to fish it carefully with one of Bob's Grasshopper flies. I rose six fish in that short, fast run, hooking three which I released. The first was a brown of one and a half pounds; the second, an acrobatic rainbow of two; and the final fish, a deep down slugger of a brown which weighed in just short of three pounds. Bob kindly returned to the boat to collect my Nikon so we could record it all and, after a number of shots, he went back saying he would collect Don and meet me at the downstream extremity of the island. As I worked my way down to our rendezvous, I held my camera in a plastic bag in my left hand while I kept midstream, casting 12 feet of line right-handed as I went.

Of course the unexpected happened! Nonchalantly strolling, fascinated by the mountains as a storm built up, and humming Hoagy Carmichael's 'Stardust', my Grasshopper fly was taken by a brown monster. Midstream, without the use of my left hand, I tried to gain the shore so that I could put my camera down and concentrate on the fish. It didn't work of course, the fish broke off and scored a well-deserved victory.

By then the thunder clouds were beginning to darken (and march their way towards our graphite rods I supposed). So we floated downstream to our final departure point, casting along the way. I missed one fish, striking too early and hard in my enthusiasm, and another—which the others had seen and were screaming advice about—simply because my polaroids had become dirty with sweat and water and I couldn't see the rise.

That wonderful day finished near to sunset when Bob trailered the boat and we drove back to West Yellowstone. It had been an extremely hot and dehydrating day; Bob had provided plenty of soft drink and iced water but, by the time we reached town, I had a vision of a frosted glass of icy-cold beer that I knew wouldn't even touch the sides as I tipped it down my throat. So we stopped at a local motel and enjoyed two such visions before filling more pancake space at the evening buffet. It had been a great day with a good friend and a first-class guide in some of the most famous and beautiful trout country in this world.

But they didn't let up on the visitor. By that stage (August 18) I was beginning to experience a creeping and growing fatigue which was even more intense than I'd felt towards the end of my southern safari. Additionally, I was so far behind in my work schedule that I had arrived at the point of saying to myself: What the heck! Enjoy what's left and work hard in the months to come at home, because you're going to have to rewrite much of your early stuff anyway in the light of your more recent experiences. Sure, they wouldn't let up, and I'm glad they didn't.

Next morning Don drove Bob, Walt and me deep into Yellowstone National Park. We took sandwiches, fishing gear, cameras and miles of film. We decided that Yellowstone could only be measured in miles of Ektachrome per minute. There was no other way!

At first I was shocked by the condition of the park; the bushfires of 1988 had laid waste more than half of it. But charcoal soon gave way to rugged mountains, an abundance of spruce, quiet meadows, obvious regrowth, beautiful rivers and a traffic-stopping parade of wildlife. On seeing my first bison close up, I said: 'Can we stop? Or will I see more that I can photograph later?' 'Maybe a thousand', came the the laconic reply from the backseat.

We made a brief stop at a place from which we could walk in to see the Yellowstone River Falls. They have probably been described, photographed and painted millions of times, and I had seen them thus in magazines and on postcards. But to see it all in reality, not only belittled our writers, photographers and artists, but gave me an impression of such starkly contrasted, colourful layers of rock strata that I spent most of my viewing time photographing the reverse, or downstream view, away from the falls, where the conglomerate of earth colours, to me, more accurately expressed the chasm.

The favourite fishing and picnic spot chosen by my friends at Buffalo Ford was further into the park, on the banks of the Yellowstone upstream from the falls. On the way, a massive old bull bison ambled unconcernedly down the centre of the road, a car's length away in bright sunlight and blue shadows. He was the one to be photographed and he was.

We unpacked our picnic, rigged our rods and waded into the deep, aquamarine green of the Yellowstone in search of indigenous cutthroat trout. Summer fishing pressures must have been very heavy because, although the old master, Bob, took one on a Green Nymph Emerger, the rest of us, content in that environment, didn't disturb the inhabitants. On the other hand, I had been told (and I don't think I believed it at the time) that late summer cutthroats would swim right up to one's waders, to eat the food one's feet disturbed and to take shelter from the current, content in the knowledge that they could outwit any angler. And they did just that.

Six of the damn things, all two pounds or more, followed me in three feet of water from behind a rock and took shelter, feeding, right in front of my knees. The cheeky bastards!

I touched them with my rod, I waved my hands above them, I cursed them, and I even tried to drop weighted nymphs in front of them (shame!), but in the end I found I loved them. With some forethought (I guess I really did believe the story about them), I had my underwater Minolta around my neck and spent that morning 'catching' fish after all . . . six fish on 24 shots of ASA 100 print film. And, believe me, it was just as exciting as catching them on a size-20 Emerging Olive. Unfortunately, a good deal later when I was using the Minolta to photograph sharks at Christmas Island, I discovered that the camera was malfunctioning to the extent that the photos of these cutthroat (and the sharks) were not good enough for publication.

After lunch in the sunshine we left the park, taking the route around the lake and stopping regularly for roadside traffic jams as cars halted suddenly to film elk and other creatures. Any chance I had of getting back early to work was lost. When Bob made a curry of the leftover lamb for our farewell dinner, I tried to thank them for their hospitality but, in my view, the words were entirely insufficient.

Don's efficiency and planning were up and running at six-thirty the next morning: 'Howya doing Buddy? We gotta pack, eat, an' hit the trail! I've finished in the bathroom, it's orl yors!'

The fatigue-scrambled brain registered, the body rose, but its actions were automatic for the first hour while we packed the brown LTD, had farewell huckleberry pancakes and eventually left West Yellowstone for yet another fascinating journey. For five hours we drove through mountains and meadows along the Gallatin River to Bozeman, then east on Highway 191 through Livingstone where we picked up the Yellowstone River again, and on to Billings where we refuelled and had lunch. From Livingstone onwards we left the Rockies to emerge on undulating prairie; shimmering hot grassland, pioneered in the nineteenth century, fought over by the Sioux, the Cheyenne and the white man, immortalised by Gary Cooper, Errol Flynn and John Wayne, and eventually settled by ranchers, sportsmen and Indians (in and out of reservations where the suicide rate sadly is often high).

These are a few of my favourite things . . . fly-fishing in Idaho, Montana and Yellowstone National Park.

Yellowstone National Park with the falls and the imposing backview.

Finally we reached Hardin and turned south, crossing the Big Horn River to reach Fort Smith around mid-afternoon when the thermometer on the Kingfisher Lodge verandah was registering 108 degrees Fahrenheit. I'd said to Don, as we left Hardin: 'How would you like to be on your horse now, with 2,000 Sioux chasing you, no John Wayne, and 40 miles to go to Fort Smith?' He replied: 'There are some spare horses in that paddock over there, and, anyway, I still have Tom Mix with me!' For the rest of the trip we argued whether or not I was old enough to remember Tom Mix.

After that long drive, Kingfisher Lodge was heaven. George Kelly, our host and an international fly-fishing guide (he caught his first permit, first cast on his first attempt and had written about it in *Fly Fisherman*), put us in the farm cottage which had three bedrooms, a kitchen and a bathroom—all air-conditioned—and enough room for me to write a sequel to the New York Telephone Directory had I wanted to. The whole town, however, including Polly's Restaurant, was under Prohibition,

being situated in an Indian Reserve. I wondered that night, after chicken dinner at Polly's, whether Prohibition was a good omen for fishing. It certainly had been north of the Arctic Circle where an equatorial fly—the Crazy Charlie—had done wonders. Perhaps an Arctic fly would do well in a Montana summer? The only trouble was I didn't know if there was such a thing as a true Arctic fly, and smuggled Johnnie Walker seemed more attractive anyway that first evening when I finished writing well after midnight and dropped into bed with a thought that continued to worry me. Up until Sun Valley, my visits had been largely one place, one stay, one story, one map, one major watercolour. Now, Don was driving me, with complaisance on my part, through four major areas, countless famous rivers, and 20 different scenes worthy of equally as many maps and paintings, all in one scheduled two-week visit.

After breakfast the next morning, we left for the river with George towing a floatboat similar to the one we used on the Madison. The scenery was less mountainous than that I'd seen so far in America. The Big Horn, in that part between three and 12 miles downstream from Fort Smith, is a medium sized, crystal-clear river with some white water but mainly long glides, set about with thick groves of aspen and occasional Russian olive trees. There were prairie hills in the distance but of no great height, and the water was very cold because of damming control upstream from Fort Smith. After the heat of the day of our arrival it was most welcome; but as the day went on, the wind rose, black clouds built up and it became obvious that a change was on the way.

That morning there was no discernible hatch, so George advised nymphing. Again it was a new experience for me. One was invited to rig one's leader as follows: to the normal point nymph (say a size-16 Caddis Emerger), a further leader of eight inches of 5X was blood-knotted to the curve of the hook, then a further point fly (say a size-18 Green Stick Caddis) was tied to the end of that tippet. Ten inches above the first fly, a small lead shot was attached, and strike indicators then clipped into position near the leader/fly-line connection.

I didn't like it. I don't go for those complicated circuses that gyrate around one's head when trying to cast, and I've generally believed that one man, one rod, one fly and no extras is a pretty fair way to catch trout. Nonetheless, I must admit that the multi-rig was very successful on the Big Horn where the water is fast, dead drifting requires at least a weighted nymph, and where sunlight on the broken water makes indicators necessary to ensure success for all but the eagle-eyed.

I took three good browns on this complicated rig before lunch, and probably lost as many; each was around two pounds. Then the first of the storm hit as we sheltered, munching salad and sandwiches. Thankfully it was short-lived and we resumed fishing in bright sunshine amidst a good hatch of black caddis. Swapping the complicated leader for a simple leader, tippet and Black Caddis fly (and making a mental note to be better prepared the next day), I cast from the shore to a riser and, after five minutes, he took my fly, raced off midstream and promptly broke me off.

Back in the boat again and we drifted into a long deep pool. Trout were rising midstream, whitefish could be seen under the boat, and carp (!) up to 15 pounds were jumping clear of the water and smashing at caddis close to the bank—an amazing, if not sickening, sight. I took two good browns on the Black Caddis fly and lost another before we moved downstream into the faster water, reverting

to the complicated rig as thunderclouds built up once again. I took two more good fish, a rainbow and a brown both close to three pounds, before we raced to outrun the rain and get back to the lodge before dark.

Don had also had a good day but always insisted on giving me the cream as his guest, an extremely kind gesture which he kept up throughout my visit.

On the second day, George allocated another guide to us to drift the same section of the Big Horn, concentrating on different pools and runs. The morning started very quietly; the water was extremely cold and covered in floating green weed, an indication that the dam had probably been opened after the rain and the fish had not yet settled. This assumption was further supported when Don took a good sized whitefish from a run which looked ideal water for trout.

After lunch the scene changed. The weather warmed up, caddis started to hatch, and the weed seemed to have passed. Then trout started to feed on the emerging caddis. At this point we were drifting a short, fast shallow run and I was still rigged for nymph fishing. My line hesitated in the run and I thought I was snagged until I saw it shoot out downstream under the control of a heavy fish. After several minutes of deep underwater struggle, I caught my first glimpse of the fish: an old brownie of four pounds or more with a broad back and a snout that looked as though it had been digging for stick caddis for years. I played it nearly out and moved it towards John, our guide, who had the net ready. But between him and Don it was a miracle that I landed it: one would yell for me to lower the tip, the other would say: 'No, raise it!' '. . . on to the left side! No! the right . . .' and so on. At last John scooped it into the net and four pounds of excellent brown was duly photographed and gently released.

Switching to the dry fly, I left the boat to move into a quiet backwater where trout were feeding hard off the surface. On the third cast I found myself connected to a rainbow tornado which tried very hard to fly ashore before it threw the hook and raced downstream, jumping with its new-found freedom as it went. A pity, because I believe it was probably bigger than the brownie.

So ended another day, my seventh since arriving in America and I had fished five different areas. My head started to spin as I knew we were moving on again the next morning for our final stop on the famous South Fork of the Snake.

It was a long day in the car, backtracking through cowboy country, the towns of Hardin and Billings;

Fishing the Big Horn. A four pound brownie is taken and released . . . and the author's (by now perpetual) grin grows even bigger! (*Don Haines*).

then smoke started to obscure the horizon as we continued west towards Bozeman. We found out later that it was caused by forest fires hundreds of miles away near Boise in Idaho. The diffused light continued as we drove south through Yellowstone, and onwards, always to the south, until we reached the South Fork of the Snake River at Swan Valley that afternoon, where the smoke remained. Crossing the river three miles downstream, we pulled up at South Fork Lodge and Outfitters, where we had agreed to meet with Don Siegel, a very old friend of Don Haines' and our host for the next three days. In convoy, we followed the Snake downstream to Antelope Flat where we turned north, in towards the river, passing through wheat country and aspens to our host's cabin at Fisher Bottom.

Secluded, hidden by aspens, only five minutes' walk from the river, and the original cabin of Harper Prize-winning author, Vardis Fisher, this was a real fisherman's haven. Don Siegel had rebuilt the place, adding modern facilities and generated power. We unloaded our victuals and drink, and set about behaving like a group of Huckleberry Finns let loose

in a candy store—remarkable for men between the ages of 55 and 77!

Don had invited another old friend, Joe Brainard, to complete a fairly dangerous fishing foursome for the weekend, and we planned to use Don's outboard-powered dinghy which was moored in a nearby backwater. Haines took charge in the kitchen, Siegel immediately countermanded all his orders, I remained upstairs working, folded up with laughter, and Joe eventually did the work—directed by the other two. Nonetheless, we ate extremely well and Don Siegel provided an apparently never-ending supply of excellent Napa Valley reds and whites. It was one of the highlights of my safari.

The Southfork of the Snake is home to rainbows, browns, indigenous cutthroats and whitefish. From the wide, clear, fast-flowing water that had carved strata in the cliffs over thousands of years, we took predominantly browns, fishing spring-fed tributaries at first, in icy water of exceptional clarity. We seemed to do better later, in the main river, however, when hatching duns appeared in large numbers. I took three browns on nymphs, fishing a side stream, when Don Siegel called me over to

Don Siegel's cabin at Fisher Bottom.

the main river where he was happily pulling good browns from the edge of the current. On the bank close to him, a good hatch of duns was producing splashes and circles everywhere—small fish to be ignored in favour of the bigger browns closer to the main current. I took a beautifully conditioned brown of about three pounds from that current just

before we returned to the cabin for lunch.

On the way back I noticed a small spiral of white smoke curling slowly skywards from a gully hidden by cliffs on the far bank. During lunch the smoke increased markedly, becoming darker with upwardly convected charcoal. Don Siegel displayed concern, but there was little we could do about it. We had

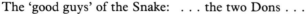

The 'good guys' of the Snake: . . . the two Dons . . .

. . . and Don Haines with the author. (*Don Siegel*).

no telephone, the fire was on the other side of the river, and Don was aware that there were other farmers in the area. But by the time we resumed fishing, I estimated that 20 to 30 acres of pines were well and truly alight.

Minutes later, a Parks' helicopter flew over the area to investigate, followed closely by a P3 Orion disgorging fire fighters by parachute. This workforce, supported by helicopter water-bombing (taking water from the river very near to where we were fishing), soon had the situation controlled and was mopping up within three hours. Superb official response which I couldn't help comparing with the wet sacks and spades of the Brindabella Volunteer Bushfire Brigade.

On the second day, I missed the morning session so that I could catch up with my work. Don Siegel very kindly drove me into South Fork Lodge so that I could phone Keith Corbould at Bella Coola in British Columbia to discuss my next visit. As luck would have it, Don and Keith were old Bella Coola neighbours of long standing; the fishing world was beginning to contract around me, or my travels were, inevitably, disclosing a world-wide network of acquaintances.

After a short afternoon session, when I landed my hundredth fish over two pounds for the Northern Hemisphere period—a three-pound cutthroat on a dry fly—we hauled Don's boat from the water and started to pack up for departure the next day.

That was my last fishing in America. Two days of travel and farewells were to follow, then I would fly to Vancouver on my way to Bella Coola. As in England, I was spoilt rotten by good friends who introduced me to some very famous fly-fishing and to the life which goes with it. I must say those storybook streams in Idaho and Montana lived up to everything I had read about them, as did the organisation behind this biggest single sport in America. It may be under pressure, but it is exceptionally well controlled.

The day before I finally departed from Idaho and America, Don and I drove from the South Fork of the Snake, though Idaho Falls and Arco, reversing our steps across Silver Creek, to arrive in Sun Valley in the afternoon. After a very comfortable night staying with Don's friends, Herb and Minerva Kunzel, including an excellent farewell dinner at Sun Valley's most famous nightspot, I flew out on the afternoon of Wednesday 26 August to Boise then, via San Francisco, to Vancouver.

The airline mislaid my big suitcase out of San Francisco, but delivered it intact 12 hours later after I told them it was full of three-week-old, filthy fishing clothing that ran a good chance of starting a major epidemic if I couldn't get it to a laundry quickly.

Don Haines—selecting a fly on the Southfork of the Snake.

If this isn't happiness, I'm damned if I know what is! Southfolk of the Snake, August, 1992. (*Don Haines*).

22
Tweedsmuir Lodge, Bella Coola, British Columbia

I guess I chose the wrong time to visit and fish the Bella Coola area in British Columbia. Keith Corbould, Brigadier General (retired) and owner of Tweedsmuir Lodge, had warned me, when I was organising the B.C. segment of my travels, that spring and autumn were best for steelheads, summer for trout, spring for chinooks and autumn for cohos. I was advised to arrive three to four months earlier than my planned dates, or three to four weeks later. I could have started my northern safari on the west coast of the North American continent, but that would have put paid to Idaho, Montana, Labrador, Baffin Island and most parts east, and was thus out of the question. Alternately, I could have tarried somewhere just prior to my arrival in B.C., and delayed my subsequent visit to Kiribati and arrival home. But, I knew I would be running out of steam (physically, mentally and economically) by that stage of my travels, so I stuck to my plan to visit Tweedsmuir Lodge during the first week of September, accepting as my own fault any paucity in the fishing at that time.

Having stored half my luggage at my Vancouver hotel, I flew in a light twin to Bella Coola on Monday 31 August. Those who know the area north and west of Vancouver will be aware of the high, jagged mountain peaks and, even having seen it all many years before and notwithstanding the barrage of natural beauty with which I had already bombarded myself, I marvelled once again at those mountains. Great craggy, cold cliffs jutting haphazardly through the cumulus; cold grey-blue in colour, contrasting with the pure white of snow and glaciers, and the dark green of fir trees, they are truly awe inspiring.

Keith met me at Hagensborg, the airport for Bella

Coola, and we drove eastwards for half an hour, through mountain valleys along the banks of the Bella Coola River. After crossing it from south to north, we continued following its course until it split to become the Atnarko and the Talchako. While the Bella Coola was fast, wide and murky with turquoise-shaded snow melt, the Atnarko, being lake-fed, was crystal clear. The Talchako, on the other hand, being a small, rocky, fast-flowing mountain stream which was glacier-fed, was milky and unfishable. We followed the clear waters of the Atnarko to Tweedsmuir Lodge, built on a private enclave within Tweedsmuir National Park.

Keith stopped at a fish viewing and counting platform just short of the lodge to have a look at the river (I'm convinced he does this for all his first-time guests). No matter how many films and video clips one may have seen showing Pacific salmon on their spawning migrations, spawning and dying in British Columbian rivers, it is not until one views it at first hand that one gains some idea of the magnitude of this extraordinary phenomenon. We looked down on a moving sea of pink salmon. Hundreds of them at one glance, tens of thousands each day, several million each season, moving up the river, jumping clear, thrashing the water to a fly-fisherman's foamy dream, completely uninterested in anything but spawning. I could never quite adjust to fishing among them; trying to ignore them; casting to fast water behind rocks in the hope of taking a steelhead, an early coho maybe, or at least a rainbow or two, without foul-hooking a pink; and retrieving fast and early from the same lies for the same reason. It was all so exciting in that steep mountain scenery, fishing that

The beautiful Atnarko River in Autumn, close to Tweedsmuir Lodge.

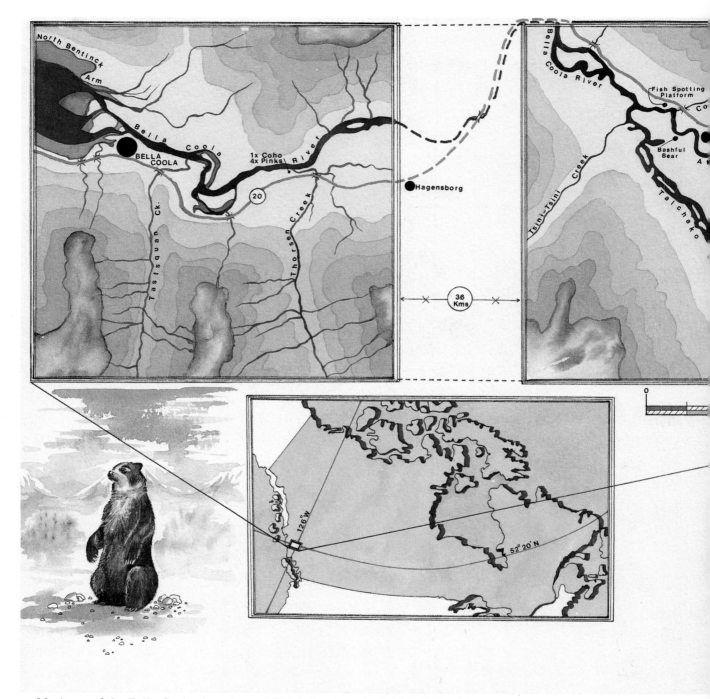

Mudmap of the Bella Coola, Atnarko and Talchako rivers in British Columbia.

bubbling river, set about with firs, aspens, red cedars and brambles, all in autumn colours, with 30-pound chinooks jumping clear of the water close by, while keeping an ever watchful eye open for grizzly bears.

But I get ahead of myself. At that stage I had only looked down on the river and its wall-to-wall fish. We parked at the lodge a few minutes later, unloaded the car, unpacked my gear and set up my rods. I was immediately struck by the similarity of this lodge with the one at London Lakes in Tasmania. Both are big and comfortable, relying on huge living areas constructed about heavy wooden beams, big fireplaces, subdued lighting and a highland atmosphere. Tweedsmuir offers twin accommodation for 14, it has a huge lounge and dining area decorated with three generations of family memorabilia, and a sweeping verandah and decking area facing down the lawns to the firs and

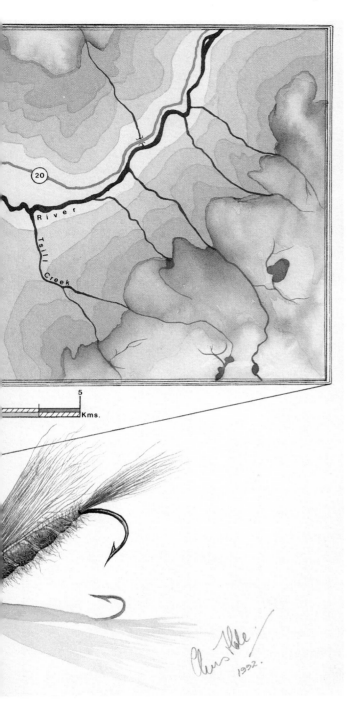

Tweedsmuir Lodge, British Columbia.

aspens which hide the river. In the near distance, overpowering snow-clad peaks rise to 8,000 feet above the trees.

Tweedsmuir, the oldest established lodge in the park, was opened in the 1930s as Stuie Lodge; the name was changed to Tweedsmuir when the then Governor-General of Canada, Lord Tweedsmuir (John Buchan, the author of *The Thirty-Nine Steps*), visited in 1937. It has been a Corbould family operation since 1947, the present building being completed in 1950 after the original was destroyed by fire. In my opinion, it compared very favourably with the many other lodges I had stayed in during my 1992 travels.

On the first evening, Keith took me to the river, a few minutes walk down the track in front of the lodge. An old wooden bridge had partially collapsed there, creating calmer backwaters and eddies where the pinks were schooled in thousands for spawning. Spawning chinooks were also visible in lesser numbers, huge fish averaging over 20 pounds, black and red in their spawning livery, with wickedly hooked jaws. Already, spent carcasses were dotted along the banks, food for the bears Keith advised, answering any query I might have been about to raise about fishing after sunset.

It was all wet-fly salmon fishing, with the hope of taking a fresh-run fish, an early steelhead, or a trout. Weight was needed to get the fly down to the fish in the moderately fast current, but too much weight vastly increased the chances of accidentally foul-hooking a spawner. This was sometimes unavoidable, but I took no joy whatsoever in dragging in tail- or fin-hooked four-pounders to gently release them as quickly as possible. It was all licensed fishing, predominantly catch-and-release, with very detailed provincial and regional regulations published in a comprehensive booklet which was issued to anglers at the time of licence purchase. For those species allowed to be taken for consumption, daily, seasonal and possession limits were imposed. The whole system is actively policed, and supported by the vast majority of anglers; there is a very evident awareness of the need for conservation.

I did not take a fish that first evening, but Keith's brother, Ken, took me on a guided fishing tour of the area the next morning, pointing out the fast water and pockets where I would probably avoid the spawners and have a good chance of picking up a fresh-run fish or trout. I took half a dozen rainbows and returned them all that morning as well as, regrettably, foul-hooking one or two pinks. In the afternoon I revisited those areas on my own with about the same level of success. It was a reasonable start, all things considered; I was getting to know something about the area and how to fish it, and I had talked to a number of other anglers along the way, swapping stories with Germans, Norwegians, Americans and Danes, as well as the locals.

The following day, Ken and I drifted the river in a boat very similar to the ones we had used on the Madison and the Big Horn in America. I took a nice sea-run cutthroat of about two pounds and, a little further down the same run, was hit by something very fast and very solid. It was unquestionably a mouth take, and not a foul-hooking, followed by unbelievable weight and speed until, seconds later, there was a PING, and my hookless flyline came whistling past my ear. I was using my #5 weight Orvis outfit, a sinktip line, two feet of ten-pound tippet and a weighted size-eight Red and Black Fuzzy Wuzzy. It was probably all too light, but I was after controlled sport, not skull-dragging. Sometime later, when we repassed the place where I was broken off, both of us sighted a silver torpedo . . . a coho salmon!

A very pleasant English couple, John and Esmé Cope, arrived at the lodge that evening and, the next morning, John had a day's drifting with Ken, joined by Esmé after lunch, while I drove to Bella Coola. Keith had suggested that I should have a look at the confluence of Thorsen Creek and the Bella Coola River, saying that although the main river would probably still be fast and milky, the creek would be clear and could hold some fresh-run coho and certainly some cutthroat trout. I arrived in pouring rain so sidetracked into town for an hour to buy maps and postcards. On returning to the creek I found the rain had stopped but the water was a writhing mass of spawning pinks, chinooks and dog salmon. The banks were covered in the carcasses of spent spawning fish, the stench was appalling and the whole mess was a brightly lit restaurant sign for hungry bears. One or two locals were trying vainly to take cutthroats, said to be in the area, but I saw them only foul-hook spawners.

Holding my nose and keeping a wary lookout for grizzlies, I made my way down to where the creek joined the Bella Coola. It was, as expected, a fast flowing torrent of turquoise milk.

Then I stopped and started to think (occasionally we fishermen do): The creek only holds spawners and it is fast becoming a very smelly graveyard; any fish bypassing the creek are probably not ready to spawn and could be silvery, lively and fresh-run; salmonids have remarkable eyesight for food (flies) even in milky water; and milky water could obscure the angler and prevent super-spooky cohos from spooking. Therefore, let me fish the edges of the main river with a large, dark, colourful fly.

Tying on a size-four Purple Ugly, I started to work the rocky edge at the outflow of the creek, fishing into the main river itself. But, first, a brief description of the fly:

Hook: Size four, black salmon, up-eye.
Tying Silk: Black.
Body: Fluorescent, dark purple dubbing.
Rib: Three turns broad, flat silver tinsel.
Tail: Deer hair dyed bright red.
Wing: Same as tail , tied in at the eye.
I walked that edge only five times, casting probably 12 times each lap, and took: four fresh-run female pink salmon (a total weight of 14 pounds),

Wall-to-wall spawning salmon, and the sad aftermath

. . . food for the bears.

and one fresh-run female coho salmon of just under eight pounds. All fish were released and I felt very satisfied with my morning's work.

On return to Tweedsmuir Lodge after lunch, I stopped again at the fish spotting platform to talk to the resident spotter. He told me that, an hour earlier, a large grizzly had lumbered up out of the river, walked under the spotting platform, stopped on the road to eat a salmon it was holding and ambled back to the river to catch dessert. It had then, a few moments before my arrival, crossed the river to shamble slowly upstream on the far bank.

I raced back to the lodge to collect my camera and, with Keith, embarked on an extensive bear hunt. We saw no bears but sighted, below us by a cliff edge, John, Esmé and Ken drifting and fishing from the boat. We warned them of the possibility of a bear a little further downstream and continued on our way. Two hours later the fishermen returned to report that they had taken two good chinook (one of 15 pounds on the fly, and one of 25 pounds on hardware), *and* they had come face to face with the bear! Apparently, when it saw them about 50 paces away, it stood up, dropped its fish and covered its private parts with its front paws. John and Esmé took some good photographs before he took off into the bushes, but we were all left to wonder about its very unusual antics. Surely, it was the most bashful Canadian any of us had ever met.

I spent most of Friday 4 September working in the lodge, although I broke for an hour before lunch to check the spotting platform in case the bear had returned. He hadn't. Eventually I packed away my notes and my paints and wandered down to the river for one last session before my return to Vancouver the next morning. I managed only two more foul-hookups before snowclouds hit the mountains, the wind increased and spots of snow appeared in the air—a good sign for further frozen conditions which would stop the melt and help to clear the Bella Coola. That evening, my last, I bought the wine for dinner, Australian chablis which complimented Keith's baked coho to perfection.

I was very sorry to leave the next morning. I wished I had given myself longer there in that very comfortable lodge, to chase coho and then steelhead as autumn deepened. But I had to leave, and I returned by lunchtime to Vancouver without incident. As we flew out of Bella Coola in quite tricky conditions that morning, another light aircraft was involved in a fatal accident in the mountains nearby.

Mid-Pacific was next on my list. I could almost smell the salt and feel the heat and excitement as I began to scent the aroma of home in my nostrils. Although I didn't know it at the time, more of the Pacific than I had bargained for was to pass me by before my final return to Australia.

Casting for early coho along the edges of a milky Bella Coola at the mouth of Thorsen Creek.

23
Christmas Island Bonefish and Other Distractions

From the moment of return to Vancouver, until touchdown at Christmas Island 11 days later, I was convinced that the gods had contrived to stop me . . . or at least to prove, once and for all time, that fly-fishing was rather more than just catching fish.

I was made aware of the first setback when I arrived at the hotel in Vancouver to find urgent messages asking me to telephone Frontier Tours, hotels and connections in Honolulu, and Nauru's national airline. Apparently the mid-Pacific island of Tarawa had run out of jet fuel and, because the weekly Air Nauru service joining Nauru to Honolulu and Christmas Island also called at Tarawa where it refuelled, it had been temporarily suspended. As a result I had no way of getting to Christmas Island as planned, my major salt-water fly-fishing episode would need to be reprogrammed at the very least, Chris Hole was operating in limbo, and 'the old man couldn't get over the stile and wouldn't be home for dinner tonight.'

Running up a horrific international telephone bill, I determined that the Pacific islands in which I was interested were serviced for their petroleum requirements by two small bulk tankers operated by two major international oil companies. Apparently one of the tankers was being refitted and the other was operating on a priority basis which, at the time, had allowed Tarawa to run out of JP5. I was told, moreover, that once bulk fuel arrived, it would be a week before it could be used as it first had to be tested—in New Zealand! Whether it was my stirring of the pot I'll probably never know, but I was telephoned a little later by the PR department of the oil company concerned and

advised that alternate arrangements were being made, including the provision of pretested fuel in drums, and that the Air Nauru service should resume within the week.

As I had planned two weeks in the area, the first at Christmas Island and the second in Waikiki, it was a relatively simple task to swap them and to fly to Honolulu as planned for a week in the sun before visiting Christmas Island. Indeed, the more I thought about it, the more attractive the prospect became. A week of resting, getting my notes up to date, sipping mai tais and lying on the sand at Waikiki sounded just like heaven on a stick. Then to have a week fly-fishing for bones on Christmas Island as a final adventure . . . Perhaps the gods had miscalculated after all?

The flight to Honolulu went like well-oiled clockwork; my baggage remained with me, once again I avoided excess luggage charges, and by midnight on Monday 7 September I was gazing out across Waikiki beach to Diamond Head, sipping rum punch, 20 storeys above the ground and congratulating myself on being flexible.

Seventy-two hours of pure lotus existence later, a bombshell dropped at sunrise. The hotel klaxon wailed into life, followed by a metallic voice announcing a full hurricane alert and asking guests to remain in their rooms to await further instructions!

The night had been heavy and very still, holding an uncomfortably high level of humidity; moreover, a tropical disturbance to the southeast had been tracked and reported for two days. Looking out the windows that morning, the view was very grey; low skidding stratus clouds were building up, the wind was blowing steadily at 25 knots from the south, and the surf had built up on the south shore of Oahu higher than I had ever seen it before, attracting a bunch of brainless surfers who rode the waves throughout the day despite an amplified recall from the beach patrol. The television revealed that Hurricane Iniki, with sustained winds of 125 knots, gusting to 160, was 120 miles south and moving north to pass between Oahu and Kauai around five in the afternoon!

How far south had it begun? Was Christmas Island affected? Were the gods still after me? There were no immediate answers to those questions and unlikely to be any until after the weekend. The next 12 hours would be taken up sheltering, followed by hours of damage assessment and repair before normal life could be resumed.

The hurricane reached the Hawaiian Islands at three-thirty in the afternoon, but by then it had swung northwest towards Kauai. In my hotel, the guests sheltered in the third-floor ballroom where we remained cooped up from midday until six. Oahu didn't suffer too badly, although winds reached 90 to 100 knots on the west coast. Poor old Kauai, however, took one hell of a pounding; four people were killed, settlements lost up to 95 per cent of their houses, and the overall damage was estimated to be in excess of one billion dollars.

When Saturday morning dawned on Waikiki, the clean-up began—mainly sand ingress at basement and ground-floor level—leaving Sunday as a rest day before a full working day on Monday when I could sort out my plans, reprogramming if necessary. Early advice indicated that all would be in order and that the flight would depart for Christmas Island as planned, albeit a week late. But I couldn't help thinking that troubles supposedly come in threes and that I'd managed to sidestep only two so far.

The third was announced at Honolulu Airport at 8 o'clock on the morning of Tuesday 15 September. The Air Nauru flight was delayed another 24 hours, 'because of further severe tropical storms to the south' the official statement read but the aircrew, on later questioning, revealed that the mid-Pacific needed yet another day to sort out its fuel problems. I booked into a nearby hotel, decided that it was time to go fishing and chartered a game boat for the afternoon, selfishly and impatiently trolling the cobalt currents off Waikiki. Fly-fishing it wasn't, but under the circumstances it was the only available alternative which 'regrettably' produced a 40-pound dolphin fish for me—some small satisfaction after hanging around for nine days.

Flight 219 for Christmas Island finally left Honolulu more or less on time the next day. After an uneventful flight over some of the bluer expanses of the Pacific, it landed at Casady Airport on Christmas Island mid-afternoon, where I spent an hour with mid-Pacific backwater officialdom obtaining a visa, which I had been told previously I would not require. Anyway, by 4 p.m. I was up to my knees in the balmy, turquoise waters of the Pacific, searching for bones on the flats of the lagoon. A guide and two Americans, Richard Humphrey and Edmund Cheng, were with me (although afterwards I fished with their companions, Tim Merrihew, Jerry Heiman and Darrell Mendenhall for the remainder of the visit). Most of these anglers were on their sixth and seventh visits to Christmas Island and their combined knowledge of fishing in the area was extensive. They willingly shared this with me and, for that advice and their companionship, I remain very grateful.

Christmas Island (not to be confused with the Indian Ocean Christmas Island, south of Sunda Strait) was discovered by Captain James Cook on Christmas Eve, 1777, and remained a British protectorate until Kiribati gained independence in 1979. During the Second World War it was a staging area for the Pacific Theatre, although no actual fighting took place in the area. It was also occupied by British and American forces for the purpose of testing nuclear devices between 1954 and 1965 and many villages and geographic points on the island—London, Paris and M-site, for example—retain their code-names from that era.

Situated 2,000 kilometres south of Hawaii and 190 kilometres north of the Equator, the island is part of the Line Island group, which was known as the Central Polynesian Islands before the formation of the Republic of Kiribati. It has the largest land area of any coral atoll in the world, its highest elevation is 12 feet and its landmass is predominantly one of sand, coral, mangroves and coconuts which overlook lagoons, flats and reefs offering outstanding fishing.

A quiet Pacific backwater, forgotten—if ever known—by most, its colouring is a brilliant kaleidoscope of vivid strips. Cobalt skies (exploded by ever-present blobs of mashed-potato cumulus), becoming purple and pink on the horizon overshadow shades of turquoise in the water, broken by the foam of surf and the brilliant white of sand; and these in turn are eclipsed by the lush greens and yellows of vegetation above the highwater mark. The only jarring note is the oxide red and brown

Waikiki from the author's hotel room . . .

. . . and the same view as Hurricane Iniki built up.

of ancient rusting military scrap left to rot in the mangroves.

The remoteness of Christmas Island, its unpredictable communications and its lackadaisical administration all add to its wonder. Its remoteness also results in little pressure and its salt-water fly-fishing must be some of the best in the world. How long it will remain thus is hard to say. My American friends, who had visited often before, talked of population increases and growing fishing pressures during the northern winter, which left me with the feeling that it might not remain a paradise forever. Moreover, I couldn't come to grips with the fact that there was only one hotel (the Captain Cook Hotel where we stayed), only one immediate way in and out of the island, only one major external tour operator, and (really) only one control of fishing guiding, when the area, despite its remoteness, had so much to offer the fly-fisherman. I'm not saying that I want to see changes, I'm only forecasting that they will probably occur, that is: attractive places attract people, and who knows, the Phoenix Island Group may be next?

In addition to the fishing, the island offers excellent scuba diving in clean clear waters and it is the base for one of the most popular ham-radio operations in the world. Operators world-wide, from Eastern Europe to the Arctic Circle, from Kerguelen Island to the Falklands, jostle for position to answer when the Christmas Island callsign is heard on the radio waves. The flight on which I finally left Christmas Island subsequently brought a world-wide team of operators to the island for an international hookup competition. I wondered whether this facet, too, might lose its unique attractiveness if the island were further developed; it is difficult to foretell.

Whatever the final outcome, in 1992 I found the salt-water fly-fishing to be the best I had ever

An impatient, post-hurricane departure for fishing . . .

the return . . .

. . . and the result!

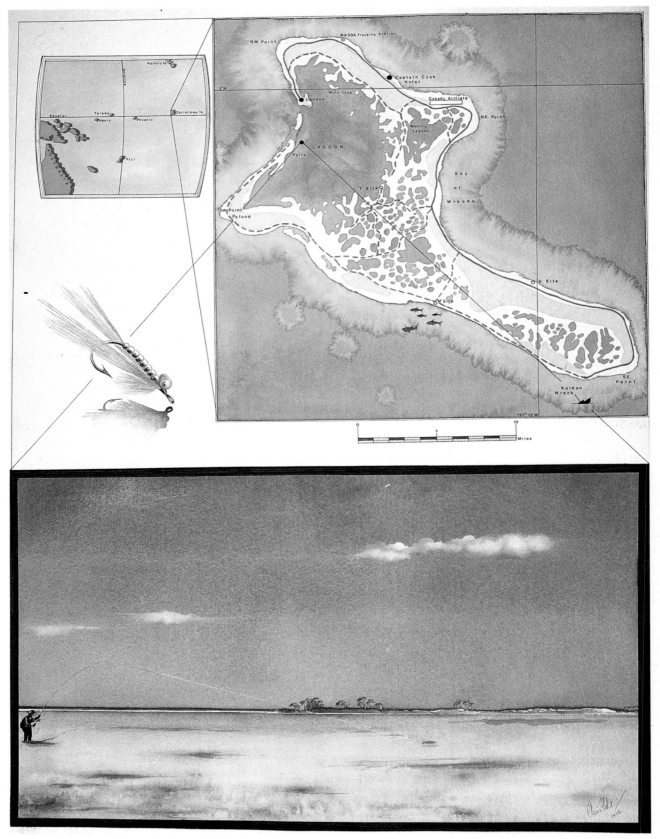

Mudmap of Christmas Island, Kiribati, with an angler about to take an accelerating bone on the reel.

The Captain Cook Hotel's accommodation . . .

. . . and fishing transport.

experienced . . . and that includes the Great Barrier Reef in Australia.

As I waded the crystal flats off Paris on the morning of my first full day, I spotted the monster bonefish inshore of me, only ten feet from the beach. It was angled away but I could see its shadow and, at first, thought it might be a huge milkfish. Then it turned side-on and I knew it was a bone—the like of which I would probably never see again.

Ten pounds? Twelve pounds? Fifteen pounds? More? I don't know. It was certainly over 30 inches long which my length/weight ration graph put at 10.8 pounds (rising to 18 pounds for a three-footer).

Out snakes the eight-weight, bonefish-taper fly line, the big old Hardy delighting in the strain. Two, three, four false casts, and SHOOT . . . the Crazy Charlie! PLOP! It drops into the water, on its ten-pound tippet, six feet in front of the bone. I let it sink, then start a slow, strip retrieve.

He follows!

I count down the distance as he approaches: 50 feet . . . 40 . . . 30 . . . 15 . . . surely he must take the fly . . . or see me and depart? Almost at my feet (probably 15 feet away in reality) he takes the fly and turns slowly, 90 degrees from me as I tighten. Then, with extraordinary acceleration and with at least twice the speed of a trout, he heads seaward in an unwavering straight line.

I thought my flyline was coral coloured, but I am looking at white! It is only seconds from hookup and already 50 metres of backing are out, and the rest is following quickly. Soon he is nearly 200 metres from me but slows, momentarily; I decide to apply pressure to recover some line, although I know the pressure may induce another run and I've hardly any backing left. The pressure does indeed start another run, but he swims towards me

and it is all I can do, keeping the rod high and winding the little Princess Multiplier as fast as I can, to keep in contact.

Momentarily, because of the slack caused by his inward run, I think he is off but, remembering Doug Stewart, I keep recovering fast. He is still there; the weight comes on again inducing yet another run, this time away from me again. Out, out, out and out he goes until there are less than five turns of backing left on the spool. Suddenly there is much increased weight. Then nothing. I have, for the first time in my life, been *spooled*!

Somewhere out there 200 metres of dacron backing, an expensive flyline, a nine-foot leader, and a size-eight Crazy Charlie are being towed around the Pacific by a very irate bonefish of 15 pounds or more. Indeed, he seems to have enough energy to tow it all the way to the Antarctic, devour two penguins and return by sunset.

I had read magazine articles about bonefish before my visit; about their strength and ability to smash up fishing tackle, yet I don't think I really quite believed them. And so, on that first full day's fishing, I rather stupidly carried only one rod and no spare reels or spools. I'd learnt an important lesson; but there was more to come.

I waded over in the direction of our guide, Tuna (who was helping Jerry spot fish), to tell my sad story and to find out if there was some way I could get back to the hotel for more tackle (we were fishing from a punt at least two hours out). The guide took it all as a fairly normal occurrence. What was more he gave me his rod to continue fishing. There were fish everywhere, too; hundreds of bones schooling close to the surface in the deeper water, and others patrolling the flats in fewer numbers, close in.

Jerry took a seven-pounder as we were talking and I followed with one around six. Moments later, when we had drifted apart in our search, I spotted another monster which I duly hooked. His initial run seemed even harder than the fish which had spooled me, but I managed to bring him towards me only to induce another torpedo run. As this second run started, there was an audibly explosive POP and the top eight inches of Tuna's rod snapped to run free down the taut flyline!

As the fish broke off I began to conclude that this was, indeed, an extremely expensive way to go fishing!

The incidents of the two big bones took place on the morning of our first full day's outing. Before that, until sunset on the afternoon of our arrival, I had waded the flats of the lagoon, not far from the hotel, and took my first-ever bonefish (a two-pounder) in the first five minutes. Several more (up to four pounds) followed. It was all very exciting to see these fish head down and tail and dorsal fin visible as they tailed for food, silhouetted by the setting sun.

But the morning of that first full day was a bonanza the like of which even the old-timers like Richard, Tim and Darrell had seldom seen. We'd had breakfast at 5 a.m. and, with our tackle and lunch, were driven in a pick-up to London to board a flat-bottom, outboard-powered punt. A 40-minute trolling run put us on the flats at Paris, where between 8 a.m. and midday we hooked (and released) probably 15 to 20 bones apiece (including my two tackle busters). It was, for once, the right place, the right tide, the right conditions, and bonefish everywhere. Despite the tackle losses, I had again fluked a Thursday, when 'You should have been here on Thursday!'

As the activity waned with the tide around lunchtime we moved further into the lagoon to fish other flats with mixed success before returning to London mid-afternoon. It had been a hot and very successful day and a cool shower, drinks and dinner were very welcome before an early start for a repeat punting day.

As is so often the case with fly-fishing, one can go to the same spot, with the same timings, in the same conditions, and on the second day draw a blank. We fished Paris flats hard that second morning and saw hardly a bone. Shifting location to a number of other flats, we didn't really meet with any great success until towards the end of the day when we anchored on flats off Moto Upua (Bird Island), to take a number of bones, but all these were relatively small fish. Once again, after an early start, we finished mid-afternoon; eight hours fishing in that

heat and brilliant glare was more than enough for me, even though it was excellent fishing. What is more, after eight months I was tiring and could already sniff the scents of home.

For the third day we decided on a 7 a.m. start to fish the southwest side of the island, fishing the reef surf and the flats inshore of the reef between M-site and the Korean wreck. It was a hot day, with little relief from the very light breeze.

The normal fishing costume in that part of the world is lightweight shirt and long trousers—Tarpon Wear, or similar—which gets wet and keeps one cool as one wades, but which dries out quickly. Footwear is normally purpose-designed coral wading (or diving) booties, and a hat is essential, as is good sunscreen. Polaroid glasses are necessary to see through the water, and tackle is kept in shirt pockets, clipped or hung from the shirt, or put in trouser pockets if getting it soaked doesn't matter.

We were all wearing such outfits that day, but I had followed Tim's lead in wearing shorts because I'd found that long, salt-encrusted trousers were causing some chafe. I'd applied plenty of sunscreen but I was getting more and more careless about it; after eight months fishing in the sun I was pretty well tanned anyway. So I forgot to screen the back of my legs and paid dearly for it that evening, and for several subsequent days as the lobster-pink skin turned to blisters and eventually peeled off.

The Korean wreck was our initial stop that morning, and Tim was the first to reach the water's edge, carrying a plug-caster: a good-sized sturdy outfit that, until then, he had used for trolling behind the punt. Because of the trolling, when he made his first cast the line twisted badly and he had to stop to take out the rotated section. While he was so engrossed I joined him with my fly rod and pointed out that his plug was still some distance out, floating in the water. He said something like: 'May as well recover it before I straighten out this mess', and jerked it back toward the beach while concentrating on getting rid of the twisted section of his line.

Three or four huge, flashing shapes nearly devoured that moving plug.

A strangled cry from me brought Tim's attention up and, although the fish were not hooked, we determined that they were very big trevally. I moved down the beach a little, cast a Crazy Charlie some 70 feet out and started a slow retrieve. JOLT! and I was hooked to one of those monsters which rocketed out towards the reef, went once around a rock, and broke me off at the tippet. By then, Tim was back in action again and suggested that

I should use four or five feet of his leftover 30-pound line as a shock-tippet, which I did. As I was making up my new leader, I glanced up to see Tim casting his plug again. It hit the water and was immediately struck with frightening aggression by a huge trevally.

It took off, in a dead straight line for the reef and the Pacific; Tim was leaning back into the rod with the drag up to maximum but making no impression whatsoever; the line was almost parallel to the water. Moments later, the trevally disappeared over the reef cutting the 100-pound shock tippet, and that—as they say—was that!

After our initial excitement, the four of us spread out and moved slowly up the beach, in a northwest direction, casting into the flats for bones. We must have taken at least half a dozen each, and other species—redtailed snapper, spotted swallowtails, and small trevally— before meeting the repositioned pick-up for a lunch break.

After sandwiches and iced water we drove to M-site to be greeted by a perfect surf-to-shore flat at a good stage of the falling tide. The only trouble was that seven or eight sharks, up to eight or nine feet long, were casually patrolling the edges.

The locals assured us these were very timid black-tipped sharks which were of no danger, although my Australian upbringing indicated otherwise. Anyway, whether it was too much sun or too much fishing I don't know, but somehow I found myself with Tim wading waist-deep among them. Tim had the fly rod with popper, and I had my Weathermatic Minolta. We must have been stark staring mad!

Tim started flailing the popper around and the sharks became quite excited. Often he would have two or more go for it at once, while I almost walked on the water to get photographs. This went on for some little time, then two of the sharks took but both missed; subsequently the popper came adrift and we found the swivel chewed to an unrecognisable mess. Finally a big fellow chased it up (and I started to move inshore only to see another shark between me and the beach!); he became quite aggressive as he circled the popper, and finally spun round and round it in a real frenzy . . . and remember, the popper has to be dragged towards the angler to produce the attractive surface movement.

Suddenly the shark had had enough (and so had I), and it headed out to sea. At that stage I became aware of a huge, dark shape in my peripheral vision, only feet from me!

'GEE-ZUZ!', I exclaimed, almost covering the distance to the shore on top of the water as only

He could . . . to find my companion was a giant turtle.

That was it. I'd had enough and I stomped back to the beach, oblivious of the smaller shark I had to pass on the way. Tim joined me, laughing so much that all I could do was to join in. What a crazy half hour, and how fortunate that the locals' advice about black-tipped sharks was apparently correct . . . or was it? I certainly wasn't going back to test it further.

It was later that I discovered my Minolta was not working properly and the evidence of this little piece of madness was unfortunately not suitable for publication.

We finished that day, fishing northwest up the beach to the pick-up point taking and releasing a vast number of bones as we went. None was very big but we had two further incidents of big trevally break-offs. It was then that I began to feel the backs of my legs and smothered them in blockout—all too late of course.

The hotel put on a magnificent and delicious open-air luau that evening: barbecued pig and lobster, salads and ice-cream. It was followed by Pacific dancing, beautifully performed by the staff and locals, ending another wonderful Christmas Island day.

On the final full day, Sunday 20 September, I simply had to catch up with my sketching and notes. This was not a hard choice, even though the fishing was excellent and the weather perfect. My blistered calves needed soaking in ice and rest.

There was a set routine on our final morning: fishing (if desired) until 10 a.m., back to the hotel by eleven, checkout and lunch at midday, and transport to the airport at 1.30 p.m. for the two forty-five flight to Honolulu. All very detailed but highly changeable stuff.

I have said that Christmas Island offers the best salt-water fly-fishing I have known, and I reiterate that view. It does, however, in my opinion, have some problems: communication, including travel to and from the island, is not totally reliable, and management and administration suffer from a similar mid-Pacific *laissez-faire*. Additionally, in my case, it came at the end of a long line of fly-fishing experiences. Something has to be at the end just as something must be at the beginning, but enthusiasm is at its peak in the beginning, accurate impressions are most often gained around the midpoint, and at the end, enthusiasm wanes and the want to criticise increases.

If that is the case, and I still believe what I have

Tim connected to a 'monster' trevally . . .

. . . not far from The Korean Wreck.

said about the island, it must surely be part of that heavenly stick.

And so back to Honolulu, without further incident, thank heaven. I had allowed myself 24 hours at the Airport Holiday Inn to catch up before taking the 'red-eye' special to Sydney at half past midnight on Wednesday 23 September. I must say that the inn was very good to me in accommodating all my many changes in plans and doing everything possible to make life comfortable. The same should also be said of Frontiers, the tour operator for Christmas Island.

It's midnight, 22 September 1992. And what now, at the end of a grand safari? A summation, of course, but not here. These chapters must be amended, edited, re-read and probably rewritten often. It cannot be even attempted now, in the departure lounge of Honolulu International Airport. Much better that, after all the revisions, it is written slowly in the light of remembered experiences, with the cushion of time and with the vivid recall of my illustrated diaries which I maintained daily throughout eight months, 150,000 kilometres, 16 countries, 41 fishing locations and 260 fish over two pounds—all of which, save nine Atlantic salmon, four trout and a couple of Arctic char—were released.

Dancing at the Luau . . .

. . . watched by a very interested observer.

Christmas Island, the greatest coral atoll . . .

Christmas Island bonefish.

The Incurable Disease

I remain convinced that the most penetrating short description of the quintessence of fly-fishing is that written by Robert Traver when he wrote 'Testament of a Fisherman'.

It is quoted in Chapter 5, and says, in one paragraph, what many others have tried to express over the years in much extended prose. Like 'The Fisherman's Prayer' ('which one?', you may well ask), and those often quoted phrases from Izaak Walton's *The Compleat Angler*, I would be prepared to bet my last surviving dollar that Traver's words will become immortal, and will be hung from the walls of hundreds of huts, cabins, angling clubs and back-country hotels throughout the world of troutdom. I only hope that, without being foolish enough to try to write a similar one-paragraph summation of my own feelings at the end of my travels, the words I have written will support Traver's 'Testament'. They were meant to.

There is another piece of angling prose that I like. Until now it has not been published; it certainly isn't a testament, nor was it ever meant to be. It is, quite simply, a particularly descriptive statement from the soul of fly-fishing, about a very particular place at a very particular time. Ambrose Streatfeild wrote it for Christmas 1990, having just visited Brindabella:

Why I Believe in Fairies
(A Midsummer Dawn's Dream)

Now, for the first time since childhood, I believe in fairies and Father Christmas. Today, at an hour when most mortals are abed, I parted a screen of bushes and entered a place of magic, mystery and unsurpassed beauty. My little world (round which both Ariel and Puck had put a girdle of silk, which they tightened, together with my heart-strings, for an hour) was known, graphically but perhaps prosaically, as Outward Bound Deep. To me it became, at once and forever, Merlin's Grotto. On one side was a small cliff of purple, brown, green—or was it golden?—stone which shifted colour by the minute as the rising sun dappled through the leaves of a thousand eucalyptus trees. Their silver and grey trunks rose, like Doric columns, until they were lost in the dark green canopy, through which I glimpsed, from time to time, a cobalt sky. Below, alternately gliding, rushing and laughing flowed the river, from which there arose wraiths of silver mist as the day dawned, triggering off mysterious spirals from unknown depths.

The dancing ephemerids were not mayflies but fairies. Didn't I see Merlin himself cast with his wand a line of spider's web at a sipping trout at the top of the pool? Companies of crimson rosellas and king parrots patrolled the lower layers of the canopy above which, no doubt, wheeled a pair of wedge-tailed eagles, guardians of this blessed plot, but to me, for once, invisible. I wished momentarily that I had brought my camera, then was glad that I hadn't. The click would have broken the spell, and the resultant colour-slide would have been, quite properly, blank.

As I reluctantly parted my scene to leave for the real world of breakfast and packing (for all too soon we had to return to Canberra), a golden whistler, ten feet above my head, saluted me with his three fluting notes and a whipcrack. I burst, quite involuntarily, into the last verse of the old Hundredth, not generally one of my favourite hymns. My singing provoked an outburst of protest from a pair of kookaburras—weren't these Merlin's familiars, bidding me farewell?

As I reached the track, five minutes from home, it dawned on me, with a sudden and startling clarity, that it was Christmas Eve. No wonder the trout hadn't risen this morning; they, too, were content to greet His birth.

Whereas a rolling stone may gather no moss, the further this rolling stone travelled, the more people he seemed to collect who would ask: 'Where is the best fly-fishing in the world?' 'What is the most beautiful country you have visited?' 'Which lodge was the most comfortable?' 'What is the best?' 'What is the best?' 'What is the best?' There was an almost urgent desire to know the answers to these questions; whether it was to balance my opinion against theirs, to seek reassurances about their own favourite locale, to name-drop some other area I hadn't visited and to laud its fishery (and their knowledge), or simply to seek an opinion without reservation, I was never quite sure.

It was easy enough to make diplomatic and entirely acceptable replies. In the early days I would respond by saying that all I had visited so far was superb but that I had much more ahead of me and it would be unfair to make comparisons until later. Later on, while maintaining a suggestion that all places on my itinerary were wonderful (which was true enough, and easily accepted because it almost always included the questioner's home water), I would make vague distinctions saying that such-and-such had superb trout fishing, another place was great for salmon, a third might have very unusual scenery, and so on, allowing others to pick up the conversation and follow it without me having to give definite answers.

On the one or two occasions when I was foolish enough to risk considered criticism, I found myself quickly and unconditionally rebuffed by the locals; I do not believe there is a place on this earth that does not suffer from parochialism to a greater or lesser degree. I found my view was frequently not welcomed even when I joined in criticism initiated by others about their own, and occasionally it caused the original critic to change tack, to oppose what I may have suggested, even if it meant refuting his own initial argument. Other than heaping praise, I found it best to keep my own counsel.

In any case, the words I have written in this book already give a good indication of my opinions, all of which are high, my criticism of local trout management in my own country not withstanding. I believe the areas I most enjoyed, nonetheless, were the very remote ones: parts of the South Island of New Zealand, Patagonia, Iceland, Baffin Island, Labrador and Kiribati. These areas also provided examples of the very best fisheries management, or were so remote that the presence of man had not yet caused the need. That is not to say that other places were much less enjoyable, particularly those areas under heavy fishing pressure like Norway, Idaho, Montana, Wyoming and British Columbia, where detailed management continues to maintain salmonid fisheries of exceptional appeal.

If I had to make some very hard decisions, I would say that I think the best wild trout fishing in the world is to be found in the South Island of New Zealand. Other places, many may argue convincingly, are better for other reasons. Patagonia, for example, offered me an almost unsurpassed quality of life in addition to its excellent trout fishing. Others may say that lake fishing in the North American continent, or fishing rivers in the wilds of Tierra del Fuego can produce monster fish. Maybe, but if I wanted consistent wild trout fishing, with little risk of failure, in wonderful scenery and in the knowledge that my average fish would be in the vicinity of four pounds, I would go to New Zealand; a view, that was incidentally supported frequently by other internationals in the many lodges I visited.

If I had to make a choice about salmon, first of all I would choose in favour of Atlantic salmon. To me, they offer a greater challenge than their Pacific cousins, and I am much more attracted to their shape, silvery appearance and firm flesh. The sight of Pacific coast rivers, chock full of spawning fish who subsequently die, saddens me immeasurably; and, in this knowledge, I get little excitement from taking these fish relatively easily, earlier as they make their way up the rivers, fresh-run.

While I thought that Iceland offered the ultimate in salmon fishing, the fish were not very big (this could change positively) and costs were astonishingly high. Labrador offered comparable fishing (although I struck a mediocre period), but it didn't have quite the same *je ne sais quoi* mystique of the top price bracket. Whatever, it was much more affordable. Norway, on the other hand, offered very big fish in small numbers at the beginning of the season, changing to greater numbers of relatively smaller fish later. Geographically it is easier of access than Iceland or Labrador so it is more subject to heavy fishing pressures, but management is very good and costs can be quite reasonable.

I found the scenery and animal life in southern Africa outstanding, and its people some of the most kind and hospitable I have ever met. But I'm not sure I would return exclusively for the salmonid fishing. I am prepared to be convinced otherwise and know that I haven't forgiven myself for not spending longer in those parts to try other areas. Particularly I should have given myself time to try to take a tiger fish on the fly from Lake Kariba. The thoughts I expressed concerning local politics at the time of my visits need rethinking also. They were, of course, subsequently overtaken by events.

I have not, however, edited them to extinction, preferring to leave them as examples of the constant and often undesirable fluctuations of life in those countries.

England, what I saw of it, was both a wonder and a worry for me; the latter (because we have always had very close and affectionate ties) I feel obliged to comment on. The days I spent with Ambrose and his friends on the chalkstreams in the south were simply wonderful; I wished at times that they, and the balmy, early English summer that went with them, would never end. On the other hand I observed, after an absence of 15 years (and temporary removal from a scene can sharpen one's vision), that fishing pressures in England were colossal, not only from the point of view of the increasing number of anglers, but from other human pressures affecting the environment. Pollution generally, agriculture, the effects of drought and water management, the disposal of effluent and chemicals, heavy construction programs and clogged roads, all seemed to be adversely affecting fishing life. Maybe an entirely new management approach might be necessary; after all, these environmental pressures are all within man's control.

Far removed from this, on the roof of the world, I enjoyed some of the greatest fly-fishing experiences that I have ever been lucky enough to know; and all of those in exceptional and remote territory, and in perfect weather. I know that I'll have to live a very long time to experience again the equivalent of those four days fishing for Arctic char, above the Arctic Circle, in Clearwater Fjord. Similarly, Kiribati was almost the tropical equal, 7,500 kilometres further south and roughly the same distance west on the Equator. The remarkable common denominator, of course, was the success of the Crazy Charlie fly in both extremes

In addition to being extremely spoilt with private invitations and accommodation, I must have stayed in close to 20 dedicated lodges (or their equivalent) during my travels, and all were very good indeed. They varied, of course, in both type and function. At the top end of the scale were those which provided a degree of luxury as well as catering for the fisherman's needs. In this bracket I include (in the order I used them); in Australia: The Outpost II and London Lakes; in Patagonia: Estancia Huechahue and Estancia Cerro de Los Pinos; in Iceland: Nordurá Lodge; in Labrador: Michael's River Lodge; and, in British Columbia: Tweedsmuir Lodge. They were all first-class fishing lodges offering the best accommodation and amenities together with excellent fishing.

Next, but of no less charm and comfort, even though offering a rudimentary lifestyle more associated with fishing in the wild, were (again, in order of appearance): in New Zealand: the Glenruth Motel at Lake Hawea and the Ranfurly Motel at Ranfurly; in South Africa in Natal: the Underberg and Himeville Hotels; in Norway: Øverkil House (this has an additional historic charm); in Baffin Island: Auyuittuq Lodge at Pangnirtung and Clearwater Fjord Camp (very basic, but comfortable and efficient); in Montana: Kingfisher Lodge at Fort Smith on the Big Horn; and at Kiribati: the Captain Cook Hotel.

There were also one or two other places—multi-function hostelries for want of a better description—where I stayed during my travels and which I found very comfortable: the Troutbeck Inn in Nyanga National Park in Zimbabwe, and the Arundell Arms in Devon in England. Every one of these lodges, hotels, motels and camps was ideal for its purpose, and often far more than that. They all impressed me, I found little to fault and much to praise in them, and in every case—forgetting for a moment the cost of fishing—their tariff for bed and food was always extraordinarily reasonable.

And what of my own country, and New South Wales inland fishery management of which I have been consistently critical?

During my travels I maintained the level of criticism, submitting articles to newspapers and magazines, and finally corresponding direct with the responsible minister in the government of New South Wales. I endeavoured to give examples of management overseas, I drew attention to the growing tide of opinion in favour of reform at home, and made some suggestions for improved management in the future. The outcome was an invitation to visit the minister for discussions on my return.

Progress? I believed so.

The minister was polite, approachable and apparently in sympathy with some of my views which I hadn't realised had been so heavily supported during my absence overseas by literally thousands of letters from like-minded anglers. Nonetheless, Inland Fishing Licences had not been reintroduced (although a poorly constructed attempt—proposing an all-types inland licence—had been made and rejected on party political lines), and the need for more complex regulations was still being reviewed by yet another committee. (If I'd had a committee planning my safaris I'd have got no further than Tasmania!) It was apparent that the opinions of the unconcerned and uneducated majority of occasional weekend anglers and voters—the numbers and belly fishermen—still carried the day; moreover, that a few of the minister's public staff were still keen on administrative shortcuts, more interested in political futures than issues and, one or two, like some others in that overpopulated public service arena that I had met and sometimes worked with over two score years, particularly keen to maintain their own perceived level of importance.

It was obvious that the education process must not be allowed to decline. On my return I found that there were rumblings also in the next-door state of Victoria where inland fisheries management was, if anything, worse, but where a growing groundswell of educated anglers' opinion was at last beginning to make itself felt.

In contrast (but hopefully in parallel someday), I couldn't help thinking about the astonishingly successful efforts of those organisations in Norway, Iceland, Newfoundland and British Columbia which had managed to influence public and political thinking so effectively. In essence, I concluded that fishing organisations in Australia were disparate, self-centred, divided and thus conquered (probably to the relief of politicians and their staffs), whereas anglers overseas had long since risen above any differences to present a unified voice speaking out for the biggest single participatory sport in the history of mankind.

Was not Peter a fisher of men . . . and John, the favourite, a dry-fly fisherman?

Now a word about guides.

Theirs is a difficult lot. Their problems range from instructing beginners, when the path to ultimate success and conversion to adequacy—if not true belief—is strewn with frustrations and days of observing monumental rises from the boughs of trees from which a fly needs to be released, to being forced by law to look after experienced fly-fishermen resentful of an enforced presence.

The accolade that I willingly bestow on them collectively, is that they are very good at sizing up newcomers, and in imparting just the right level of assistance and advice. For example, in America they wouldn't be awarded a licence if they could not do this.

I took guides in most new places unless I was fishing privately with friends. I always took them for the first time when advised by friends or locals to do so (often dispensing with their services once I had found my feet) and, of course, when it was mandatory to do so. In Labrador, for example, overseas visitors may not fish for salmon without a local guide.

Nevertheless, I found it best to establish some ground rules myself from the very start. These will differ depending on the experience and attitude of the individual angler, but most guides I met seemed to appreciate this little concern, very few falling into the category of the all-knowing-Guru, inflexible and steeped in too much experience.

My ground rules were pretty simple:
- Let's talk before we go fishing, and please keep plying me with local advice along the way.
- Let's assume that your eyesight, locally, is better than mine.
- Don't pamper me with fly and tippet tying, netting, hook removal and other niceties, I enjoy doing my own.
- If I don't like a local custom (about which I have been advised) because I believe it is an unfair practice (multiple flies, huge trebles . . . etc.), grin and bear it as I go my own way—even if unsuccessfully.
- Please fish with me if you want to (but, if I'm paying, let me try the pool first); I want this fishing experience to be a friendly one and not a master/slave relationship.

I thoroughly enjoyed fishing with all those who were good enough to guide for me during my travels. I always acknowledged their superior local knowledge, and eagerly looked forward to a drink or two and a chat at the end of the day. The only thing that ever really upset me was when a guide would join my other companions in screaming conflicting advice when I was hooked up, playing a big one. Good guides would read my face very quickly under such circumstances, and remain silent with me as I did it my way, oblivious to the continued screaming of my friends ('enthusiastic encouragement' might be a more kind and truthful description).

One final thing: I would *always* determine costs and the standard tip rate (if any) from my friends or locals before committing myself.

My *bête noire* during these travels (and the reader will have probably grasped this by now) was international airports. To me they exist as vast barns of headache and confusion, lorded over by customs and immigration procedures, baggage checking, forms in triplicate, officials (plural), security people, X-ray machines, an absence of trolleys and mile after never-ending mile of walkways. No matter how hard my travel agent tried (and she did a superlative job covering 150,000 kilometres), I always seemed to end up with approaching nightfall in pouring rain, at one end of a place the size of Montreal International or Heathrow, to find my next flight was due to depart in 30 minutes from the opposite end of the terminal.

Although that may be a minor exaggeration on my part, it has been a recurring nightmare of mine for some weeks after each major international leg.

It is a truth, however, when I reveal that, under very similar circumstances at Chicago's O'Hare airport, I said to the smiling face behind the Information Desk: 'You know, there is only one thing wrong with this magnificent airport'.

Smiling face: 'And what might that be, Sir?'

Me: 'The taxis are on the *Outside*!'

Do fishermen really lie?

I suppose they bend the truth more than some others but, in doing so, harmlessly add to the mystique and fun of fishing. 'Always multiply by point eight for each year passing the date of the event,' someone once said to me.

I have said that a number of my fellow lodge guests agreed with my views regarding New Zealand. Enthusiastically, during such conversations, they would recount tales of regular seven- and eight-pound fish, caught almost daily. It was as if each was striving to outdo the next possible speaker, safe in the knowledge that such fishing was very likely if the glossy ads were to be believed—even though many a six and a half pounder is known to grow to 'a little under seven' on first recall, 'a good seven' later, and finally the reality and the glossy seem to merge around the eight-pound mark! In eight visits to New Zealand I have caught a mass of three-pounders, a number of good four and a half to five and a half pound fish, the occasional six-pounder and a few fish in excess of six and a half. My best fish topped eight pounds, but the average is somewhere around four—top fishing in anyone's language.

I mention this, not to poke fun at my fellow anglers, nor to call them liars. (Maybe they were utterly truthful and *my* fishing in New Zealand has been either unskilful or unlucky.) Nor do I want to belittle the trout fishing in that country, fishing which I still believe to be the best there is. I simply wish to establish a datum. Readers may like to apply a factor to my own fish weights in this book, but they are given with respect to that datum, and I guarantee their accuracy to the nearest quarter pound . . . I think!

Which brings me back, naturally, to my six most remembered fish (although there *was* a seventh)—all lost of course!

Two of them I never even hooked!

The Rakaia Monster in the Hydra Waters off Mount Algidus Station, near Mount Hutt in the South Island of New Zealand; we chased him for two years and never even pricked him. In truth he must have been a 25-pounder, which is not bad for a brown trout.

The other radio-controlled monster (that I did not hook) was the Atlantic salmon that played with Reg and me in the Michael's River in Labrador. He *must* have been over 20 (and once one reaches the score, I think it's fair to ascend in fives!) The remarkable thing about these two fish, apart from their size and refusal to take a fly, was that we actually eyeballed each other. I'm certain they *knew* I was fishing for them, and probably felt a responsibility to humour me but not to endanger themselves—or so it seemed. I couldn't help feeling that I was as visible to them as they were to me; it was as though a bizarre communication link had been established between quarry and hunter.

On the other hand, I actually managed to hook the other four monsters before losing them. And I think the one I was most sorry about was the brown trout I hooked that magical morning in the secret part of the upper Murrumbidgee. He was the first fish that would have gone beyond the stretch of my pocket spring-balance: in truth a 12-pounder (?); and he would have been my best ever fish in Australia. It was his loss that forced me, such was my sorrow, to take sustenance at the Snowgoose Hotel at Adaminaby, and I hold him entirely responsible for my sickly condition the next morning.

My biggest loss was the behemoth Atlantic salmon which, after days of frustration in perpetually hot Norwegian summer sunlight, I hooked using a nine and a half foot trout rod, at five-ten that Sunday morning in the white water below the falls on the Fossen beat of the River Forra, only to have the hook pull out 40 minutes later. I saw that fish as he rolled to take my fly before he sounded. I really do believe he is the biggest I've ever hooked on a fly, and I think I can safely describe him as 'a little under 30'!

The remaining two monsters were undoubtedly lost through bravado, carelessness, foolishness . . . call it what you will. First, there was the big Atlantic salmon on the horseshoe bend of the Nordurá in Iceland. The reader will recall that, full of victory and red wine the evening before, two of us—a Norwegian and an Australian—had foolishly agreed to fish super-light the next morning to prove some ridiculous and forgotten point. I enjoyed every moment of the 40-minute fight with that fish, but he deserved his freedom much more than I would have deserved any acclaim had I luckily landed that 20-pounder, on a trout rod and seven-pound tippet, from white water.

Finally there was the monster bonefish at Kiribati, the 15-pounder(?) last seen accelerating towards the Antarctic, towing about $150 worth of fly line, backing, leader and Crazy Charlie because I'd used inadequate tackle (and hadn't even bothered to carry a spare spool). These last two monsters I never really deserved.

Oh, the secret seventh?

I never saw him properly so I can't put a figure on his size. He was the leviathan Arctic char which, as I stood rooted to the spot in Clearwater Fjord, took off with such acceleration that my fly reel backlashed for the first time in my experience. He is but a blur rather than an indelible stain on my memory and, in recalling the story, I can probably play with his size as much as I like!

The big fish landed during my travels were less memorable. There were good trout (over five pounds) in New Zealand, and the four and a half pound rainbow from the little feeder stream under the shadow of Vulcan Lanin in Patagonia. There were a number of very healthy Atlantic salmon in Iceland and Labrador; there was a four-pound brownie from the Big Horn, and a good coho salmon from the Bella Coola, not to mention some exceptional bones at Kiribati. But I don't dream of these; they are not haunting memories like the others. The only fish which were close to recurring dream material were the double-figure Arctic char in Baffin Island, and even these have faded with time.

The lost monsters will always haunt me like some incomplete love affair. If anyone ever hears me retell one of those stories, I ask forgiveness in advance for any gain in weight I might inadvertently apply. But, remember, those monsters are still on the loose and they have every natural reason to grow bigger.

As it was during my travels, so it was after my return: questions; inevitable, anticipated, intelligent and welcomed questions.

On my return, however, these were unexpectedly directed more towards the degree of total success, the countries I considered worthy of a second (or more) visit, the changes I would make (given the opportunity again), and whether I would indeed do it all again, given the chance, rather than inquiries about which part was individually the best.

Given a second opportunity I would certainly make changes in order to see additional areas. In the Southern Hemisphere I would take a round-the-Pacific ticket to fly, via Honolulu and Kiribati (for bones again), to Chile: a new adventure. I would then, with much pleasure, repeat Patagonia (probably concentrating on different rivers and some of the lakes) before flying to Buenos Aires. In BA I would take the Aerolineas Argentinas flight to Auckland in the knowledge that this flight goes through Tierra del Fuego where I would stop for some days to seek the legendary searun browns of the Rio Grande. And, once in Auckland, I'd just *have* to fly south to fish for wild browns again in the South Island of New Zealand.

In the north I would go direct to Europe, where I would need to do more research before making any decisions. Germany maybe(?), and one other stop perhaps before the Kola Peninsula in Russia; then Sweden and a return to Norway (the Forra, after all, owes me one), would be the start of my planning. Thereafter I would face a real dilemma. I can't imagine being in that part of the world again without revisiting Iceland, Baffin Island and Labrador; but at what expense? Maybe Ireland and Scotland should be visited instead followed by a direct flight to America? And, once in the States, I would feel obliged somehow to examine the eastside, the Catskills and Lee Wulff territory. A further dilemma would follow: to go south for bones, tarpon and permit, or north into other parts of Canada's Northwest Territories, followed by more appropriately timed steelhead fishing, and Alaska on the way home?

When I returned to Australia in September 1992, I informed my travel agent that my family would exist on bread and water for two years and that I would ask her to book us three square metres of water frontage on the local lake for an annual two-day holiday during the same period. What I'm trying to say is that I doubt whether I'll actually get another opportunity to repeat 1992 (with amendments). I was extremely fortunate that year and want, very much, to share those extraordinary experiences. Another adventure is but a dream; but where would we be if we couldn't dream?

Was it all a dream?

Well, maybe it was, and maybe it wasn't.

Apart from my notes, my sketches and my slides, I find it very hard to convince myself that I was really up there, north of the Circle, fighting huge Arctic char in storybook scenery and weather. On the other hand, I now take New Zealand almost for granted. Would Ross Peyton and Bill Bennett do likewise?

One of those who questioned me on my return once asked: 'If you hadn't done it; if you were starting from scratch again, would you do exactly what you did?'

'Baby,' was my reply, 'you betcha sweet bippie I would!'

Salmo trutta

APPENDIX

Some International Fly-fishing Addresses

This list covers only those venues that I visited during my travels where the activity concerned was carried out commercially, and where the owners or managers agreed to their addresses being published in this book. Prices are not included because they will vary with time and can be ascertained by contacting the venue direct.

While it cannot, of course, include the addresses of the private hospitality that I was fortunate enough to enjoy, in some cases mention is made of outfitters operating in the same areas.

Occasionally there is a need to amplify some of the information given; where necessary, this is done in parenthesis.

Argentina

Estancia Huechahue (Jane Wood)
Apartado Especial 12, 8371 Junin de Los Andes
Provincia del Neuquen, Argentina
PHONE: 944 91303 FAX: 972 27111

Estancia Cerro de Los Pinos, (Pedro Larminat)
8371 Junin de Los Andes
Provincia del Neuquen, Argentina

Frontiers, PO Box 959, Wexford, PA 15090
U.S.A. PHONE: 412 935 1577
Tollfree (U.S.A.): 800 245 1950 FAX: 412 935 5388

(Frontiers is an international tour operator covering many parts of the world. I used them most satisfactorily for Kiribati. In Australia they normally work through the Australian Fly Fisherman—see Australian section.)

Australia

The Outpost II, (Peter and Jill Blackman)
Yaouk, Adaminaby
New South Wales 2630, Australia
PHONE: (0)64 542293 FAX: (0)64 542612

Australian Fly Fisherman, (Andrew Brzoz)
143 Bayswater Road, Rushcutters Bay
New South Wales 2011, Australia
PHONE: (0)2 360 2830 FAX: (0)2 331 2149

(For local and overseas fishing tours, and for tackle.)

Aus-Fly, PO Box 1233, Queanbeyan
New South Wales 2620, Australia
PHONE: (0)6 299 4846 FAX: (0)6 299 4397
(Orvis distributor)

London Lakes, (Jason and Barbara Garrett)
Post Office, Bronte Park,
Tasmania 7140, Australia
PHONE: (0)02 891159 FAX: (0)02 233992

Chris Hole Fly Fishing Art, PO Box 26
Monaro Crescent, Red Hill,
Australian Capital Territory 2603, Australia
PHONE: (0)6 295 3287 FAX: (0)6 239 7141

Baffin Island

Clearwater Wilderness Lodge,
(Jeff. R. Peyton Enterprises Ltd),
Box 303, Pangnirtung, North West Territories,
XOA ORO Canada
PHONE: 819 473 8719 FAX: 819 4738924

Auyuittuq Lodge, (Donna Copeland)
Box 53, Pangnirtung, North West Territories
XOA ORO Canada
PHONE: 819 473 8955 FAX: 819 473 8611

England

The Rod Box, (Ian Hay)
London Road, King's Worthy, Winchester
Hampshire SO23 7QN, England
PHONE: (0)962 883600 FAX: (0)962 883419

(For tackle, and provision of fly-fishing on
Hampshire chalk-streams.)

The Arundell Arms, (Anne Voss-Bark)
Lifton, Devon PL16 OAA, England
PHONE: (0)566 784666 FAX: (0)566 784494

Iceland

The Angling Club of Reykjavik, (SVFR)
Haaleitisbraut 68, 108 Reykjavik, Iceland
PHONE: 354 1 813425 FAX: 354 1 32060

Kiribati (Christmas Island)

Frontiers, PO Box 959, Wexford, PA 15090
U.S.A.
PHONE: 412 935 1577
Tollfree (U.S.A.): 800 245 1950
FAX: 412 935 5388

Australian Fly Fisherman, 143 Bayswater Road
Rushcutters Bay, New South Wales 2011, Australia
PHONE: (0)2 360 2830 FAX: (0)2 331 2149

Holiday Inn Honolulu International Airport
3401 Nimitz Highway, Honolulu, HI 96819
U.S.A. PHONE: 808 836 0661 FAX: 808 833 1738

(Very convenient when travelling to and from
Christmas Island.)

Labrador

Gander Aviation Ltd, (Bill Bennett)
PO Box 250, Gander
Newfoundland A1V 1W6 Canada
PHONE: 709 256 3421 FAX: 709 256 2413

(Responsible for Sandhill, Wulff Lake and Michael's
River Lodges.)

New Zealand

Glenruth Motel, Lakeview Terrace, Lake Hawea
Otago, New Zealand
PHONE: (0)3 443 1440 FAX: (0)3 443 1709

Ranfurly Motel, 1 Davis Avenue, Ranfurly,
Otago, New Zealand
PHONE: (0)3 444 9383

Brian Thomson, The Balmoral Dairy
17 Northland Street, Ranfurly, Otago
New Zealand. PHONE: (0)3 444 7001

(Brian is one of the best guides in the South Island
but only guides on an 'as available' basis because of
his busy work in the dairy. He is always willing to
give good advice, and hopes to be able to provide
inexpensive accommodation in the future.)

Norway

Norwegian Fly Fishers' Club, (Manfred Raguse)
Lerchenstrasse 3 and 7
D-2000 Hamburg 50, Germany
PHONE: (0)40 430 2529 FAX: (0)40 430 2599

South Africa

Underberg and Himeville Trout Fishing Club, (Bob
Crass)
PO 134, Underberg, Natal 4590,
Republic of South Africa
PHONE: (0)33 701 1041

Underberg Hotel, Underberg, Natal 4590
Republic of South Africa
PHONE: (0)33 701 1412

USA

South Fork Lodge and Outfitters, Box 22,
Swan Valley, Idaho 83449, U.S.A.
PHONE: 208 483 2112

(South Fork of the Snake River)

Kingfisher Lodge, (George Kelly and Jo Newhall)
Box 524, Fort Smith, Montana 59035, U.S.A.
PHONE: 406 666 2326

(Big Horn River)

Bob Jacklin (Outfitters)
Box 310, 105 Yellowstone Avenue, West Yellowstone
Montana 59758, U.S.A.
PHONE: 406 646 7336 FAX: 406 646 9729

(Madison, Yellowstone, Gallatin, Snake, Firehole
and other rivers, Hebgen Lake etc.)

Silver Creek Outfitters, Box 418, Sun Valley
Idaho 83353
and
507 North Main Street, Ketchum, Idaho 83340
USA.
PHONE: 208 726 5282/8348 FAX: 208 726 9056

(Silver Creek)

Zimbabwe
Zimbabwe Sun Hotels, (Eric Jones)
PO Box 8221, Causeway, Harare, Zimbabwe
PHONE: 737944 FAX: 734739

Troutbeck Inn, (Trish Lee)
PO Box 1, Troutbeck, Zimbabwe
PHONE: Nyanga 305 and 306

* If a phone or fax number is preceded by (0), omit this digit
if dialling from another country.

Bibliography

Armstrong, R., *The Painted Stream*, 1985, J. M. Dent & Sons.

[Berners, Dame, J.], *The Treatyse of Fysshynge Wyth an Angle*, 1496, William Caxton Press, St Alban's House.

Collis, B., *Snowy*, 1990, Hodder and Stoughton.

Crass, R. S., *Trout Fishing in Natal*, 1971, Daily News.

Farson, N., *Going Fishing*, 1983, Hamlyn Paperbacks.

Ferris, G., *The Trout and I*, 1970, Heinemann.

Francis, F., *A Book on Angling*, 1920, Herbert Jenkins.

Haig-Brown, R. L., *Bright Waters, Bright Fish*, 1980, Douglas & McIntyre.

Haig-Brown, R. L., *A River Never Sleeps*, 1974, Douglas & McIntyre.

Halford, F. M., *The Dry-Fly Man's Handbook*, 1913, George Routledge & Sons.

Hemingway, E., *The Old Man and the Sea*, 1952, Jonathan Cape.

Hunter, C. J., *Better Trout Habitat*, 1991, Island Press.

Leitch, W. C., *Argentine Trout Fishing*, 1991, Frank Amato Publications.

Maclean, N., *A River Runs through It*, 1990, Picador, Pan Books.

Patterson, G., *Angling in the Andes*, 1961, K.G. Murray Publishing Company.

Pawson, A., *Fly Fishing Around the World*, 1987, Unwin Hyman.

Ritchie, J. G., *The Australian Trout*, 1988, The Victorian Fly-Fishers' Association.

Ritz, C., *A Fly Fishers' Life*, 1959, Max Reinhardt.

Sautelle, J., *Fishing for the Educated Trout*, 1978, Murray Book Distributors.

Sautelle, J., *Champagne Fly Fishing*, 1990, Tas-Trout Publications.

Schwiebert, E. G., *The Compleat Schwiebert*, 1990, Truman Talley Books/Dutton.

Schwiebert, E. G., *A River for Christmas*, 1988, Stephen Greene Press.

Skues, G. E. M., *The Way of a Trout with a Fly*, 1949, Adam & Charles Black.

Sloane, R. D., *More About Trout*, 1989, Tas-Trout Publications.

Stewart, D., *The Seven Rivers*, 1966, Angus and Robertson.

Sutcliffe, T., *My Way With a Trout*, 1989, Shuter & Shooter.

Theroux, P., *The Old Patagonian Express*, 1980, Penguin Books.

Tichborne, B., *Anglers' Paradise* (illustrated by Nancy Tichborne), 1990, Bush Press of Auckland.

Tilzey, R. D. J., 'Repeat Homing of Brown Trout (*Salmo trutta*) in Lake Eucumbene, New South Wales, Australia', 1977, 34 (8), reprinted from the Journal of the Fisheries Research Board of Canada.

Traver, R., *Trout Magic*, 1989, Fireside, Simon & Schuster.

Voss Bark, C., *A Fly on the Water*, 1986, Allen & Unwin.

Walton, I., *The Compleat Angler*, 1653. A facsimile of the first edition, reproduced from the copy in the Grenville Collection at the British Museum, and published by A. & C. Black, 1978.

Index